LINKING LEADERSHIP
TO STUDENT LEARNING

LINKING LEADERSHIP TO STUDENT LEARNING

Kenneth Leithwood and
Karen Seashore Louis

With contributions from Stephen E. Anderson,
Kyla Wahlstrom, Blair Mascall, Molly F. Gordon,
Emanda Thomas, and Doris Jantzi

Foreword by Michael S. Knapp

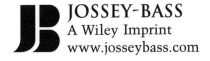

JOSSEY-BASS
A Wiley Imprint
www.josseybass.com

Published by Jossey-Bass
A Wiley Imprint
One Montgomery Street, Suite 1200, San Francisco, CA 94104-4594—www.josseybass.com

Jossey-Bass books and products are available through most bookstores. To contact Jossey-Bass directly call
our Customer Care Department within the U.S. at 800-956-7739, outside the U.S. at 317-572-3986, or fax
317-572-4002.

Wiley also publishes its books in a variety of electronic formats and by print-on-demand. Some material
included with standard print versions of this book may not be included in e-books or in print-on-demand. If
the version of this book that you purchased references media such as CD or DVD that was not included in your
purchase, you may download this material at http://booksupport.wiley.com. For more information about Wiley
products, visit www.wiley.com.

Library of Congress Cataloging-in-Publication Data

Leithwood, Kenneth A.
　　Linking leadership to student learning / Kenneth Leithwood, Karen Seashore Louis ; with contributions
　from Stephen E. Anderson . . . [et al.].
　　　p. cm.
　　Includes bibliographical references and index.
　　ISBN 978-0-470-62331-2 (pbk.)
　　　1. Educational leadership.　2. School management and organization.　3. Achievement motivation
　in children.　I. Louis, Karen Seashore.　II. Anderson, Stephen E.　III. Title.
　LB2806.L3854　2011
　371.200973—dc23

2011032062

Printed in the United States of America
FIRST EDITION
PB Printing　10　9　8　7　6　5　4　3　2　1

CONTENTS

v

FIGURES AND TABLES

Figures

Tables

ACKNOWLEDGMENTS

This book is based on the evidence collected as part of a large, Wallace Foundation–funded research project. Without the careful reviews and long-standing support for that research provided by our Wallace Foundation project officers, Dr. Mary Mattis and Dr. Edward Pauly, this book would not be the thorough and comprehensive document that we believe has been produced. We value, in particular, all of the feedback that Mary gave us as we moved into our analysis phase, and her skill at creating consensus about what was needed, both from the perspective of the Wallace Foundation and from the members of our research team.

This book would still be hidden somewhere in our computers if it were not for Gabrielle de Montmollin, whose editorial assistance and general ability to keep things rolling in a large and complex project have been valuable assets since this project began in 2003. A number of people who are not primary chapter authors made substantial contributions to the research in a number of ways. At the University of Minnesota, a very special thanks goes to Dr. Michael Michlin and Judy Meath, who assisted in the development of our sample and of state and local databases, coordinated all survey data collection activities, and provided support for data analysis, and also served as team leaders for site visits. Dr. Beverly Dretzke provided excellent and thoughtful work in conducting path analysis of our data. Additional support has been provided by Dr. Judy Hornbacher and Diane Cirksena, whose expertise in on-site data collection was invaluable. Graduate research assistants at the University of Minnesota have been essential partners as well in the data collection and analysis activities; they include Sarah Berman-Young, Chad Schmidt, Monica Jacob, and Sarah Frederickson. Andrea Peterson provided excellent administrative and technical support for a myriad of clerical and computer-related tasks throughout the entire project. At the University of Toronto, Dr. Suzanne Stiegelbauer played a substantial role in site-visit data collection and analysis in Texas and New Mexico. Doris Jantzi, Robin Sacks, and Jing Ping Sun contributed significantly to the analysis of our survey results. We are also grateful to professor Stephen Jacobson (SUNY) for his help with first-round site visits in New York. Finally, successful execution of the site visits would not have possible without the assistance of several research assistants from the University of Toronto, including Leanne Foster, Carol Brayman, Carol Slater, and Joelle Rodway Macri. In the end, we produced a long and scholarly document, which was ably edited by Dr. Richard Western.

From start to finish, the project on which this book is based was about teamwork. As a team, we have shared our wisdom, skills, and voices, with each person stepping forward when such leadership was most needed. We have grown in knowledge of ourselves and within our discipline. In the end, our deepest thanks goes to the Wallace Foundation for supporting us in this work, which we hope will be valuable to many others.

                                   Ken Leithwood and Karen Seashore Louis

ABOUT THE AUTHORS

Kenneth Leithwood is Professor Emeritus at the Ontario Institute for Studies in Education (OISE) at the University of Toronto. His research and writing are about school leadership, educational policy, and organizational change, and he has published many dozens of articles and books on these topics. His most recent books, with colleagues, include *Leading School Turnaround* (2010), *Distributed Leadership: The State of the Evidence* (2009), and *Leading with Teacher Emotions in Mind* (2008). Professor Leithwood is a Fellow of the Royal Society of Canada.

Karen Seashore Louis is Regents Professor of Organizational Leadership, Policy, and Development, and Robert H. Beck Chair in the College of Education and Human Development at the University of Minnesota. Her recent books include *Aligning Student Support with Achievement Goals: the Secondary School Principal's Guide* (with Molly Gordon, 2006), *Professional Learning Communities: Divergence, Depth, and Dilemmas* (with Louise Stoll, 2007), *Building Strong School Cultures: A Guide to Leading Change* (with Sharon Kruse, 2009), and *Educational Policy: Political Culture and Its Effects* (forthcoming). She is a Fellow of the American Educational Research Association, where she also served as the president of Division A (Educational Administration). In 2007 she received the lifetime Contributions to Staff Development award from the National Staff Development Association, and was the recipient of the Campbell Lifetime Achievement Award from the University Council for Educational Administration in 2009.

ABOUT THE CONTRIBUTORS

Stephen E. Anderson is an associate professor in the Department of Theory and Policy Studies in Education at the Ontario Institute for Studies in Education (OISE) at the University of Toronto. His research and publications focus on school district and school leadership and strategies to improve teaching and learning in North America, Africa, South Asia, and Latin America.

Kyla Wahlstrom is the director of the Center for Applied Research and Educational Improvement in the College of Education and Human Development at the University of Minnesota. Her research focuses on educational leadership, professional development of teachers, the politics of school change, and the role of standards in school reform. Dr. Wahlstrom is an experienced school administrator and teacher, and she is the recipient of the Minnesota Association for Supervision and Curriculum Development (MASCD) National Research Award for her ground-breaking study of the effects of later starting times for high schools. Publications include one book, several book chapters, and numerous journal articles and technical monographs used by educational leaders to shape policy decisions across the United States.

Blair Mascall is an associate professor and associate chair in the Department of Theory and Policy Studies at the Ontario Institute for Studies in Education (OISE) at the University of Toronto. His research examines the processes one can use to help guide and monitor the implementation of a variety of educational changes, and the work that leaders can do to help develop people and their organizations during a time of change. Most recently, his research has focused on building evidence about the outcomes associated with distributed leadership in Ontario schools.

Molly F. Gordon is a research associate at the Center for Applied Research and Educational Improvement at the University of Minnesota. Her recent research has focused on educational leadership, parent and community engagement in education, and how educational policies are interpreted and enacted in practice.

Emanda Thomas is a research associate in WestEd's Evaluation Research Program. Dr. Thomas's work involves education research, policy analysis, and program evaluation predominantly within the state context. Recent works with colleagues include *How Do States Influence Leadership in Small Districts* (Educational Policy and Leadership, 2010) and *State Leadership for Learning: An Analysis of Three States* (Educational Administration Quarterly, 2008).

Doris Jantzi is a senior research officer emeritus of the Ontario Institute for Studies in Education (OISE) at the University of Toronto. Her research interests include school leadership, educational reform, and the effects of accountability policies on elementary and secondary schools. Recent research activities include participation in external evaluations of various programs developed within accountability contexts; for example, an intervention aimed at improving educational potential for disadvantaged students and a professional development program for principals intended to help their students meet local achievement standards.

FOREWORD

Leadership and learning. The two terms have been in close proximity within educational discourse and national conversations about educational reform for a decade or more now. Rolling off the lips of a number of educators and scholars, the two have been juxtaposed in ways that presume a connection. And long before any scholars tried their hand at demonstrating any such links, the field has long felt intuitively that they belonged together. Why wouldn't the way a school was led have something very basic to do with how much—and what—its students learned? Why wouldn't "good" leadership (whatever that means) be essential for "good" outcomes from schooling, once the nonschool contributors had been stripped away?

The assumed answer has long been: of course it would. But therein lies the challenge to scholars or reformers who would base their ideas and actions on more than hopes, intuitions, and dreams. The flurry of demonstration projects and scholarly activity they have undertaken to meet this challenge seek answers to the next logical questions: *how*—and *how much*—does leadership contribute to teaching practices and the outcomes of schooling, especially those that reside in student learning? *Under what conditions* might these contributions be enhanced or diminished? And *what forms of leadership* are we talking about, exercised at what levels of the system?

Now, moving into the second decade of the twenty-first century, with a significant investment by The Wallace Foundation and others, we have a wide range of writings that have begun to answer these questions in one or another way. Dozens of reports have probed these matters, and as many or more journal articles. Numerous books, some with titles barely distinguishable from one another—such as *Leading Learning, Leading for Learning, Learner-Centered Leadership, Leadership for Learning: How to Help Teachers Succeed, Connecting Leadership and Learning: Principles for Practice,* and *Connecting Leadership with Learning: A Framework for Reflection, Planning, and Action*—purport to explore the territory (though not always with the goal of demonstrating empirically how what leaders do influences what learners learn).[1] A similarly named non-profit group—The Leadership and Learning Center—regularly beams its messages and services toward schools and districts wishing to work on improving the impacts of leadership on learning. And a flood of international scholarship, now crystallized in a soon-to-be-released *International Handbook on Leadership for Learning,* assembles current understandings on many aspects of this wide ranging territory in sixty-six chapters from scholars around the world, in ways that sensitize us to the different meanings of "leadership," "learning," and their interaction, across national contexts.[2]

In all this talk, it is easy to lose meaning (prompting some to wonder: *How many more books do we need with titles such as these?*). And it is even easier to lose sight of the hard conceptual and empirical bridge-building that will always attend efforts to convincingly link organizational-level activity, which is one or more steps removed from the actual encounter between teacher and learner, to the demonstrated outcomes of that encounter. Anyone who has spent significant time trying to demonstrate these connections knows that compelling "hard" evidence—or even "soft" evidence—connecting the two is exceedingly difficult to come by.

But this book comes closer to meeting that elusive goal than any others to date, and as such it represents a major new landmark in the open space between leadership and learning, one that fully deserves the two terms in its title. In a more comprehensive and rigorous way than any other scholarly work in this line of inquiry, this book explores the "critical connection" between leadership, exercised collectively by formally anointed administrators, teacher leaders, and others, and the teaching and learning that takes place in classrooms. It does so with particular attention to the distribution of leadership that recent scholarship has so aptly underscored as central to the exercise of leadership in complex organizations like schools. Then, to situate these connections in the larger context of reform activity and concern, the study charts various ways that districts and states seek to energize the connection, enhance leaders' sense that they can affect student learning, and develop systems of support for leaders' work.

A scan of the chapter topics in this book and a deeper dig into their contents will reveal the broad scope of contemporary issues related to instructional improvement and educational reform that these analyses touch. In addition to questions of leadership distribution, and the possibility of constructive district and state roles in educational reform, noted earlier, consider this short list of contemporary issues that this study informs:

- Where principals exert their greatest leverage over the improvement of student achievement
- What "instructional leadership" looks like and how it is supported
- How the leadership for reform of high schools necessarily differs from that for schools at other levels
- How community engagement figures in the leadership equation for educational reform
- How rapid turnover of school principals relates to student achievement and how it can be mitigated
- How school and district leadership contributes to the possibilities for evidence-based practice in schools

These matters and more are explored through judicious combinations of quantitative data and comparative case-based examples that help the reader see the leadership dynamics and its consequences at work. The scope of these analyses is strikingly comprehensive.

The study addresses these matters in a well-constructed, representative sample and with sufficient data, both quantitative and qualitative, collected across a long enough period of time, to represent leadership-learning links in a wide range of contexts in which leaders seek to shape the learning environment and outcomes. Not many scholarly teams have the resources and time horizon to attempt such an effort. The authors of this volume have done so.

As we go forward from here, continuing to explore what will always be a rich and elusive domain and trying to translate our understandings of it into terms that actually improve teaching and learning, this volume will occupy a prominent place in educators' and scholars' thinking, no less in their bibliographies, frameworks, and new attempts to lead education toward more powerful forms of schooling. It will not answer all the questions we have or will continue to devise. But it will answer some of the most fundamental questions and will provoke new thinking by educators for many years to come.

Michael S. Knapp
Center for the Study of Teaching and Policy
University of Washington

PREFACE

This book is an outgrowth of what was, at the time it was conducted, one of the most ambitious studies of educational leadership and its contributions to student learning ever undertaken anywhere in the English-speaking world. Situated in the United States and generously sponsored by the Wallace Foundation, the study was conducted in a large number of states, districts, and schools and collected many different types of evidence. The starting points for the study have been described in Leithwood, Louis, Anderson, and Wahlstrom (2004). A technical report of results can be found in Louis et al. (2010), and a non-technical summary of those results can be found in Wahlstrom, Louis, Leithwood, and Anderson (2010). Some of our results also have been published, by now, in academic journals, and these articles are cited in relevant chapters of the book.

We, of course, are not alone in trying to examine the way in which leaders and leadership affect schools, and we have been explicit in how we draw on the work of those who went before us—and also those who were carrying out investigations during the same period during which our study was conducted (2004–2010). In addition to its scope, we believe that we have also made some important theoretical contributions. The tradition in leadership studies tends to fall into two camps. The first examines leaders, paying some attention to their context but emphasizing investigations of what they do and who they are. The second starts by examining the context or the organizational setting and then explores the ways in which leadership may be intertwined with either the processes or the outcomes of the many events and behaviors that can be observed. This study was explicit in its efforts to do both. A second contribution is our explicit attention to integrating perspectives derived from studies carried out in noneducational contexts. We draw on research carried out in for-profit settings, non-profit and government contexts, and in countries other than the United States in order to frame our questions and interpret our findings. Finally, our contribution is important because of our efforts to consistently examine the multiple outcomes of leadership—both on the "bottom line" of student learning and development and also on the adults who work in schools and the communities in which they are located.

For many of our readers, this information will provide sufficient assurance that the claims, recommendations, and guidelines provided within the chapters are well founded. If you are one of them, jump to Chapter One. If you are more curious about how we did our work, read on.

Noteworthy Features of the Research

As compared with most previous studies of educational leadership, particularly noteworthy features of our study include the size of the database, the use of multiple theoretical and methodological approaches to the research, and the comprehensive sources of leadership examined.

Size of the Database

We collected data from a wide range of respondents in 9 states, 43 school districts, and 180 elementary, middle, and secondary schools. Although not a focus of this book, at the state level we conducted interviews with legislators, stakeholders, and members of state education agencies. In districts, we interviewed senior district leaders, elected board members, representatives of the media, and other informants. We used survey instruments and interviews with teachers and administrators, and we conducted classroom observations with most of the teachers we interviewed. Survey data were collected in the first and fourth years of the study, and interviews in districts and schools took place in three cycles over the five years of the project. These efforts yielded, by the end of the project, survey data from a total of 8,391 teachers and 471 school administrators; interview data from 581 teachers and administrators, 304 district level informants, and 124 state personnel; and classroom observation data from 312 classrooms. Finally, we obtained student achievement data for literacy and mathematics in elementary and secondary grades, using scores on states' tests for measuring Adequate Yearly Progress as mandated by the No Child Left Behind Act of 2001.

Multiple Methodological Approaches

We used qualitative and quantitative methods to gain certain advantages associated with multiple-methods research. The advantages typically include "rich opportunities for cross-validating and cross-fertilizing . . . procedures, findings, and theories" (Brewer & Hunter, 1989, p. 13). Our particular use of multiple methods offered opportunities that we had not fully appreciated in the early stages of our work. These included the discovery of significant patterns and relationships in our quantitative evidence, which we then were able to pursue in greater depth, thanks to our qualitative evidence.

For example, from the analysis of our first-round survey data we found that one of the most powerful sources of districts' influence on schools and students was through the development of school leaders' collective sense of efficacy or confidence about their jobs. With this connection well established quantitatively, we then mined principal-interview data to learn in greater detail what districts actually did to develop a sense of efficacy among principals.

Multiple Theoretical Perspectives

In collecting data and working to make sense of our results, we drew on conceptual tools from sociology, sociopsychology, political science, and organizational theory. Sociological concepts informed our understanding of shared leadership, contexts for leadership, and community engagement. Sociopsychological perspectives helped us analyze leader efficacy and (along with organizational theory) the nature of successful leadership practices, as well as the use of evidence in districts and schools, and leader succession. Political science concepts framed our research about state leadership.

Our goal with this seemingly eclectic approach was to draw on the theoretical perspectives best suited to the question at hand—an approach especially useful for a project like ours with multiple principal investigators who had studied and used each strand of theory in their prior work. We shared the view that using multiple methods and theoretical perspectives can provide a powerful antidote to the unintended self-deceptions or oversights that sometimes arise from the use of more unitary approaches. Our approach, however, also challenged us to develop a valid and coherent story line from the data. In that effort, inevitably, we have sacrificed some measure of coherence in order to present a rich account of our findings.

Comprehensiveness of Leadership Sources

Many leadership studies in education focus on a single institutional role. The bulk of it focuses on the principals' role,[1] with a growing but still modest body of attention to district-level leadership.[2] Over the past decade, researchers have also begun to study leadership provided by teachers.[3]

The recent flurry of attention to a broader spectrum or distribution of leadership sensitized us to the remarkable array of people who exercise formal or informal leadership in schools and districts. Research of this sort also shows that the influence of leadership on organizational outcomes arises from the behaviors of these various people acting as leaders in either an "additive" or a "holistic" manner.[4] We could not push our understanding of leadership influence much further without considering the many sources of leadership in the education system and also the web of interactions created by these sources. At the time, our study was one of only a few to have examined leadership at each organizational level in the school system as a whole—state, district, school, classroom, and community.

This comprehensive approach acknowledges an important reality for all leaders: no matter one's hierarchical "level," every leader is at the same time constrained and enabled in some measure by the actions of others, including other leaders, and by the consequences of those actions. Without a better understanding of such antecedents and consequences, we are left with an impoverished appreciation of why leaders behave as they do. Invoking social theory, this more comprehensive perspective has the potential to shift the field of educational leadership research from a dominant preoccupation with "agency" (explaining leaders' behaviors as a function of individual capacities, motivations, and traits) toward a more balanced understanding of how the structures within which leaders work also shape what they do.

Framework Guiding the Study

The framework guiding our study emerged from a review of evidence that Leithwood et al. (2004) completed prior to our data collection and summarized in Figure P.1.[5] As this figure indicates, features of state and district policies, practices, and other characteristics interact with one another and exert an influence on what school leaders do. These features also influence conditions in schools, classrooms, and the professional community of teachers (for the sake of simplicity, we do not connect these variables in Figure P.1). Other stakeholder groups—including the media, unions, professional associations, and community

FIGURE P.1 LEADERSHIP INFLUENCES ON STUDENT LEARNING

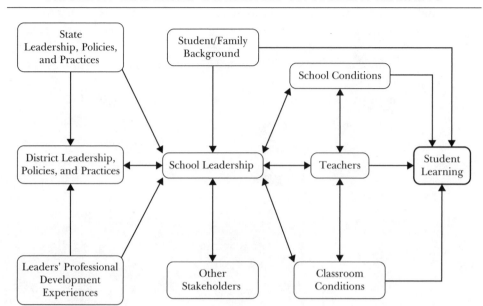

and business groups—also influence school leadership practices. And of course leaders are influenced by their own professional learning experiences and by student and family backgrounds.

School leadership, from formal and informal sources, helps to shape school conditions (including, for example, goals, culture, and structures) and classroom conditions (including the content of instruction, the size of classrooms, and the pedagogy used by teachers). Many factors within and outside schools and classrooms help to shape teachers' sense of professional community. School and classroom conditions, teachers' professional communities, and student/family background conditions are directly responsible for the learning of students.

Three Important Features of the Book

How, you might well ask, is this book any different from the final reports and journal articles already published from the study? First, we have "stripped away" much of the technical information demanded of a research study while preserving our basic results. Second, the book includes only results from our study that have significant implications for policy and practice, leaving most of the implications for future theory and research to our other publications. Finally, we have written the book in a form that we think would make it appropriate not only for individual readers but also for use in continuing education and graduate course contexts.

We hope you will find the fruits of our considerable labor helpful.

LINKING LEADERSHIP
TO STUDENT LEARNING

CHAPTER ONE

LEADERSHIP AND LEARNING

The Critical Connection

Education is widely held to be crucial for the survival and success of individuals and countries in the emerging global environment. U.S. politicians of all stripes have placed education at the center of their political platforms, and education has been at the center of many European and Asian policy agendas. Comparable agreement is also evident about the contributions of leadership to the implementation of virtually all initiatives aimed at improving student learning and the quality of schools. It is therefore difficult to imagine a focus for research with greater social justification than research about successful educational leadership. That was the broad focus for the five-year study on which this book is based, a study generously funded by the Wallace Foundation. We aimed to identify the nature of successful educational leadership and to better understand how such leadership can improve educational practices and student learning.

More specifically, we sought to do the following:

- Identify state, district, and school leadership practices that directly or indirectly foster the improvement of educational practices and student learning.
- Clarify how successful leadership practices directly and indirectly influence the quality of teaching and learning.
- Determine the extent to which individuals and groups at state, district, school, and classroom levels possess the will and skill required to improve student

learning, and the extent to which their work settings allow and encourage them
to act on those capacities and motivations.

- Describe the ways in which, and the success with which, individuals and groups
at the state, district, school, and classroom levels help others to acquire the will
and skill required to improve student learning.

- Identify the leadership and workplace characteristics of districts and schools
that encourage the values, capacities, and use of practices that improve student
learning.

The Educational Leadership Effect

Although leadership is widely thought to be a powerful force for school effectiveness, this popular belief needs to be justified by empirical evidence. There
are five types of such evidence, each offering its own estimate of the size of
leader effects.

One type is evidence from *qualitative case studies*. Studies providing this type
of evidence typically are conducted in exceptional school settings, selected as
exemplars of effectiveness.[1] Some studies report large leadership effects—on
student learning and on an array of school conditions. Other qualitative studies
focus on "typical" schools rather than outliers; these studies often produce
complex pictures of how leadership operates in different settings.[2] Many educators
and scholars find the descriptions provided by case studies to be interesting and
informative. But descriptions of a small number of cases do not yield explanations
of leadership effects for a more general population of schools.[3]

The second type of evidence has been derived from *large-scale quantitative
studies of leadership effects on schools and students*. Evidence of this type, as reported and
reviewed since about 1980,[4] suggests that the direct and indirect effects of school
leadership on student learning are small but significant. Leadership explains
5 to 7 percent of the variation in student learning across schools (not to be con-
fused with the very large within-school effects that are likely). Five to 7 percent,
however, represents about one quarter of the total across-school variation (12 to
20 percent) explained by all school-level variables, after controlling for student
intake or background factors.[5] Classroom factors explain more than a third of
the variation. To date, research of this sort has done little to clarify how leaders
achieve the effects in question, and the implications for leadership practice are
therefore limited.

A third type of evidence arises from studies (also large-scale and quantitative) focused on the *effects of specific leadership practices*. Some evidence of this sort
can be found in the research just summarized. But a meta-analysis conducted

by Marzano, Waters, and McNulty (2003) extends our understanding of the explanatory potential of this type of research. Marzano et al. identify twenty-one leadership "responsibilities" (behaviors) and then calculate an average correlation between each responsibility and the measures of student learning used in the original studies. From these data they calculate estimated effects of the respective responsibilities on student test scores. For example: there would be a 10 percentile-point increase in student test scores resulting from the work of an average principal if she improved her "demonstrated abilities in all 21 responsibilities by one standard deviation" (p. 3). Extending this line of inquiry, Marzano and Waters (2007) provide a comparable analysis of research on district-level leadership, identifying five broad categories of superintendent leadership. Robinson, Lloyd, and Rowe (2008) have provided a more recent meta-analysis of evidence identifying specific school-level leadership practices along with estimates of their independent contributions to student learning. Robinson's work may be distinguished from Marzano and colleagues in two ways: first, the quality screen used for inclusion in the analysis was more stringent; second, the purpose was to locate a smaller number of factors (five) that had the strongest evidence, across multiple studies, for achievement effects.

A fourth type of evidence has been provided by studies of *leadership effects on student engagement,* as distinct from effects on student learning; some evidence suggests that student engagement is a strong predictor of student learning.[6] Recently, at least ten large-scale, quantitative studies, similar in design, have assessed the effects of leadership behavior on student engagement, and all have reported significant positive effects.[7]

Finally, a different but quite compelling sort of evidence about leadership effects comes from research on leadership succession. Unplanned principal succession, for example, is a common source of adverse effects on school performance, regardless of what teachers might do. Studies by Macmillan (2000) and Fink and Brayman (2006) demonstrate the devastating effects of rapid principal succession, especially on initiatives intended to increase student learning. And rapid succession is very common. Clearly, leadership matters.

In developing a starting point for this five-year study, we claimed, based on a preliminary review of research,[8] that leadership is second only to classroom instruction as an influence on student learning. After five additional years of research, we are even more confident about this claim. To date we have not found a single documented case of a school improving its student achievement record in the absence of talented leadership. Why is leadership crucial? One explanation is that leaders have the potential to unleash latent capacities in organizations. Put somewhat differently: most school variables considered separately have only small effects on student learning.[9] To obtain large effects, educators need to create synergy across the relevant variables. Among all the parents, teachers, and policy makers who work hard to improve education, educators in leadership positions are uniquely well positioned to ensure the necessary synergy.

Meanings of Leadership

Leadership can be described by reference to two core functions: *providing direction* and *exercising influence.* Whatever else leaders do, they provide direction and exercise influence. This does not imply oversimplification. Each of these two leadership functions can be carried out in different ways, and the various modes of practice linked to the functions distinguish many models of leadership.

In carrying out these two functions, leaders act in environments marked variously by stability and change. These conditions interact in complementary relationships, and while stability is often associated with resistance and maintenance of the status quo, it is in fact difficult for leaders and other educators to leap forward from a wobbly foundation. To be more precise, stability and *improvement* have a symbiotic relationship. Leaping forward from a wobbly foundation may well produce change, but not change of the sort that most of us value: falling flat on your face is the image that comes to mind. Wobbly foundations and unwise leaping may help to explain why the blizzard of changes adopted by our schools over the past half century has had little effect on the success of our students. School reform efforts have been most successful in schools that have needed them least.[10] These have been schools with well-established processes and capacities in place, providing foundations on which to build—in contrast to the schools most often of concern to reformers, those that are short on essential infrastructure.

How do these concepts come together in a clarification of *leadership*? Leadership is all about organizational improvement. More specifically, it is about establishing agreed-upon and worthwhile directions for the organization in question and doing whatever it takes to prod and support people to move in those directions. Our general definition of leadership highlights these points. Leadership is about direction and influence. Stability is the goal of what is often called management. Improvement is the goal of leadership. But both are very important. One of the most serious threats to stability in a school district is frequent turnover in the ranks of superintendents, principals, and vice principals. Instability at the school level often reflects a failure of management at the district level.

Alternative Models of Leadership Reflected in the Literature

The broad literature on leadership includes an extensive set of models and approaches, many of which overlap. But this full array of models and approaches is only partly reflected in the educational leadership literature, and it has its own models and approaches purpose-built for leadership in school contexts.

Leadership in Nonschool Contexts

Research on leadership in nonschool contexts is frequently driven by theories described by one of our colleagues as "adjectival leadership models." A recent review of such theories identified twenty-one leadership approaches that have been objects of considerable theoretical and empirical development.[11] Seventeen have been especially attractive, and some of them have informed research in school contexts.[12] Here are some examples.

- *Contingent Leadership.* Encompassing research on leadership styles, leader problem solving, and reflective leadership, this two-dimensional conception of leadership explains differences in leaders' effectiveness by reference to a task or relationship style and to the situations in which leaders find themselves. To be most effective, according to this model, leaders must match their styles to their settings.
- *Participative Leadership.* Addressing attention to leadership in groups, shared leadership,[13] and teacher leadership,[14] this model is concerned with how leaders involve others in organizational decisions. Research informed by the model has investigated autocratic, consultative, and collaborative sharing styles.
- *Transformational and Charismatic Leadership.* This model focuses on how leaders exercise influence over their colleagues and on the nature of leader-follower relations. Both forms of leadership emphasize communicating a compelling vision, conveying high performance expectations, projecting self-confidence, modeling appropriate roles, expressing confidence in followers' ability to achieve goals, and emphasizing collective purpose.[15]

Leadership in Education

Leadership research also has been informed by models developed specifically for use in school and district level settings. Of these, models of "instructional leadership" are perhaps the most well known. These models bear some resemblance to more general, task-oriented leadership theories.[16] The instructional leadership concept implies a focus on classroom practice. Often, however, the specific leadership practices required to establish and maintain that focus are poorly defined. The main underlying assumption is that instruction will improve if leaders provide detailed feedback to teachers and include suggestions for change. It follows that leaders must have the time, the knowledge, and the consultative skills needed to provide teachers in all the relevant grade levels and subject areas with valid, useful advice about their instructional practices. Although these assumptions have an attractive ring to them, they rest on shaky ground at best. The evidence to date suggests that few principals have made the time and demonstrated the ability to provide high-quality instructional feedback to teachers.[17] Importantly, the few well-developed models of instructional leadership posit a set of responsibilities for principals that goes well beyond observing and intervening in classrooms—responsibilities touching on vision, organizational culture, and the like.[18]

In addition, studies of school leadership are replete with other adjectives purporting to capture something uniquely important about the object of inquiry; for example, learning leadership,[19] constructivist leadership,[20] and change leadership.[21] Few of these conceptions, however, are the products of a sustained line of inquiry yielding the sort of evidence needed to justify their claims. This observation influenced our approach as we began our study. Eschewing any particular model of leadership, we examined the actual practices across models for which there was significant evidence of desirable effects.

Overview of the Book

Results of our five-year study reported in the two Parts of this book focus on leadership at the school and district levels. Our evidence about state-level leadership can be found in our final research reports. The five chapters in Part One are about school-level leadership in particular. Chapters Two, Three, and Four summarize our evidence about several forms of, and approaches to, shared school leadership and the effects of such leadership on teaching and student learning. Two Chapters (Five and Six) describe in some detail those individual leadership practices with the greatest influence on schools and students.

Part Two of the book is about district leadership and its relationship with school and state leadership. Chapter Seven describes ways in which districts engage parents and the community in their school-improvement efforts and explores the impact of such engagement on students. Chapters Eight and Nine are about leadership efficacy or confidence—its contribution to school improvement and what districts do to develop it. Evidence described in Chapter Ten clarifies the mostly negative effects of rapid principal succession and offers advice to districts about how to ameliorate such effects. Chapter Eleven is about data-use practices in schools and what districts do to help make those practices useful for instructional improvement. Chapter Twelve paints a broad and integrated picture of district approaches to improving leadership, teaching, and learning; Chapter Thirteen unpacks the relationship between district and state-level leadership. We conclude the book with a selected summary of key findings from our study and draw attention, in particular, to key features of successful school leadership.

PART ONE

SCHOOL LEADERSHIP THAT MATTERS FOR STUDENTS

CHAPTER TWO

COLLECTIVE LEADERSHIP

The Reality of Leadership Distribution Within the School Community

Kenneth Leithwood and Doris Jantzi

Claims Supported by Evidence in This Chapter

- Collective leadership has a stronger influence on student achievement than individual leadership.
- Almost all people associated with higher-performing schools have greater influence on school decisions than is the case with people in low-performing schools.
- Higher-performing schools award greater influence than low-performing schools to teacher teams, parents, and students, in particular.
- Principals and district leaders have the most influence on decisions in all schools, and they do not lose influence as others gain influence.
- School leaders have an impact on student achievement primarily through their influence on teachers' motivation and working conditions. Their influence on teachers' knowledge and skills produces much less impact on student achievement.

Collective leadership, as the term is used in this chapter, refers to the extent of influence that organizational members and stakeholders exert on decisions in their schools. This relatively narrow but fundamental perspective on leadership focuses attention on the combined effects of all sources of leadership, along with possible differences in the contributions made by each of these sources (for example, administrators, teachers, students, parents). Guided by this conception of leadership, the analysis described in this chapter addressed the following factors:

- The relative influence on school decision making of each of the individuals or groups potentially contributing to a school's collective leadership.
- The impact of collective leadership on teacher knowledge and skills, motivations, and working conditions.
- Whether different levels of influence on the part of those involved in school decisions are associated with differences in the levels of student achievement across schools.
- Whether differences in the extent of influence exerted by the respective participants is related to differences in levels of student achievement.

Our Starting Points

There were three starting points for the research described in this chapter: a conception of leadership as the exercise of influence, an explanation of leadership as a collective act, and an explanation about the importance of leaders' contributions to teacher performance.

Leadership as Influence

The conception of collective leadership used for this study overlaps with Rowan's conception of "organic" management,[1] defined as follows:

> a shift away from conventional, hierarchical patterns of bureaucratic control toward what has been referred to as a network pattern of control, that is, a pattern of control in which line employees are actively involved in [making] organizational decision[s,] [and] staff cooperation and collegiality supplant the hierarchy as a means of coordinating work flows and resolving technical difficulties.
>
> [Miller & Rowan, 2006, p. 219–220]

Conceptualizing collective leadership as a network of influence and control also locates our study in relation to other research about organizational control structures. A seminal paper by Tannenbaum (1961), for example, introduced the "control graph" as a means of displaying patterns of control in formal organizations. The horizontal axis of a control graph designates each of the "levels" (designated positions) in the organization, while the vertical axis represents the degree of perceived influence or control exercised at each level. Tannenbaum used the control graph to illustrate four prototypical control modes or approaches to leadership:

- *Autocratic* (influence rising with the hierarchical level of the role)
- *Democratic* (higher levels of influence ascribed to those in hierarchically lower levels or roles)
- *Anarchic* (relatively little influence by any level or role)
- *Polyarchic* (high levels of influence by all levels or roles)

Reflecting Rowan's (1990) expectations for organic management under conditions of uncertainty, Tannenbaum also hypothesized that organizational effectiveness will be related to (1) more democratic and (2) more polyarchic forms of control.

The first of these hypotheses arises from two sets of expectations. First, more democratic forms of control will be more consistent with employees' beliefs and values in a democratic society and contribute to higher levels of job satisfaction and morale, whereas autocratic forms of control are expected "to reduce initiative, inhibit identification with the organization and to create conflict and hostility among members" (Tannenbaum, 1961, p. 35). Second, more control by those lower in the hierarchy will lead to greater acceptance of jointly made decisions, along with an increased sense of responsibility for accomplishing organizational goals and increased motivation to accomplish them. Such participation may also contribute to more effective coordination through mutual influence mechanisms.

The second of Tannenbaum's hypotheses, sometimes called the "power equalization" hypothesis, is justified, Tannenbaum claims, by certain results: the improved organizational efficiency realized when more control is exercised by those lower in the hierarchy, and the improved motivation and identification with the organization on the part of those whose power is enhanced. Reasons offered in the current literature on distributed leadership are quite similar to the justification Tannenbaum offers for his two hypotheses.

Collective Leadership Effects

What evidence is there to show that democratic, supportive, and shared forms of leadership are effective? Some empirical evidence may be found in research on teacher participation with peers in planning and decision making[2] and in research on transformational leadership.[3] Several lines of related theory also give rise to expectations of a positive association between organizational effectiveness and the distribution of influence, including theories connected with organizational learning,[4] distributed cognition,[5] and communities of practice.[6]

Nonetheless, there is substantial evidence to the contrary, especially from research in which organizational effectiveness is defined as the organization's bottom line (some measure of productivity) and is assessed using objective indicators, such as student test scores. Tannenbaum (1961) was able to provide only limited support for his hypotheses about organizational control structures. And after about fifteen years of programmatic research about "organic" management, Miller and Rowan (2006) reported: "the main effects are weak[,] and positive effects appear to be contingent on many other conditions" (p. 220). A recent, comprehensive review of research on teacher leadership found only a small handful of studies in which researchers had actually inquired about effects of teacher leadership on students, and the results were generally not supportive.[7]

To date, most research about school leadership has focused on the work of teachers and school administrators. It is certainly possible, however, to conceive of other people—including parents, students, and interested members of the community—as exercising influence in schools as well. The work of Pounder, Ogawa, and Adams (1995) provides one example (there are not many) of research that examines leadership exercised by a broader array of participants. Pounder et al. tested a model of the influence of principals, teachers, parents, and secretaries on a number of mediating variables as well as on a range of school outcomes, providing a useful model for our approach a decade later.

Evidence reported in this chapter looks beyond the school setting to examine leadership from multiple partners, including the superintendent, other district office administrators, principals, other school administrators, teacher leaders, teacher teams, individual teachers, parents and students. We are interested, in particular, in reexamining Tannenbaum's notion that polyarchic influence—more influence from more different individuals and groups—will affect the work of teachers and student learning. However, we are also interested in how the influence of groups and individuals outside the school affects teachers and teaching. For example, staff members in district roles also have an obligation to influence what schools do, although most studies of collective, shared, and distributed leadership have not examined the contribution of district personnel.[8] This chapter is concerned with all of these potential sources of influence.

The Effect of Leadership on Teacher Performance

The effects of leadership on student learning are largely indirect.[9] Studies designed to explore direct effects of leadership rarely detect significant effects, whereas many studies of indirect effects do. The reasons for this are obvious: people in formal leadership positions rarely have a great deal of interaction with students that is directed at learning. Instead, the effects of formal leaders are felt because, as we noted in Chapter One, they create the conditions in which teachers are able to perform well in their classrooms. Most studies since 1996 have been guided by complex causal models, which include a wide array of potential mediators, ranging from effects on individual teacher self-efficacy to changes in the level of trust among school members.

Our analysis in this chapter assumed indirect leadership effects and conceptualized as mediators a set of teacher performance antecedents or causes, including (1) their motivation, (2) their knowledge and skills, and (3) their working conditions. Some combination of these antecedents, we assume, accounts for what teachers actually do.

New Evidence for this Chapter

Evidence for this chapter is based on one set of data collected in the first round of surveys for our larger study, including responses by 2,570 teachers (a 77 percent response rate) from a total of ninety schools in which seven or more teachers completed usable surveys and for which usable student achievement data were available.[10] Student achievement data consisted of three years' school-wide results on state mandated tests of language and mathematics at several grade levels.

Teacher responses to 49 items from a 104-item survey provided the remaining data for this chapter. These items measured the teacher performance antecedents described earlier, as well as the extent of influence of all those in, or associated with, the school. These measures were highly reliable. Remaining sections of this chapter report evidence relevant to each of the three questions addressed by the study: the impact of collective leadership on key teacher variables and student learning, the relative influence of different people and groups engaged in the collective leadership of the school, and the relationship between student achievement in schools and different levels of influence by those people and groups.

Collective Leadership Effects on Teachers and Students

Our analysis indicated that collective leadership was significantly related to all three teacher variables. The strongest relations were with collective leadership and teachers' work setting, followed by teacher motivation. All variables except teachers' knowledge and skill were significantly related to student achievement. Teachers' work setting had the strongest relationship, followed by teachers' motivation and collective leadership. These data also indicated significant relationships among the teacher variables.

A relatively precise indication of our findings can be found in Figure 2.1.[11] This figure summarizes the results of a relatively complex form of statistical analysis (structural equation modeling), a full explanation of which is not needed for purposes of this chapter. It is sufficient to know these facts:

- The model illustrated in the figure explains 20 percent of the variation in student achievement across schools.
- Collective leadership has significant direct effects on all teacher variables. Its strongest effects are on teachers' work settings, followed by teacher knowledge and skill, and motivation (weakest effects).
- Collective leadership accounts for only 13 percent of the variation in teacher knowledge and skills.
- The paths linking the three teacher variables to student achievement indicate:
  - Collective leadership influences student achievement through teacher motivation and work setting.

FIGURE 2.1 THE INDIRECT EFFECTS OF COLLECTIVE LEADERSHIP ON STUDENT ACHIEVEMENT

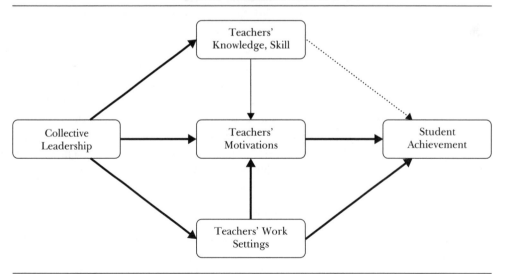

Bold line = significant positive relationship
Solid line = positive relationship
Dotted line = negative relationship

- The effect of teachers' work setting on achievement is significant, but the effect of teacher knowledge and skill is insignificant.
- Total effects on student achievement are greatest for work setting, followed by teacher motivation, and the indirect influence of collective leadership. The higher effect for work setting is explained by its indirect effect through teacher motivation.

We also examined the contribution of students' socioeconomic status (calculated as the percentage of students in a school eligible for free or reduced lunch) to relationships between the three teacher variables and student achievement shown in Figure 2.1. Socioeconomic status is almost always an important predictor of differences in student achievement across schools, and this remained true in our analysis as well.

The measures of teachers' capacity, motivation, and work setting that we used in this study are drawn from a previous research effort.[12] Instead of examining collective leadership, however, the earlier study examined individual leaders' transformational practices. In that study, as in the present one, leadership was more strongly related to teachers' work setting, and it had weaker effects on teacher capacity than on teacher motivation. The effects of individual transformational leadership on student achievement were, however, weaker than the effects of collective leadership as we have measured it here. This suggests some support for the claims about the benefits of more widely distributed leadership in school settings.

Another related earlier study also differed in several important respects from the present study but addressed several of the same questions.[13] Student engagement rather than student achievement was used as the dependent (outcome) variable, and the variables mediating the leadership influences on students were different from those used in the present study. The measure of collective leadership, however, was almost identical to the measure used in this chapter. In contrast to the main findings reported in this chapter, the earlier study found nonsignificant, negative effects of collective leadership on students. This important difference in results offers at least modest support for the argument that the choice of mediating variables is a crucial matter in studies of how leadership affects students.[14]

A second related study addressed the effects of collective leadership on students and used a measure of collective leadership that was almost identical to the one that we used in this study. The dependent measure was, however, student engagement rather than achievement. In addition, the mediating variables differed from those reported earlier, and they included ADD. In contrast to the main findings reported in this chapter, the earlier study found the effects of collective leadership on students were insignificant. This suggests that the choice of mediating and outcome variables may be crucial in investigating how leadership affects students.

The differences we have noted among our three studies might well be accounted for by nontrivial differences in their designs. Consistency among them is greatest with respect to the effects of collective leadership on teachers' internal states. Across all three studies, collective leadership has not been shown to have a demonstrable impact on measures of teacher capacity. (As we will show in Chapter Three, leadership within the school does have such effects.) Also, claims that collective leadership has a significant impact on students have received mixed support. Hiller, Day, and Vance (2006) conclude, based on studies in noneducational settings, that collective leadership is likely to be effective "when teams are engaged in complex tasks that require large amounts of interdependence, but under more routine conditions . . . the benefits of collective leadership have yet to be demonstrated" (p. 388).

The Relative Influence of Collective Leadership Sources

To address this issue, we analyzed teachers' ratings of the extent of influence on school decisions based on nine measured sources of collective leadership. Table 2.1 reports the mean or average ratings by teachers of the influence of each source on school decisions (using a six-point scale). As Table 2.1 indicates, principals and district administrators were given the highest, almost identical ratings (M = 5.30 and 5.28, respectively). Although not reported in the table, the small standard deviations (or ranges) of these ratings indicate considerable agreement among respondents about the perceived influence of people acting in these two roles. There is a significant drop in the rating of the next most influential role: building-level administrators other than the principal, typically the assistant principal (M = 4.75).

TABLE 2.1 SOURCES OF INFLUENCE ON SCHOOL DECISIONS RANKED FROM WEAKEST TO STRONGEST

	Mean
Parent Advisory Groups	3.84
Some Individual Parents	3.96
Some Individual Teachers	4.28
Staff Teams (e.g., departments, grade levels)	4.36
Teachers with Designated Leadership Roles	4.43
Other Building-Level Administrators (not principal)	4.75
District-Level Administrators	5.28
Principals	5.30
Collective Leadership Aggregate	**4.42**

(N = 90 Schools)

Rating Scale: 1 = None, 2 = Very Little, 3 = Little, 4 = Some, 5 = Great, 6 = Very Great

Among teacher sources of influence, teachers with designated leadership roles were perceived to have the strongest influence (M = 4.43), followed by staff teams (M = 4.36), and then some individual teachers (M = 4.28). Our analysis of the significance of the differences among these ratings indicated that teachers with formal leadership roles were considered significantly more influential than staff teams or some individual teachers, and the rating of staff teams was significantly higher than the rating of individual teachers.

Ratings for parents (parent advisory groups and some individual parents) were considerably lower than for teachers, ranging from means of 3.84 to 3.96, a statistically significant difference. Respondents perceived students to have the lowest level of direct influence on school decisions. The very low standard deviation of ratings (not shown) for all sources of influence, especially for principals, reduces the potential strength of relationships with any other variables in our study.

Table 2.2 reports the relationships between each of the individual sources of collective leadership, teacher-related variables (capacity, motivation and setting), and student achievement (that is, mean annual achievement over three years). Among the teacher-related variables, work setting has a significant relationship with seven of the nine sources of leadership (not principals or individual teachers). This surprising result for principals may be a reflection of the low level of variation in the ratings. The strongest relationship is between motivation and staff teams (r = .71). Capacity was the only variable significantly related to principal influence (r = .22), teachers' work setting was the only variable related to other building administrators (r = .32) and to district-level administrators (r = .41).

TABLE 2.2 CORRELATIONS BETWEEN SOURCES OF LEADERSHIP, MEDIATING VARIABLES, AND ACHIEVEMENT[15]

	Capacity	Motivation	Setting	Achievement
Collective Leadership	.36**	.55**	.58**	.34**
District Admin.	.04	.13	.41**	.09
Principal	.22*	.20	.12	−.06
Other Bldg. Admin.	−.01	−.02	.32**	−.11
Teachers Formal	.35**	.54**	.34**	.09
Staff Teams	.44**	.71**	.44**	.28**
Individual Teachers	.23*	.24**	.17	−.08
Individual Parents	.16	.10	.34**	.43**
Parent Advisory	.32**	.44**	.40**	.56**
Students	.17	.55**	.52**	.30**

*Significant at the .05 level.

**Significant at the .01 level.

The influence ascribed to teachers in formally designated roles was significantly correlated with all three teacher-related variables but not with student achievement. The influence of staff teams, individual parents, parent advisory groups, and students was significantly related to student achievement. Student leadership is most strongly related to teacher motivation ($r = .55$). Parent advisory teams are most strongly related to motivation ($r = .44$) and achievement ($r = .56$). Individual parents are most strongly related to achievement ($r = .43$) and weakly to setting ($.34$). There appears to be a differentiation between those leaders who are members of the school staff and those who are not. Staff teams have stronger relations with all three teacher variables than any of the others within school collective leadership sources, and staff teams are the only in-school source of collective leadership related to achievement ($r = .28$).

We were intrigued to see that the two sources of leadership consistently showing significant relationships with all three teacher-related variables and with student achievement were groups. Staff teams and parent advisory groups had significant correlations with all our mediators and with student achievement. In schools with high levels of student achievement and high ratings for capacity, motivation, and setting, we are more likely to see higher levels of influence from staff teams and parent advisory groups. This suggests there may be something about the collective nature of these roles that adds to their influence in the schools.

In sum, our results indicate the following:

- School decisions are influenced by a broad array of groups and people, reflecting a distributed conception of leadership.
- The degree of influence exercised by these people and groups reflects a traditional, hierarchical conception of leadership in organizations. Teachers rate the influence of traditional sources of leadership much higher than they rate nontraditional sources.
- Among teacher roles, the more formalized the leadership expectation, the greater the perceived influence.
- Nonetheless, the influence of parents and students is significantly related to student achievement. This result may reflect the well-known effects of student socioeconomic status on achievement.

If the profession has become enamored of distributed forms of leadership, as one might infer from current scholarship, the responses of teachers surveyed here suggest that few changes detectable by teachers have actually occurred in schools. The groundswell of support for distributed conceptions of leadership may well be a kind of meta-rhetoric denoting little reality on the ground. This possibility is consistent with a familiar criticism of schools: as a means of legitimizing their work, they are more concerned with the appearance than the substance of change.

Despite a decades-long effort to restructure schools, in part to give parents a greater voice in school decisions, we see little evidence that teachers perceive much influence from parents or from students.[16] This outcome probably reflects the well-known and persistent challenges teachers and administrators face in creating authentic relationships with parents for school-improvement purposes.

Our results also reinforce two other claims. First, significant change in schools requires much more than encouragement and rational argument,[17] the strategies that have often been relied on to promote greater parent influence. Second, as Jaques (2003) has long maintained, hierarchy is a necessary, unavoidable feature of any large organization, even when participants add structures and procedures to encourage lateral influence within the hierarchy. If Jaques is correct, current expectations regarding the extent to which leadership distribution is either possible or desirable in schools will need to be severely modified.

Patterns of Collective Leadership and Student Achievement

As we reported earlier, on average, teachers perceived influence in their schools to be exercised in a distributed but still hierarchical manner. Nevertheless, prompted by widespread claims from many organizational theorists about the benefits of more distributed forms of leadership, we wanted to know whether variations in these perceptions of influence were related to levels of student achievement in schools. To address this question, we returned to Tannenbaum's early work (reviewed earlier) on control graphs.[18]

To distinguish schools by mean levels of achievement averaged over three years, we constructed a control graph of our own. As Figure 2.2 indicates, we first divided the schools in our sample into quintiles on the basis of mean annual student achievement scores. Then we compared teachers' ratings of each source of collective leadership influence across quintiles.

Results displayed in Figure 2.2 indicate that teachers in the highest-achieving schools (Quintile 5) generally attributed higher levels of influence to all people and groups than did teachers in lower-achieving schools. Even though teachers in higher-achieving schools attributed greater influence to nontraditional leadership roles, they also perceived that those in traditional leadership roles had the same *relative* amount of influence. For example, an increase in the influence of staff teams or parents does not mean less influence for principals and district administrators. Furthermore, teachers in schools whose students achieved in the highest and second-highest quintiles attributed significantly more relative influence to

FIGURE 2.2 RELATIONSHIPS BETWEEN SOURCES OF COLLECTIVE LEADERSHIP INFLUENCE AND STUDENT ACHIEVEMENT

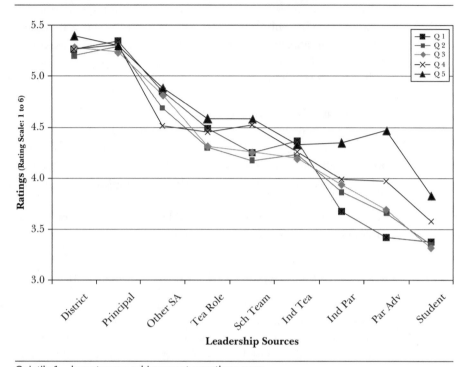

Quintile 1 = lowest mean achievement over three years

staff teams. Teachers in the highest-quintile schools attributed significantly more relative influence, as well, to individual parents and to groups of parents.

Although we do not include a table reporting all correlations, we found student socioeconomic status (SES) to be significantly, although unsurprisingly, related to student achievement—a possible explanation for the high level of influence parents and students apparently exercise in schools in the higher quintiles of performance, which generally serve higher SES students. Three correlations seem especially interesting: those between SES and the influence of (1) individual parents ($r = .35$), (2) parent advisory committees ($r = .53$), and (3) students ($r = .36$). The influence of staff teams was also related to student SES as strongly as student influence was ($r = .34$).[19] Others also have reported evidence of the relationship between SES and parental involvement and, more interestingly, between SES and levels of collegial control in schools.[20] Schools in high SES communities tend to build collegial professional practices among teachers and to have a particularly strong focus on student learning.

This evidence indicates, in sum, that participants acting in traditional leadership roles remain very influential in higher-performing schools—a result not evident from the correlation analyses reported in Table 2.2. In the highest-performing schools, everyone seems to have more influence than participants in low-performing schools, where leadership may be "laissez-faire," an approach to leadership almost invariably found to be ineffective.[21]

What Might We Conclude?

Evidence described in this chapter highlights three claims. First, collective leadership has a stronger influence on student achievement than does individual leadership. This suggests that the current emphasis on distributing and sharing leadership might have the potential for real payoffs. At the very least it confirms the assumption that increasing the influence of many actors in a school system will not undermine effectiveness and accountability, but potentially enhance them.

Second, in higher-performing schools, principals and district leaders retain the highest levels of influence, but almost all people are granted greater influence than is the case in low-performing schools. The big "winners" in the influence "lottery" in higher-performing schools are parents and teachers acting together, a topic that will be explored more fully in Chapter Seven. But with these two exceptions, the overall hierarchical control structure of schools remains largely unchanged. It is a structure that conforms, we believe, with Jaques' (2003) claim about requisite hierarchy in social organizations large enough to place significant demands on the coordination of its members' actions.

Third, collective leadership is linked to student achievement indirectly, through its effects on teacher motivation and teachers' workplace settings. As in several of our previous studies,[22] we found significant but much weaker relationships between leadership and teacher capacity. The way in which we measured teacher capacity may help to explain these results. It was primarily a measure of professional development opportunities—that is, opportunities to learn from colleagues in a variety of ways—rather than a direct measure of the knowledge and skills teachers need to foster student achievement. In effect, although principals and their coleaders exert a significant influence on teacher access to professional learning opportunities, their power to influence the quality and impact of those activities on teacher knowledge and skills may be more limited. This qualification, however, does not diminish our finding that motivation and work settings—factors subject to leadership influence—have significant effects on student achievement. In light of this, a narrow focus on leadership efforts aimed at building teacher capacities would be misguided.

Implications for Policy and Practice

Three implications for policy and practice are suggested by the evidence described in this chapter:

1. In their efforts to improve student achievement, school- and district-level leaders should, as a matter of policy and practice, extend significant decisional influence to others in the school community. This implication for practice is also justified by evidence in Chapter Three. Other justification for distributed influence can be found in many other sources; for example, in studies of collaborative cultures and professional learning communities.

2. District leaders and principals working to extend influence to others should not be unduly concerned about losing their own influence. Our data depict the hierarchical structure of influence typically associated with roles and responsibilities in schools and districts—a structure that conforms, we believe, with Jaques' (2003) claim about requisite hierarchy in social organizations large enough to place significant demands on the coordination of its members' actions.

3. In responding to demands that they focus sharply on improving their teachers' instructional capacities, school and district leaders should not overlook the influence they can have on classroom practice through their efforts to motivate their teachers and to align their teachers' work settings with what is known about effective instructional practice.

Reflections

1. Who has influence in your setting? Of the five influence patterns displayed in Figure 2.2, which most closely matches the pattern in your school (or district)?
2. How do the working conditions in your school contribute to the instructional practices of teachers? Which ones seem to aid teachers in doing their best work and which ones seem to impede them?
3. What could a school leader do to significantly influence the motivation of teachers?

CHAPTER THREE

SHARED AND INSTRUCTIONAL LEADERSHIP

When Principals and Teachers Successfully Lead Together

Karen Seashore Louis and Kyla Wahlstrom

Claims Supported by Evidence in This Chapter

- Leadership practices targeted directly at improving instruction have significant effects on teachers' working relationships and indirectly on student achievement.
- When principals and teachers share leadership, teachers' working relationships are stronger and student achievement is higher.
- Leadership effects on student achievement occur largely because effective leadership strengthens professional community—a special environment within which teachers work together to improve their practice and improve student learning. Professional community, in turn, is a strong predictor of instructional practices that are strongly associated with student achievement.
- The link between professional community and student achievement may be explained by reference to a school climate that encourages levels of student effort above and beyond the levels encouraged in individual classrooms.
- Leadership and improved instruction alleviate but do not eliminate the effects of concentrated poverty in schools.

The previous chapter described how leadership in school decision making affects teachers and student learning. This chapter focuses more narrowly, looking at the working relationships between principals and teachers within schools. We focus on principals and teachers for two main reasons. First, professionals acting within schools are uniquely well positioned to affect student experiences, both in and out of classrooms. Unlike district administrators or advisory groups, they work directly with students on a daily basis. Second, the narrower focus pushes us beyond a simple definition of leadership as influence, to a more explicit specification of the behaviors that may account for such influence. We begin with three specific questions:

- Do specific principal leadership behaviors—the sharing of leadership with teachers, the development of trust relationships among professionals, and the provision of support for instructional improvement—affect teachers' work with one another and their classroom practices?
- Do these leadership behaviors and attributes contribute, either directly or indirectly, to student achievement?
- Do these leadership behaviors have the potential to help alleviate differences in achievement between students from different socioeconomic backgrounds and racial groups?

Evidence for this chapter is based on the survey data collected from teachers, as well as from student achievement data. An exploration of the more nuanced interpretation of the findings from this chapter will be explored in Chapters Four, Five, and Six. In our analysis, we assumed that both principal-teacher relationships (indicated by trust, instructional leadership, and perceptions of shared leadership) will affect how teachers work with each other (teacher-teacher relationships as indicated by professional community). These in turn will affect classroom practice. Classroom practice, particularly the type of instruction that combines elements of both teacher-directed and constructivist approaches, will be the primary determinant of student learning. We emphasize the importance of classroom practice as the direct cause of increased student learning because there is little evidence, from either survey or qualitative research, that principal leadership can have a direct effect apart from changes in teacher practice. The ways in which we measured each of the constructs that are part of our analysis are documented in other published sources, and are shown in Appendix A.[1] In the remainder of this chapter we will explain what we found with respect to our three questions, and we will discuss the implications, including how the findings will be further explored in later chapters.

Our Starting Points

We began our investigation of these questions by turning to the emerging research about the importance of leaders in shaping a school's culture and climate, including (1) variables on which principals can have some direct effect, such as principal-teacher relations, trust, and shared leadership; (2) variables on which principals may have less influence, such as teacher-to-teacher relations in professional communities, and collective responsibility; and (3) variables over which the principal has indirect control, such as teachers' sense of personal efficacy and the quality of instruction.

Starting with Instruction

As in the previous chapter, we assumed that the effects of principal leadership on students are almost entirely indirect. The long line of research on school effectiveness shows that classroom environment and the quality of instruction are the variables linked most strongly to student learning (although some questions remain about the relative effectiveness of specific modes of instruction).[2] Teacher characteristics (such as type of degree or certification) have limited effects,[3] operating for the most part indirectly, through their impact on instruction.[4] In other words: *to learn how leadership contributes to student learning, we must ask how leadership affects instruction.*[5]

Various models of effective instruction have evolved over the last several decades, but controversies and differences among them remain unresolved. An early review of research showed that certain instructional practices were consistently associated with student achievement,[6] including creating academic objectives to establish learning expectations; using particular strategies for classroom management; and pacing instruction appropriately, given the content to be taught and the characteristics of the learners. Variants on these approaches have often been lumped together under the label of "direct instruction," wherein teachers' control over the learning environment is central to their ability to create learning environments for most students. Robert Slavin has been one of the strongest supporters of direct instruction over the past several decades, and he points to the importance of teacher control and pacing for the learning of struggling students.[7] In contrast, after the late 1980s, a number of scholars returned to the approaches favored by John Dewey, and they emphasized inquiry-based instructional models, in which the teacher's most important role was to design lessons or learning experiences that guided students toward new understanding through exploration and induction, an approach that is often labeled "constructivist teaching."[8] Although some approaches to constructivism emphasized modest roles for teachers (as "guides on the side"), others gave teachers clear responsibilities consistent with traditional roles, as well as for organizing learning environments that develop students' sense of responsibility for their own learning.[9]

Today, teachers often blend aspects of both direct and constructivist approaches, and only a few scholars hold to extreme positions on the direct versus constructivist debate. A growing body of evidence shows that student learning is enhanced when teachers exercise appropriate control over the pacing of classroom work,[10] at least when the activity in question is based on rich materials and stimuli. Recent reviews have begun to reemphasize the role of the teacher in directing student learning, but within an inquiry-based curriculum that gives students some personal responsibility for their own learning.[11]

Although the issue of what constitutes good teaching is far from resolved, in our work we choose to think of good instruction as requiring a blended approach, one that incorporates direct influence over the pacing and content of classroom work while also providing opportunities for students to take charge of their own learning and construct their own knowledge. We called this style of teaching "focused instruction."[12] In our view, if we overlook the theoretical debates,[13] we find that the most effective "real teachers" combine elements of a traditional teacher-centered model with elements of constructivist models, consistent with other research on instructional approaches that are linked to student achievement. This assumption is consistent with the work of Fred Newmann and his colleagues, who have looked at instructional practices that are both engaging and highly focused on important subject matter.[14]

In this chapter, we use a measure of focused instruction that combines responses to five questions, indicating the extent to which:

- The teacher enables students to construct their own knowledge.
- Disruptions of classroom time are minimized.
- The teacher assumes that most students in the classroom are capable of taking charge of their own learning (in age appropriate ways).
- The teacher emphasizes the development of deep knowledge of the core subject(s) that are being taught.
- A rapid pace of instruction in the classroom is maintained.[15]

Our initial examinations of instruction suggested that teachers who score high on the index of focused instruction are more likely to work in schools where students are achieving at higher levels. Furthermore, this instructional approach has a positive association with instruction in schools with higher percentages of students who are often less likely to succeed in school because they come from

FIGURE 3.1 RACE/ETHNICITY, POVERTY, FOCUSED INSTRUCTION, AND ACHIEVEMENT IN 138 SCHOOLS[16]

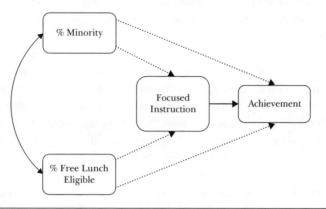

Solid line = positive relationship
Dotted line = negative relationship

poorer families or families identified with immigrant, ethnic, and minority groups. Figure 3.1 shows in a graphic way that focused instruction matters, although it does not eliminate the association between the school's demographic composition and its achievement. In this figure, a negative relationship is indicated by a dotted line, and a positive relationship by a solid line. The figure indicates that schools in our study with higher percentages of minority and poor students not only had weaker scores on state math tests, but they also were less likely to have a high level of focused instruction in all classrooms. However, when they did experience focused instruction, poor and minority dominant schools fared better on standardized tests.

Instructional Leadership

As Hallinger (2005) notes in a recent review of scholarship, *instructional leadership* is an idea that refuses to go away, although it has been poorly defined since it was first introduced in the 1970s. Research to date has provided some insight into the link between the practices of school-level leaders and the provision of high-quality instruction, whether teacher-directed or teacher-guided. In the school building, the principal is expected to understand the tenets of quality instruction and to have sufficient knowledge of the curriculum to ensure that appropriate content is being delivered to all students.[17] This presumes the principal either is capable of providing constructive feedback to improve teaching or can design a system in which others provide this support. Research shows that consistent, well-informed support from principals makes a difference,[18] and accordingly, principals face increasing pressure to deliver (or at least promote) better support for instruction.

In their efforts to act as instructional leaders, principals can benefit from support provided, for example, through professional development programs. Those who do get support are more likely than others to enact this leadership role consistently.[19] We will explore this issue in greater detail in Chapter Nine. But there are still controversies about what instructional leadership might entail. Some scholars emphasize the importance of principals' coaching and modeling that demonstrates deep understanding of curricular content and instructional materials.[20] Others pay more attention to principals' support for improved instruction through the development of improved learning and innovation contexts for teachers, focusing on the ability of principals to stimulate teachers' innovative behavior.[21] Those who emphasize the importance of deep content knowledge typically study elementary schools. However, secondary school principals cannot be coaches and in-classroom guides for the multiple disciplines that are taught in their schools. Because our study includes secondary schools, we chose, in both this chapter and others, to emphasize supportive behaviors as well as direct coaching or modeling of instruction.

Shared Leadership

As noted in Chapter Two, reform proposals have recommended the inclusion of teachers in shared leadership roles for several decades. In the late 1980s and early 1990s, efforts to promote school-based management often included formal representation of teachers in decision making. Many investigations of these efforts report weak implementation,[22] and there are mixed results regarding whether increasing teacher influence will have an impact on improvements in instruction and achievement. Some research has found that increasing teacher influence may improve schools significantly.[23] Other research suggests that teachers' involvement in formal decision making or leadership roles will have limited impact on student achievement.[24] Sharing leadership may have its greatest impact by reducing teacher isolation and increasing commitment to the common good.[25] Experiencing informal influence and feedback through professional discussions encourages a focus on shared practices and goals,[26] and it may foster organizational innovation.[27]

In spite of the mixed evidence, recent policy discussions (within, for example, the Education Commission of the States, the Council of Chief State School

Officers, and teacher professional associations) suggest broad support for expanding teachers' participation in leadership and decision-making tasks. Still, what constitutes and promotes the distribution or sharing of leadership in a school is somewhat unclear. In this paper we define *shared leadership* broadly to denote teachers' influence over, and their participation in, school-wide decisions with principals. This view of shared leadership reflects an emerging consensus among scholars about the people who are concerned with formal and informal enactments of leadership roles, and also distinguishes our approach from those who blend the concepts of *shared leadership* and *instructional leadership*.[28]

Trust

The concept of *organizational trust* has been a staple of organizational research for some time. It matters a great deal whether participants in an organization trust the decision-making capacity of the organization's leaders. Driscoll (1978) found that such trust predicts overall satisfaction with the organization better than employee participation in decision making. A recent study examined changes in levels of trust within work teams, and found the perceived ability of colleagues was a strong predictor of trust, and trust was a significant predictor for risk-taking behaviors.[29] In the past two decades, studies of trust as a factor in school improvement have begun to illuminate certain actions leaders take to positively alter the culture in a school.[30]

Supportive principal behavior and faculty trust are significantly correlated in both elementary and secondary schools.[31] In schools with higher levels of engaged teachers, moreover, teachers express higher levels of trust in their colleagues, more collective decision making, and a greater likelihood that reform initiatives are fully implemented and affect student achievement. Key leadership behaviors and specific actions are known to engender trust. For example, "competence" is demonstrated by "engaging in problem solving, setting standards, buffering teachers, pressing for results" (Tschannen-Moran, 2004, p. 34). More recently, trust has been shown to predict how educators interpret their superiors' ability to carry out more technical and transformational leadership functions.[32]

Embedded in the notion of trust is the key distinction between the trustee and the truster; that is, those having more or less power (or dependence) in a particular situation.[33] Teachers' views of trustworthy principals tend to be based on the leadership characteristics outlined earlier. However, we have much less information about why principals do or do not trust their teachers than vice versa.

Figure 3.2 summarizes our findings about the relationship between these three aspects of leadership as they are perceived by teachers, and focused

FIGURE 3.2 LEADERSHIP AND FOCUSED INSTRUCTION IN 138 SCHOOLS

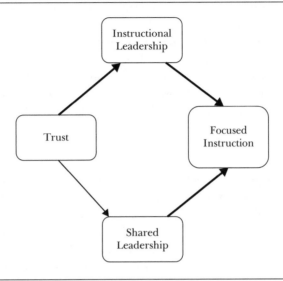

Solid line = positive relationship
Bold line = strong positive relationship

instruction. Only significant relationships are shown, and stronger relation-ships are indicated by the bold lines. As the figure shows, all of the leadership behaviors are associated with focused instruction. Their association is quite strong: together they predict a third of the variation between schools in the prevalence of focused instruction. However, trust appears to be a precondition for leadership behaviors that will affect instruction, not a direct cause. In schools with higher levels of trust, principals are also more likely to be engaged in instructional behaviors and to be actively involved in discussions about instruc-tional improvement; however, the direct effect of trust on focused instruction is insignificant.

Teacher Leadership and Professional Community

As we have focused thus far on principal-teacher relationships, we assumed, based on previous research, that teacher-teacher relationships are even more important as a foundation for how teachers work to improve instruction.[34] If principals are to have an impact on instruction by building a positive school culture, they must foster collaborative and effective working relationships among teachers.[35] Here we emphasize the importance of *professional community*, largely because accumulating evidence shows that it is related to improved instruction, student achievement,[36] and shared leadership, one of our leadership variables.[37]

York-Barr and Duke (2004) view professional community as a vehicle for the exercise of teacher leadership, a perspective that we adopt in this paper. Supportive interaction among teachers in school-wide professional communities enables them to assume various roles with one another—as mentor, mentee, coach, specialist, advisor, facilitator, and so on. However, professional community amounts to more than just support. It also includes *shared values*, a *common focus and collective responsibility for student learning, reflective dialogue about improvement,* and the *purposeful sharing of practices*—all of which may be thought of as distributed leadership.[38]

Findings from several studies cited earlier suggest that when the professional community focuses on the quality of student learning, teachers adopt instructional practices to enhance students' learning. Although many factors affect whether or not professional community exists in a school, one highly significant factor is strong leadership by principals.[39] Professional community is closely associated with organizational learning, and the term "professional learning communities" has become a common shorthand expression among practitioners. Thus the presence of a professional community appears to foster collective learning of new practices—provided there is principal leadership.[40]

Figure 3.3 shows the results of our teacher surveys. As with the previous figures, the bold lines represent stronger relationships, the solid lines positive but weaker relationships. As in previous studies, we find teacher-teacher relationships are associated with the kind of instruction that is related to student learning. However, the direct effects of professional community on student learning are limited. Most of the benefits to students that accrue because teachers are working together around issues of instruction and school improvement occur because there are actual changes in classroom practice moving toward more focused instruction, blending constructivist and teacher-directed approaches. In other words, the development of teacher teams that take responsibility for improvement stimulates the development of effective learning environments for students. But professional community still has a modest direct relationship with achievement. This suggests, we argue, that in schools where teachers work together intensively on instruction and learning, they also create a school climate that is supportive of student learning outside the classroom.

FIGURE 3.3 PROFESSIONAL COMMUNITY, FOCUSED INSTRUCTION, AND STUDENT LEARNING IN 138 SCHOOLS

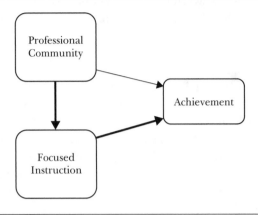

Solid line = positive relationship
Bold line = strong positive relationship

Additional Evidence: Do Principal Behaviors and Attributes Affect Student Achievement?

As noted earlier, our data suggest that principal behaviors and attributes, as assessed by teachers, have very strong associations with how teachers work together. However, the evidence presented so far does not fully address the question of whether the effects of leadership on student achievement are significant, or whether they provide any levers for improving the achievement outcomes for the many students who apparently are still being left behind. In order to understand these issues, we need to dig behind the visual summaries that we have presented so far.

We initially assumed that the effects of leadership on student achievement are largely indirect, operating through other variables. We first examined this assumption by looking at simple correlations, presented in Table 3.1. The results indicate that achievement scores in mathematics are significantly associated with focused instruction, professional community, and teachers' trust in the principal. They are not significantly associated with principal behaviors (instructional leadership and shared leadership), which provides some support for our assumption.

Two other features of this table stand out. First, we look at the measures we have been examining as possible mechanisms by which adult relationships might affect what happens to students in classrooms. Clearly, they are all strongly

TABLE 3.1 RELATIONSHIP BETWEEN SURVEY VARIABLES AND STUDENT ACHIEVEMENT: CORRELATION COEFFICIENTS

	2004–05 Mean Math Proficiency for That Building	Building Mean Focused Instruction	Building Mean Instructional Leadership T2	Building Mean Trust T2	Building Mean Shared Leadership	Building Mean Professional Community
2004–05 Mean Math Proficiency for That Building	1					
Building Mean Focused Instruction	.269** .006	1				
Building Mean Instructional Leadership T2	-.071 .475	.310** .001	1			
Building Mean Trust T2	.249* .011	.436** .000	.490** .000	1		
Building Mean Shared Leadership	.170 .052	.330** .000	.106 .276	.256** .007	1	
Building Mean Professional Community	.198* .023	.510** .000	.420** .000	.451** .000	.597** .000	1
% Free Lunch	-.399** .000	-.124 .199	.156 .068	-.053 .586	-.133 .124	.004 .96
% Minority	-.398* .000	-.123 .206	.133 .121	-.209 .03*	-.041 .633	.060 .488

(N=138 Schools)
*Significant ≤.05
**Significant ≤.001

FIGURE 3.4 EFFECTS OF PRINCIPALS' LEADERSHIP BEHAVIOR ON TEACHERS AND STUDENT ACHIEVEMENT

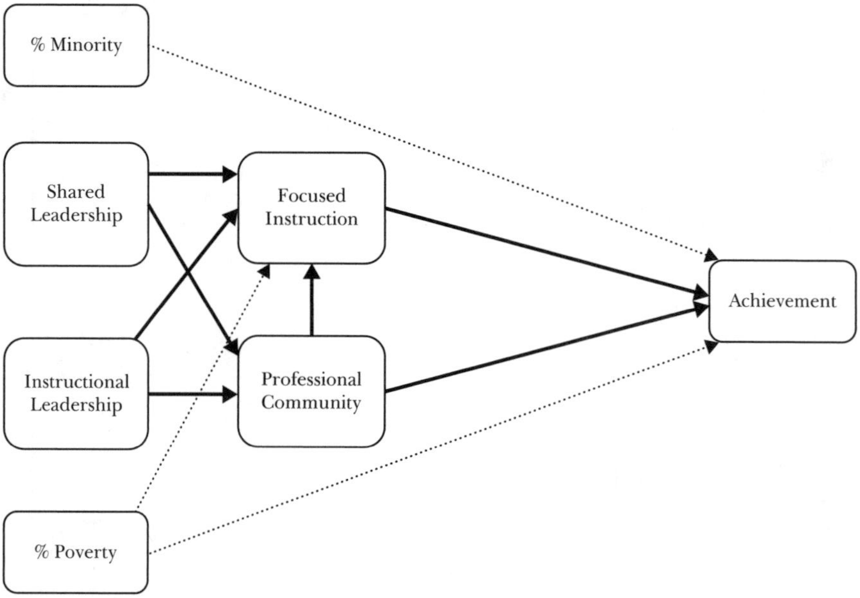

Bold line = strong positive relationship
Dotted line = negative relationship

associated. In addition, teachers whose experience with other adults is positive on one of our dimensions tend to have similarly positive responses on the others. In sum, although the results are confirmatory, they suggest a need for further analysis to investigate how the relationships among the variables may combine to affect teachers' classroom practice and student learning.

Figure 3.4 presents the model that illustrates the least complicated approach to answering the questions motivating our inquiry. Note that the figure does not include the trust variable. Our results in this analysis confirmed what we noted earlier; namely, that trust seems to add relatively less to the explanation of the effect of leadership on professional community, focused instruction, and achievement than the principal's behaviors. Bold lines indicate strong and significant relationships. Dotted lines indicate a negative relationship. We have eliminated all lines that are insignificant.

The model makes the simplifying assumption that we do not know enough to examine a causal relationship among the measures of leadership behavior and characteristics. Thus they are positioned at the left of the figure, along with the variables reflecting the percentage of students who are eligible for free and reduced-price lunches and the percentage of students belonging to ethnic or minority groups. In light of prior research, we assume that leadership behaviors and characteristics are the factors most likely to create the conditions necessary for professional community to develop among teachers, and to stimulate more focused instruction.[41] We can summarize the findings of the structural equation model as follows:

- Both *principal instructional leadership* and *shared leadership* have significant effects on teachers' working relationships (professional community), and on focused instruction. Neither has a significant direct relationship with student achievement.
- *Student poverty* is negatively associated with the prevalence of focused instruction.
- Both the level of *student poverty* (as measured by eligibility for free and reduced-price lunches) and the *percentage of students from ethnic and minority families* have a strong negative relationship with achievement. Neither has an effect on the level of professional community.
- Both *focused instruction* and *professional community* have significant positive associations with achievement.
- As a brief summary, the analysis suggests that leadership—whether from principals or teachers through their work in professional communities—matters for student achievement. In addition, principal leadership provides a solid foundation for both teacher leadership and higher quality instruction.

What Might We Conclude?

Efforts to determine how principal leadership affects student achievement have a rich, albeit recent, history. Our analysis provides the most extensive empirical test to date of whether instructional leadership, shared leadership, and trust in the principal, when considered together, have the potential to increase student learning. The answer is an unqualified *yes*, but the findings are complex and suggest a need for further analysis.

First, the emotional side of principal behavior, which we have assessed by reference to teachers' trust in the principals as ethical, caring, and competent, has on its own been shown to have a strong relationship to student outcomes. In our study, however, its relative significance diminishes when we take into consideration principal behaviors, as measured by our constructs of instructional leadership and shared leadership. Still, we are not prepared, based on a single study and a simple structural equation model, to discount the importance of the emotional side of leadership, which has been shown in studies in industry as well as education to have powerful effects on the way in which people engage with their work.

Because trust is highly correlated with other key measures used in this study, we are inclined to say that any assumption that trust has limited effects in creating a climate for improved instruction is unwarranted. Further investigation is required to determine how the emotional side of leadership interacts with other leadership behaviors and with teachers' relationships with one another. Follow-up research might build on existing work, and should also attend more directly to how trust affects instrumental leadership actions.[42]

Shared leadership and instructional leadership are important variables, but they are indirectly related to student achievement. Both seem to gain their influence because of their strong relationships to other variables: the way in which teachers organize themselves into professional communities, reflective discussions about instruction, and a sense of collective responsibility for student learning. This finding is hardly surprising when we consider the arguments for shared leadership, which generally emphasize expanding the sphere of responsibility and creativity to meet pressing school needs. The largely indirect effects of instructional leadership are, however, equally significant. Although principals may engage in classroom visits and model good teaching by working with individual teachers, individual interventions (which would have emerged as a direct effect on good classroom practice) seem less important than the detailed investigations of elementary schools suggest.[43]

This finding is important because shared leadership and instructional leadership are often regarded as alternative strategies for reaching the desired end of student learning. Those advocating instructional leadership emphasize the need to maintain a singular focus on classroom practice as the key to improving student achievement, and they point to the important role of the principal as a model. Others who look at shared leadership point to the importance of creating a learning organization in which all eyes are focused on leadership for learning. Our data suggest that these are complementary approaches and that both may be necessary. Thus, using a larger and more diverse sample, we affirm Marks and Printy's (2003) work, which emphasizes the importance of combining leadership foci (in their case, transformational and instructional).

The findings regarding the important effects of the characteristics of a school's student body are particularly important as we begin to develop theories of effective school leadership that contribute to more equitable learning outcomes for all students. Poverty and ethnic minority status are highly correlated in our sample, but our analysis suggests a number of points that are important:

- Although both poverty and ethnic minority status have strong and independently negative associations with achievement, their effects are diminished when we take into account the internal leadership and instructional practices that exist in the school.
- This finding is clearer in the case of concentrated poverty. *In other words, strong shared and instructional leadership, strong professional community, and strong instruction moderate the effects of concentrated poverty.* The extent to which internal conditions can minimize the combined effects of poverty and ethnic/minority concentration is less certain.
- Concentrated poverty is also associated with lower levels of the most effective instructional practices, even though it has no relationship with professional community. In other words, professional community in low-income schools is less likely to lead to the kind of instruction that supports learning, even under conditions in which there is strong principal leadership.

These points are pertinent to the continuing dilemma of how to create more effective instructional practices in the schools in which they are most needed.

Implications for Policy and Practice

Four implications for policy and practice emerge from this chapter:

1. Teachers and educators holding formal administrative responsibilities need to acknowledge and act on the importance of collective, shared efforts to improve instruction.

Professional learning community is regarded by some teachers as a code term for an administratively initiated program designed to encourage teachers to analyze student achievement data and turn it into improved test scores. Our analysis suggests that the reality is more complex. Teachers do need to work together to improve instruction and student learning, but administrators also need to be part of the process. The process may be as simple as having principals participate in professional development activities for teachers, or as complex as reorganizing the formal authority structure of the school. In any case, it requires a rethinking of the "bright line" that often separates administration and teaching.

2. To realize their potential as instructional leaders, principals working in middle schools and high schools need particular modes of support. They face a

distinct challenge—shaped by the large, complex settings in which they work—and they need a level of support commensurate with their distinct needs.

Simply increasing pressure on principals is unlikely to bring about real improvements in principal-teacher collaboration and achievement levels in secondary schools. Many school districts, however, lack the capacity to do more than that. We suggest that, accordingly, entities at the state or the regional/national level will need to be involved. Because we know from international studies (such as PISA [Programme for International Student Assesment] and TIMSS [Trends in Mathematics and Science Study]) that secondary schools are the weakest link in our educational system, and because they show limited capacity for improvement under current accountability policies, we suggest that designing and providing new programs to support secondary school principals must become a policy priority.

3. Principal preparation and professional development programs should continue to emphasize both the "softer" (emotional) and the "harder" (behavioral) aspects of leadership.

Although our results suggest that principals' behavior is more important than the levels of trust principals evoke, behavior and levels of trust are empirically part of a bundle that is difficult to disentangle. Trust alone, without instructional and shared leadership to support it, may be of little consequence for students, but our data suggest that teachers' relationships with each other, and their trust in the principal, cannot be easily disaggregated.

4. Although public policy and community opinion increasingly put pressure on principals to improve student performance, it is equally important to expect that principals take actions to support instructional and shared leadership that leads to improved student learning. Increasing teachers' involvement in the difficult task of making good decisions, and introducing improved practices, both must be at the heart of school leadership. There is no simple shortcut.

Reflections

1. Consider the school environment in which you work (or, if you are in a district or another organization, think about one school you work with). How would you describe instructional leadership in that setting? How about shared leadership? (You may want to look at the indicators of instructional and shared leadership in Appendix A).

2. Thinking about the same setting, in what ways does the administrative leadership support teacher leadership? Think not only about the development of identifiable formal teacher leadership positions, but also about informal leadership.

3. Can you identify any specific changes in the school's improvement agenda that can be attributed to teacher leadership? How did these come about?

4. How do administrators and teacher leaders work not only to understand but also to support the learning of lower-income and minority students? Are both administrators and teachers paying attention to students' experiences rather than focusing exclusively on tests and curriculum? What evidence do you have to support your assessment, or what additional evidence would you need?

CHAPTER FOUR

DISTRIBUTED LEADERSHIP IN ACTION

A Complex Pattern of People, Tasks, and Goals

Stephen E. Anderson

Claims Supported by Evidence in This Chapter

- Although there can be multiple sources of leadership in schools, principals remain the central source.
- Principals enact a wide array of leadership and management activities encompassing multiple goals and school improvement initiatives; other leaders in the school have narrower sets of responsibilities and influence.
- Principals typically determine the allocation of leadership responsibilities and influence, usually based on their understanding of school goals and the expertise that is available within the staff. Leadership arrangements can shift depending on the focus of improvement activity.
- The leadership responsibilities for developing people and for managing instruction involve more people in a wider variety of roles than other leadership tasks (such as setting directions or making decisions about workplace arrangements).
- The distribution of school leadership roles and tasks varies both within schools (depending on the task) and between schools, and it is contingent on particular goals, sources of expertise, and the principal's preferences.

The quantitative evidence used in the previous two chapters does not help us to describe the shared leadership practices associated with school performance. This chapter draws on interview data from principals and teachers, in a sample of elementary and middle schools, to address four questions:

- Who participates in leadership for school improvement?
- What patterns or "arrangements" does the distribution of leadership roles and actions take?
- How is responsibility for "core" leadership functions spread among people?
- How is leadership distribution related to school improvement goals?

Given the small sample of schools from which these data are drawn, the findings are intended to provide deeper insight into the *potential* nature of leadership distribution as it relates to school improvement. As with most qualitative evidence, readers will need to make their own judgments about the fit of the data to their own circumstances.

Starting Points

Scholars recently have focused considerable attention on the properties and complexities of leadership distribution in schools and districts.[1] Leadership distribution may assume different patterns, though consensus on a typology and terms remains elusive. Curiously, the role of principals in varying patterns of leadership distribution has not been a specific focus of inquiry and discussion, and we know little about how different forms of leadership task distribution (or patterns) are related to the accomplishment of organizational goals. Building on the previous two chapters, which examined the distribution of influence on school decisions of principals and other sources of leadership, this chapter looks more concretely at the distribution of leadership responsibilities and tasks in schools.

Leadership Distribution Patterns

Gronn (2002) has distinguished between holistic and additive patterns of leadership distribution. His additive model encompasses a dispersed pattern of leadership in which multiple members of an organization provide leadership in order to accomplish a variety of *distinct* goals and/or tasks. Different members may provide leadership for different purposes, without coordination or with a shared focus. Gronn's holistic model is characterized by greater interdependency and coordination among varied leadership sources focused on *shared* goals and tasks. In other words, Gronn and also Goldstein (2003) distinguish between situations in which leadership for specific tasks is enacted by multiple leaders, together or separately.

Spillane (2006) makes a similar distinction, but identifies three arrangements for distributing leadership responsibilities: division of labor (different leaders for different tasks); co-performance (multiple leaders together for same task); and parallel performance (multiple leaders performing the same tasks but in different contexts). Spillane expands on this formulation, defining three types of co-performance:

- Collaborated distribution (multiple leaders jointly enacting the same leadership practice in the same context)
- Collective distribution (multiple leaders performing separate but interdependent tasks in different contexts and in support of the same goal)
- Coordinated distribution (interdependent actions of multiple leaders being performed in a particular sequence)

Leithwood and his colleagues have taken a somewhat different approach, using a framework focused on leadership functions.[2] This framework, grounded in a research-based definition of leadership, identifies four core leadership functions: setting directions, developing people, redesigning the organization, and managing the instructional program (which is explained in more detail in Chapter Five).[3] The typology for leadership distribution emphasizes variability in the alignment of leadership functions vis-à-vis school improvement goals and initiatives: planful (a term coined by Leithwood and his colleagues) alignment, spontaneous alignment, spontaneous misalignment, and anarchic misalignment.

This chapter explores patterns of leadership task distribution in a selected sample of elementary and middle schools, focusing on sources of leadership influence, the distribution of leadership responsibilities by school improvement goals and by core leadership practices, and implications for student performance. Particular attention is devoted to the part principals play in the distribution of leadership roles and tasks in their schools.

Additional Evidence on Leadership Distribution

We selected a purposive sample of site-visit schools included in our larger study for this analysis. All site-visit schools were categorized as high, medium, or low on measures of collective leadership (see Chapter Two) and student performance. We then selected five schools for qualitative analysis of leadership distribution. These schools varied widely on collective leadership scores and student performance. The sample (Table 4.1) included elementary and middle schools, schools in high- and low-SES settings, and schools in inner-city, suburban, and rural settings across four states (Texas, Missouri, Oregon, and New Jersey).

This sample does not represent the full range of elementary and middle schools that participated in the broader study. However, selecting schools that vary in collective leadership scores, school characteristics, and student performance increases the likelihood that what can be learned from them will be applicable to a broader range of schools. All school administrator and teacher interviews from our first site visit to these schools were transcribed.[4] The findings in this chapter highlight key themes that emerged from the cross-case analysis.

Who Participates in Leadership?

Consistent with findings reported in Chapters Two and Three and by other researchers,[5] we found that school personnel rarely attributed leadership actions and influence to only a single source, and they did not always identify the principal. The individuals or groups identified as providing leadership included a mix of

TABLE 4.1 SAMPLE SCHOOL CHARACTERISTICS

School	Collective Leadership	Student Achievement[*]	Setting[**]
London Elementary	High	High	Size: 537 Pupils Diversity: High Poverty: High
Overton Elementary	High	Low	Size: 221 Pupils Diversity: Med Poverty: Med
Gregory Elementary	High	High	Size: 581 Pupils Diversity: Med Poverty: High
Playa Junior High	Low	Middle	Size: 345 Pupils Diversity: High Poverty: High
Forest Elementary	Low	Low	Size: 443 Pupils Diversity: High Poverty: Med

[*]Student achievement rankings were calculated by comparing the percentage of students scoring at or above minimum state proficiency standards on state-mandated assessments in reading and mathematics (2002–2005) relative to other schools in the states where these schools are located.

[**]Diversity (Low = 66%+ White; Medium = 18%–65% White; High = 0–17% White); Poverty (Low = 0–17% F/R lunch; Medium = 18%–65% F/R lunch; High = 66%+ F/R lunch).

principals, assistant principals, teachers in formal leadership roles (such as grade or subject team leaders), and teachers with specialist positions (such as literacy specialists, technology specialists, counselors). Teachers also identified other teachers informally recognized by peers as influential; school leadership or management committees; school program teams or committees (such as Special Education, Gifted and Talented, Limited English Proficiency); parent involvement personnel; district administrators and professional staff; and external consultants linked to particular areas of curriculum, program, and teacher development priorities at the school level.

Merely identifying the various individuals and groups contributing to school leadership provides scant insight into the actual distribution of leadership roles and tasks, however. Overall, principals were more likely than any other source to be associated with multiple leadership responsibilities. Leadership from specific teachers or other individuals (such as district or external consultants) tended to be in relation to specific school improvement initiatives, or to particular core leadership functions. Three overall patterns or arrangements of leadership sources appeared across the five schools:

○ *Pattern One* (London, Overton, and Gregory Elementary Schools). The leadership influence of the principal was evident across various focal points of school improvement activity. Principals exercised influence in planned collaboration with influential school-based teacher leaders (individuals and groups) and with outside sources (district specialists, external consultants) associated with particular goal-oriented initiatives. In these schools principals and teachers strongly emphasized teacher collaboration, including the involvement of teachers in instructional leadership roles that crossed curriculum and grade boundaries.

○ *Pattern Two* (Playa Junior High School). The leadership influence of the principal extended across various focal points of school improvement activity, but the evidence was less robust for influential sources of teacher leadership and for principal collaboration with teachers and/or external change agents. Teacher leadership was limited to traditional grade-level or program-specific structures, and there was less emphasis, school-wide, on teacher collaboration.

○ *Pattern Three* (Forest Elementary School). The principal exercised oversight on key points of school-improvement activity, but she had little influence on implementation. Key teachers or external agents were identified with support for different improvement initiatives, yet teachers attributed little influence to their enactment of those roles. Teachers did not report an emphasis on or a culture of teacher collaboration within or across school organizational structures.

The first pattern of leadership distribution was found in schools with higher student performance (London, Overton and Gregory Schools) whereas patterns two and three—in Playa and Forest schools—were associated with lower achievement scores. Of course, these suggestive associations are in need of further exploration with larger samples of schools. Nevertheless, Gronn's (2002) distinction between additive and holistic leadership is useful for describing leadership distribution here. Forest Elementary provides the clearest example of a school in which the overall pattern of leadership distribution corresponded to an additive pattern, at least in a formal, bureaucratic sense (teachers attributed little actual influence to those in formal positions of leadership responsibility). The distribution of leadership sources in London, Overton, and Gregory Schools exemplified more holistic patterns of leadership distribution. This clearly reflects the extension of the principal's leadership influence across various focal points of school improvement, as well as the emphasis on teacher collaboration in those schools, which is consistent with the findings and arguments in Chapter Three regarding strong professional community as a context for shared leadership influence between teachers and principals. Playa School did not clearly fit either an additive or a holistic pattern of distribution in leadership sources, in part because there was no strong teacher-leader presence.

Teachers' Collective Influence as a Pattern of Distributed Leadership

Teachers in several schools talked about the *collective* influence of teachers, not merely the influence of colleagues identified as teacher leaders. Collective influence, these teachers reported, was instrumental in school decisions and in broader decisions about school improvement. They framed it as a function of whether the principal and district authorities invited, valued, and acted on input from teachers. This qualitative finding reinforces the teacher survey–based findings on collective and shared leadership presented in prior chapters.

In London School, for example, teachers reported that a previous principal rarely solicited teacher input; when she did, teachers said, she rarely acted in ways that acknowledged the value of that input. They felt unsupported, and increasingly they kept their opinions and ideas to themselves, thereby decreasing the potential for broader teacher influence on decisions in the school. That changed when a new principal came in—one who was perceived as genuinely seeking and respecting teacher input and influence on school decisions. Teachers and principals in Overton and Gregory Schools also affirmed the presence and influence of a strong collective voice from teachers, facilitated by the principal's orientation to teacher input and to organizational structures enabling that input. These findings stand out in contrast to discussions about distributed leadership that focus on the contributions of individually influential teachers. They may reflect the reported strength of teachers' professional collaboration and community in these schools, and the viability of teachers' working conditions (Chapter Two) and professional community (Chapter Three) as a context for shared leadership influence on school decisions.

Formal Role Designations and the Distribution of Leadership Influence

It is tempting to associate the bureaucratic distribution of roles, responsibilities, and authority with the distribution of leadership sources and influence. Beyond the pervasive role of the principal, however, our findings paint a more complex picture.

First, the bureaucratic allocation (principal delegation) of responsibility to perform certain functions and tasks does not necessarily mean that the persons or groups so designated will be perceived as influential. Spillane (2006) argues that leadership sources and acts can be recognized as such even if they do not yield their intended effects. But that argument is not reflected in the evidence from, for example, Forest School, where people in formal leadership positions were not seen by school personnel to make much difference in what other people in the school thought or did.

Second, administrative structures do not necessarily determine how leadership influence will be enacted. The schools examined here all had multi-stakeholder school leadership committees and special program committees (such as special education or bilingual education). They all had a similar array of formal teacher-leader positions, including subject and grade team leaders. Some had teachers assigned to instructional leadership roles associated with priorities for improvement in program and instruction (such as in literacy and mathematics). However, actual patterns of influence varied from school to school. Even in single schools, we found examples of variation over time in how leadership was enacted and distributed within the same bureaucratic structures. Principal succession was a factor in each of these situations.

In London School the current principal and her predecessor both worked with a School-Based Management Team, grade-level teams, cross-grade subject teams, special program committees (gifted education, bilingual education, and so on), and specialist roles (counselor, literacy teacher, parent involvement coordinator, and so on). Under the previous principal, the leadership distribution pattern had been additive, and the principal was not closely involved with school-improvement initiatives. These initiatives were mandated by the district: they proceeded in an uncoordinated manner, guided and managed by grade team leaders, specialists, and external consultants. In contrast, the new principal took on a proactive leadership role, exercising influence within existing governance structures in a way that spanned multiple focal points of school improvement activity. That change yielded a more holistic pattern of leadership distribution, exemplifying a shift from an anarchic to a more democratic if not polyarchic form of leadership control (see Chapter Two).

In Gregory Elementary School a previous principal led an effort to implement the Accelerated Schools comprehensive school reform model. This effort entailed formation of five curriculum cadres, a school-site council, and a school improvement planning process. Although the cadres and council were chaired by teachers, and teacher influence on school directions, improvement plans, and professional development was reportedly strong, school personnel said that the previous principal played a more overt co-performance leadership role within those structures than did the current principal. The current principal and assistant principal talked about deliberately stepping back from a co-performance leadership role to a more indirect advisory role in the cadres and site council. Teachers also reported that adherence to the needs assessment and planning processes became less stringent under the new principal. These cases show that formal organizational structures create an institutional framework for the distribution and enactment of leadership, but they do not determine how leadership plays out over time.

In sum, it is important to distinguish the formal *allocation* of leadership roles and responsibilities from what Leithwood, Mascall, et al. (2007) define as the *planful alignment* of leadership sources, practices, and influence. Formal bureaucratic structures do not necessarily require or facilitate the kind of consensus building, communication, interaction, and collaboration that we would associate with the deliberate alignment of leadership influence and practices.

How Responsibility for Core Leadership Functions is Distributed

Who takes the lead in setting directions, developing people, redesigning the organization and improving the instructional program? Analyses of our elementary and middle school case study data indicate that patterns of leadership distribution and influence can vary by core leadership practices—not only between schools and districts, but also for different focal points of activity within a given school.

Overall, leadership in the five case study schools was more commonly distributed for developing people and improving the instructional program than it was for setting directions and redesigning the organization or workplace. This emphasis may reflect external policies that limit the freedom of principals and teachers to set goals or to redesign the workplace, or it may reflect the often observed tendency for school structures and goals to remain unchanged over long periods of time. Principals' beliefs about their own expertise and the expertise available from other sources also affect direction setting, and they are a key factor shaping the distribution of leadership for developing people and program management in this sample of schools.

For all the schools and districts sampled in our study, state and federal curriculum policies, standards, and accountability systems pervaded direction-setting activities. Flexibility for principals and teachers depended greatly on the extent to which state and district authorities tended to mandate programs or enable schools to select their own priorities and programs (Chapter Thirteen). Ultimately, however, leadership distribution for direction setting was shaped by how the principals viewed and enacted their roles within the context of state and district policies, priorities, and leadership traditions, as illustrated in the following contrasting examples.

The principal and teachers at Forest Elementary School portrayed themselves as complying with state- and district-mandated programs (such as in reading and mathematics) and procedures (such as curriculum mapping, student data reports). The principal described herself and the School Leadership Committee as managing the implementation of externally mandated directions, not as setting directions per se. In contrast, the state and district did not mandate commercial or local programs at Overton Elementary School. While district authorities established system priorities for improvement based on results from state testing, the principal focused her leadership influence less on setting or enforcing program or achievement targets for improvement than on structuring the workplace (such as through a Leadership Committee, curriculum teams, and coaches), facilitating teacher learning (through lesson study and book study teams), and managing the instructional program (by monitoring teaching and teachers' professional learning plans) in ways that guided teachers to establish their own directions for improvement collegially, in the context of state standards, test results, and district priorities.

Our cases highlight two circumstances in which principals may be more prone to act directly and less collaboratively to influence school directions for improvement. First, a principal who possesses specific expertise in curriculum or instruction may be inclined to press forward on the strength of that expertise. At London Elementary School, for example, the principal was well known for her expertise in reading instruction. She decided that children in her school would do better in reading if teachers were to adopt and implement a wider variety of teaching strategies. She communicated that goal to teachers, provided training herself and via an external expert, and monitored teachers' implementation of new strategies in the classroom and in grade team meetings. At the same time, she facilitated ongoing improvement efforts mandated at the district level prior to her appointment (curriculum writing, implementation of a commercial mathematics program), by collaborating with grade team and subject leaders, specialist teachers, and trainers provided by the externally developed mathematics program.

Second, a principal who believes that his or her teachers have become complacent may be inclined to press forward independently, launching efforts to set higher standards for teacher performance and student learning. At Playa Junior High School, for example, the principal sought school improvement through an effort to get teachers to be less didactic in their teaching, to broaden their repertoires of instructional strategies, and to focus on higher-order learning expectations. She explained her initiative as a strategy to motivate teachers and to help them improve student performance beyond the school's predominantly "acceptable" ratings under the state's accountability system. She reported that she coached teachers and used external consultants for in-service training with this in mind. Teachers at Playa were also involved in curriculum writing projects in response to a district mandate. The principal delegated responsibility for leading curriculum development work to traditional subject heads and teams.

These cases make clear that the distribution of leadership practices is influenced by the nature of that practice—not only between schools and districts, but also for different focuses of improvement within a given school. Here, as in many other areas of interest, professional practice is more varied and complicated than the simplified patterns of leadership that often stand out in scholarly discussions. There are several possible explanations for such variation within a small sample of elementary and middle schools. As we intimated in our sample selection, perhaps the intentional diversity of the sample captured much of what will be found in larger samples of schools. Or, less optimistically, the search for the "one best pattern of leadership distribution" may be misguided. It is more likely, we believe, that there will be future research results demonstrating that some patterns are generally unproductive while others depend for their value on school goals, circumstances, conditions, and the like.

Complexity of Leadership Distribution as a Function of Goal Type and Breadth

Leadership distribution patterns are affected by goals. Some goals (such as improving student results in mathematics, strengthening professional community) are larger in aspiration and scope than others (such as implementing a specific mathematics program, standardizing student discipline practices). The more encompassing the goal, the greater the likelihood that multiple sources of leadership will be involved, and the greater the range of activities to which leadership might be attributed.

Contrasting illustrations from Forest Elementary School and London Elementary School will help to clarify this point. Both schools were involved in implementing new, district-mandated, externally developed mathematics programs. Student performance in mathematics at Forest Elementary was below average levels for the state, and the school was not currently satisfying Adequate Yearly Progress expectations; nonetheless, school personnel did not explicitly identify improved achievement in mathematics as a goal. Instead, the goal (one of many program-specific goals in the school) was simply to implement the district-mandated sixth through eighth grade mathematics program. A district mathematics consultant visited the school weekly to assist math teachers with implementation. At the same time, two potentially related initiatives were underway.

First, the school counselor was preparing student assessment data reports at the beginning of the year to assist teachers with lesson planning and tracking student progress. These reports were intended to reach teachers prior to state testing dates so that teachers could identify students who might need additional coaching. The principal was reportedly keenly interested in student performance data, though no one could identify any actions that she had taken to influence the use of those data. Second, the school technology coordinator had been trained by district staff to facilitate the implementation of a computerized curriculum mapping and lesson-planning tool. The interview data for Forest Elementary School did not indicate that these strands of activity and the leadership sources and actions associated with them were deliberately coordinated. The result, from a teacher's perspective, was a leadership distribution pattern of anarchic misalignment.[6]

In London Elementary School, the principal's vision and goals included improving student success (not limited to mathematics), greater coherence in curriculum and teaching, and improved teamwork, focused on student learning, among teachers and with other stakeholders (such as parents). Although the percentage of London Elementary students performing at or above state standards in mathematics was acceptable (and actually high, relative to similar schools in neighboring districts), the principal's goals emphasized the success of all students and the need to boost learning outcomes beyond those touched on by the tests. Consultants working for the commercially developed mathematics program visited the school every six weeks to provide implementation training and assistance for the teachers. Not unlike the faculty at Forest Elementary, London Elementary faculty members were engaged in a curriculum project (mandated by the district but organized internally) that involved writing curriculum guides and common assessments keyed to the state curriculum in core subject areas. The principal arranged for the writers to get input from external program consultants. She relocated the writers' classrooms to ensure that all teachers had convenient, informal access to them for advice. Not only was the principal committed to the use of assessment data for identifying and addressing student learning needs, but she also delivered data-use training for teachers, and she sat in on grade-level team meetings to facilitate teachers' use of assessment data in their planning of six-week tutoring cycles. She also arranged for the parent coordinator to get trained in the mathematics program so that she could prepare ways to show parents how to help their children with mathematics homework.

With the exception of parent involvement, activities related to implementation of the mathematics program in London Elementary were similar to activities at Forest Elementary (external program with in-service training, curriculum mapping aligned to state standards, assistance with data use). At London Elementary, however, these activities and varied sources of leadership were linked in a complex, collective pattern through the principal's actions. The overall effort encompassed multiple, core leadership practices (setting directions, developing capacity, workplace arrangements, managing the instructional program) and multiple leadership sources associated with the focus on a shared learning goal. The pattern at London Elementary seems likely to produce a greater impact on student learning in mathematics than the pattern at Forest Elementary, where the focus was basically limited to program implementation. The leadership distribution scenario at London Elementary corresponds well to the concept of planful alignment across core leadership practices.[7]

Student Learning and the Distribution of Leadership Roles and Tasks

Most school and district leaders' interests in leadership distribution are motivated by the expectation that there may be some leverage in such leadership for improving student learning. Clearly, the evidence in this chapter cannot begin to satisfy this source of motivation. But it does offer a more nuanced picture of the relationship between leadership distribution and student achievement. Specific goals and leadership tasks, we found, influenced the patterns of leadership distribution that emerged in our five schools and indicated that different patterns can coexist in a school (such as improvement in mathematics and reading performance at London Elementary).

It would be unwise to assume that leadership, as it is distributed and practiced in one leadership context (leading a new reading initiative) would necessarily be similar across other contexts (changing the science curriculum). The influence of more general forms of leadership distribution on student achievement, such as collective leadership (Chapter Two), shared leadership and professional community (Chapter Three) are more easily and empirically measurable than specific forms and arrangements of distributed leadership.

What Might We Conclude?

The idea of distributed leadership overlaps with the notions of collective leadership and shared leadership addressed in Chapters Two and Three. Collective leadership was mainly concerned with identifying the relative and combined influence of different individuals and groups on school decision making, and the relationship of patterns of stakeholder influence to teacher motivation, teacher capacity, working conditions, and student achievement. Three key findings from that analysis were that:

- Principals enact the greatest influence.
- Significant influence from others need not diminish the influence of principals.
- Higher levels of collective influence are positively associated with teacher motivation, teachers' working conditions, and student achievement.

These results gave rise to the conclusion that principals should be open to, and provide constructive opportunities for, participation and influence in schoolwide decision making by other school and district office personnel as well as by parents.

Chapter Three examined, more specifically, the incidence of teacher participation in, and influence on, school decisions with principals, referred to as shared leadership. Results pointed to a positive relationship between shared leadership and teachers' professional community, in combination with instructional leadership from the principal. Professional community strongly mediated the leadership influence of principals and teachers on instructional practice and on student achievement. That analysis treated principals' instructional leadership behaviors as distinct from teacher participation in school decisions.

Evidence in this chapter broadened our understanding of leadership distribution in schools in two ways. First, it examined the distribution of leadership roles and tasks, in addition to considerations previously given to the simple distribution of "influence" on school-wide decisions reported in the preceding chapters. Second, it explored the consistency with which leadership was distributed across different school improvement contexts.

It is tempting to talk about "distributed leadership" as if it were a particular arrangement and form of leadership practice and influence. Evidence in this chapter, albeit from a small sample of schools, suggests that this misrepresents the multiple patterns of leadership distribution that are possible and perhaps likely within a school. We found that the extent to which leadership will be distributed in schools, and the forms it may take, are determined in large measure by what principals believe and feel about a handful of key factors, including, for example:

- External and internal influences on school direction setting
- The nature and scope of school goals for improvement
- Sources and uses of professional expertise required for the accomplishment of school goals

- Latitude for participation in the enactment of different dimensions of leadership practice

Indeed, evidence in this chapter suggests that the productive distribution of leadership in schools depends more on the principal's disposition toward collective influence and shared leadership than on the establishment of specific arrangements for joint enactment of leadership tasks and influence.

Implications for Policy and Practice

While acknowledging the usual limitations on what might be concluded from a study based on a small sample of qualitative data, this chapter suggests three provisional implications for policy and practice:

1. Distributing leadership in schools requires the allocation and sharing of leadership tasks by principals in light of school goals and access to requisite expertise, in addition to providing genuine opportunities for input from teachers and others in school decisions. Formal roles and arrangements can create and legitimize the distribution of leadership tasks but do not guarantee their influence on organizational directions and practices of the person(s) fulfilling those tasks, nor effective coordination amongst those enacting those tasks.

2. Coherence in the distribution of school leadership roles and tasks depends on the active involvement of principals in enacting or coordinating those leadership responsibilities. Distributing leadership more widely in schools does not reduce principals' workload.

Leadership from teacher and external sources is more likely to be goal- or initiative-specific. Principals, on the other hand, are responsible for a boundary-spanning role not typically picked up by others in the absence of active principal leadership. Principals are typically involved in many leadership initiatives in their schools, including initiatives for which others have assumed lead roles. Their role to coordinate or link others' leadership efforts is essential.

3. Efforts to promote greater sharing or distribution of leadership need to operationally identify specific or desired leadership role and task arrangements. Simply invoking the term *distributed leadership* is meaningless, given the different patterns that distributed leadership can take, even within the same school, for different school improvement goals and initiatives. To understand the distribution of leadership one needs to explore evidence of actual behaviors and influences associated with core leadership practices and specific focal points of school-improvement activity. Principals working in similar organizational

structures may enact their leadership roles and engage in distributed leadership in quite different ways.

Although we now have a better insight into alternative arrangements or patterns of school leadership roles and tasks in practice, our evidence about the effects of leadership distribution on school improvement initiatives or student learning remains modest. The broader evidence presented in Chapters Two and Three does suggest that principals' sharing of leadership with others in planful patterns of leadership distribution is probably a worthwhile way to approach improvement in student learning, but it needs to be coupled with leader efforts to motivate commitment to common directions for improvement and to develop teacher working conditions (especially professional community) that more directly support improvements in the quality of instruction and learning.

Questions for Reflection

Considering two goals or focuses of school improvement activity in your school, answer the following questions.

1. Using the four core leadership practices (setting directions, developing people, structuring the workplace, managing the instructional program) as a framework, who is providing leadership and in what ways across those practices for each goal?
2. Does the leadership role of principals and other sources of leadership influence vary depending on the goal or focus of improvement activity in your school?
3. In what ways does the availability of professional expertise in the school or district shape the sources and distribution of leadership for school improvement in your school?
4. Given your analysis, can you identify needs for greater coordination in leadership actions and influence for different focuses of improvement activity?

CHAPTER FIVE

CORE PRACTICES

The Four Essential Components of the Leader's Repertoire

Kenneth Leithwood

Claims Supported by Evidence in This Chapter

- Previous research has identified a set of core practices underlying the work of successful school- and district-level leaders. About sixteen in total, these practices can be classified as *setting directions, developing people, redesigning the organization,* and *improving the instructional program.* Almost all leadership practices considered instructionally helpful by principals and teachers are specific enactments of these core practices.
- Teachers and principals agree that the most instructionally helpful specific leadership practices are:
  a. Focusing the school on goals and expectations for student achievement
  b. Keeping track of teachers' professional development needs
  c. Creating structures and opportunities for teachers to collaborate
- Teachers who vary widely in the sophistication of their classroom instruction identify as helpful most of the same leadership practices.
- Teachers' school level (elementary, middle, secondary) makes only a small difference in the leadership practices teachers consider helpful to them.
- Successful principal leadership includes careful attention to classroom instructional practices, but it also includes careful attention to many other issues that are critical to the ongoing health and welfare of school organizations.

Chapters Two, Three, and Four examined the effects on students of different groups of (mostly) adults in schools enacting leadership practices together. Chapter Two examined something akin to the total leadership provided by all the usual suspects, Chapter Three narrowed the focus to principals and teachers working together, and Chapter Four inquired about the patterns of leadership distribution among those in schools. Departing from a primary focus on *who* exercises leadership, this is the first of two chapters focused directly on *what* leaders do. Specifically, this chapter describes the practices and behaviors that help account for the success of principals' leadership—undoubtedly the most influential leadership position in education. The chapter is based on a qualitative approach to identifying such practices, and it uses evidence from a sample of schools selected for this purpose.

In the context of prevailing national and provincial/state accountability policies, claims about successful or effective leadership practices are considered most defensible when they are justified by quantitative evidence linking the practices to standardized measures of student achievement, as was the case in the previous chapters. The evidence on which this and the next chapter, like Chapter Four, are based stems from the perceptions of principals and teachers. This approach extends a line of leadership research that has generated many useful insights in the past, even though its influence on policy and practice is muted at present.[1] The central question driving the research on which this chapter is based was: Which leadership practices enacted by principals are considered by principals and teachers to be most helpful in supporting and improving classroom instruction?

We have two reasons for making use of the multiple data sources available in this study to address this question. First, so-called "hard" quantitative evidence cannot, by itself, provide the guidance for policy and practice that many educators and policy makers now expect of it. For example, the "grain size" of this evidence is almost always impractically large; that is, the leadership practices that this sort of evidence tests are measured at a level of abstraction not directly implementable by real leaders in real organizational contexts. Furthermore, the data generated by these favored forms of research are far less conclusive than is sometimes claimed. This limitation is usually a function of (1) the constraints on research designs that can be used in field settings (experimental studies, for example, are almost impossible to manage in field settings) and (2) the weak causal claims that can be made about data resulting from such designs (because many potential "causes" of the observed effects cannot be controlled).

Second, every style of research brings with it some important advantages, but also some serious limitations. Synthesizing results across studies that vary in research style and method offers potentially more robust justification for knowledge claims.[2] However, relying on multiple methods within the same study, particularly where analyses are carried out independently, provides an even stronger basis for establishing claims of greater or lesser certainty.

Starting Points

Success in creating schools that contribute substantially to student learning depends in some measure on interaction with the specific contexts in which school- and district-level leaders find themselves working. Nevertheless, a considerable amount of evidence from district, school, and noneducation organizations points to four broad categories of *core* leadership practices that appear to be effective across varied contexts. We begin this chapter by summarizing these core practices. Then we provide a synopsis of results from our research about leadership practices perceived by teachers and principals to be helpful in accomplishing their schools' goals. Finally, we compare practices identified as helpful through this analysis with the core leadership practices identified by prior research.

The four categories of core leadership practices identified by prior research are: *setting directions, developing people, redesigning the organization,* and *improving the instructional program.* Each of these categories comprises from three to five more specific practices. Similar approaches to the classification of leadership practices are not difficult to find. Hallinger and Heck (1999) classify the practices in their instructional leadership model as "purposes," "people," and "structures and social systems." Conger and Kanungo (1998) speak about "visioning strategies," "efficacy-building strategies," and "context changing strategies." Robinson and her colleagues (2008) have generated the most recent set of categories, and they are quite compatible with those described here.

Our claim that these practices ought to be an essential part of the repertoire of school leaders is based on reviews of empirical research and on illustrative original studies carried out in educational contexts.[3] A synthesis of evidence about effective managerial skills compiled by Yukl (2002) also supports this claim.

Setting Directions

This category of leadership practices comprises four specific practices: *building a shared vision, fostering the acceptance of group goals, creating high performance expectations,* and *communicating the direction.* Overall, it is a category of practices intended to establish what Fullan (2003) and others call "moral purpose," a basic stimulant for the work in question. All of these practices are aimed at bringing a focus to the individual and collective work of staff members in the school or district.

Developing People

The specific practices in this category are *providing individualized support and consideration, offering intellectual stimulation,* and *modeling appropriate values and practices.* These practices aim to communicate the leader's respect for his or her colleagues, as well as concerns about their personal feelings and needs (Podsakoff, MacKenzie, Moorman, and Fetter, 1990). Encompassed by this set of practices are the "supporting" and "recognizing and rewarding" managerial behaviors associated with Yukl's (1994) Multiple Linkage model, as well as Hallinger's (2003) model of instructional leadership and the Waters, Marzano, and McNulty (2003) meta-analysis. The primary aim of these practices is capacity building, which is understood to include not only the knowledge and skills that staff members need to accomplish organizational goals, but also the disposition that staff members need to persist in applying such knowledge and skills. People are motivated by what they are good at. And mastery experiences, according to Bandura (1986), are the most powerful sources of efficacy. Building capacity that leads to a sense of mastery is therefore highly motivational as well.

Refining and Aligning the School Organization

The four practices comprised in this category—*building collaborative cultures, restructuring the organization to support collaboration, building productive relationships with families and communities,* and *connecting the school to the wider community*—are intended to establish workplace conditions that will allow staff members to make the most of their motivations and capacities. The organizational setting in which people work shapes much of what they do. There is little to be gained by increasing people's motivation and capacity if working conditions will not allow their effective application. People's beliefs about their situation are an important source of their motivation. People are motivated when they believe the circumstances in which they find themselves are conducive to accomplishing the goals they hold to be personally important.[4]

Improving the Instructional Program

This category includes practices intended to significantly improve the core technology of schooling: the processes of teaching and learning. These practices include *staffing the program, providing instructional support, monitoring school activity, buffering staff from distractions to their work*, and *aligning resources*. These practices have the most direct effects on students, as compared with the three previous categories of practices, and because they directly shape the nature and quality of instruction in classrooms, they are the practices typically evoked by the term "instructional leadership."

New Evidence for this Chapter

This component of our larger study aimed to ground, illustrate, and when warranted, elaborate our understanding of the core leadership practices based on the experience of teachers and principals. Evidence collected for these purposes also provided opportunities to explore differences (by school level and by level or degree of teachers' instructional expertise) in the value participants assigned to the core practices. This evidence came from a sub-sample of twelve principals and sixty-five teachers in twelve schools.

Selection of the twelve schools was based on one aspect of teachers' instructional practices assessed during classroom observations collected in the first round of site visits.[5] Six schools were designated as High-Scoring Schools (HSS) from the larger sample because at least 60 percent of the teachers who had been observed received a high score on a portion of the rating scale we used to guide our classroom observations (teaching higher-order thinking skills). We selected six additional schools, designated Low-Scoring Schools (LSS), because at least 60 percent of their observed teachers received a low score on the same standard.

Equal numbers of high- and low-scoring schools were selected to represent elementary, middle, and secondary schools,[6] and there were modest differences in the average sizes of the high- and low-scoring schools.[7] Percentage of students eligible for free or reduced lunch was used as a proxy for socioeconomic status. Schools were evenly distributed across low, medium, and high levels of socio-economic status. Average levels of student diversity were approximately the same for both high- and low-scoring schools.

Teachers were asked about these factors: their approach to teaching, the lessons we had observed, the principal's role in guiding and supporting their work, factors that had the greatest influence on student learning, district influences, professional development opportunities, the school community, the extent of parental involvement, and what they would tell a new teacher about what it is like to work at this school.

Principals and vice principals were asked about the principal's leadership in areas such as student achievement goals, vision for the school and student learning, making decisions about instruction, leadership distribution in the school, professional development experiences for principals and teachers, curriculum and instruction, school culture, state and district influences on administrators' and teachers' work in the school, and the impact of parents and the wider school community.

Subsequent sections of this chapter describe specific leadership practices that both principals and teachers identified as helpful to teachers as they worked to improve their instruction. Then we report the relationships between those practices and the four categories of core leadership practices described earlier.

Specific Leadership Practices Perceived to Help Improve Instruction

A large proportion of both principals and teachers agreed on the importance of three specific practices:

- *Focusing the school on goals and expectations for student achievement* (100 percent principals, 66.7 percent teachers).
- *Keeping track of teachers' professional development needs* (100 percent principals, 84 percent teachers). Although professional development was often prescribed, designed, and delivered at the district level, principals were involved in managing teachers' attendance at workshops offered outside the school, as well as planning for, and sometimes providing, on-site professional development.
- *Creating structures and opportunities for teachers to collaborate* (91.7 percent principals, 66.7 percent teachers). Principals supported collaboration among teachers by scheduling times for teachers to meet and discuss how they were working through the curriculum.

Other practices attracting support from a smaller but still sizeable number of principals and teachers included the following:

- *Monitoring teachers' work in the classroom* (83.3 percent principals, 37.7 percent teachers). Principals mentioned formal classroom observations carried out for teacher evaluation purposes; they also mentioned less formal ways of monitoring, such as classroom visits and checking lesson plans.
- *Providing mentoring opportunities for new teachers* (33.3 percent principals, 26 percent teachers). Some teachers and principals referred to programs initiated by the district or the school to support staff members who were new to teaching or new to the school.

- *Being easily accessible* (50 percent principals, 27.5 percent teachers). Principals spoke about how they supported teachers' efforts in the classroom in a general way.
- *Providing backup for teachers with student discipline and with parents* (25 percent principals, 23.1 percent teachers). School safety and the management of students' behavior were of concern to administrators and teachers. Teachers were particularly appreciative of administrators who could be relied on to back them up when they faced challenging situations with parents.

Finally, most principals (83.3 percent) considered *staying current* to be a very important part of their leadership, although only one teacher mentioned this practice.

Differences in Successful Leadership Practices Across School Levels

Do principals and teachers at different school levels (elementary, middle, secondary) differ in the leadership practices they believe to be helpful? Our analysis suggested almost no such differences in the minds of principals. For teachers, small differences emerged around three leadership practices:

- *Monitoring teachers' classroom work* was identified by only 30 percent of middle school teachers, by a slightly larger proportion of high school teachers (34.8 percent), and by 54.5 percent of elementary school teachers.
- *Creating structures and opportunities for teachers to collaborate* was identified by 78.3 percent of high school teachers, 70 percent of middle school teachers, and 63.6 percent of elementary school teachers.
- *Allowing teachers flexibility regarding classroom instruction* was identified by 55 percent of middle school teachers, 43.8 percent of high school teachers, and 40.9 percent of elementary school teachers.

Successful Leadership Practices and Teaching Quality

Were principals in our higher-performing schools engaged in different instructional leadership practices than those in the low-performing schools? This was the question that initially prompted the analysis described in this chapter and shaped the method used for sampling schools initially.

Principals and teachers concurred about differences in one leadership practice. *Providing instructional resources and materials* was identified as helpful by half of the principals and 25 percent of the teachers in low-performing schools, whereas only one principal and 6 percent of the teachers in the higher-performing schools identified this practice as helpful. A difference of two principals between the high- and low-scoring schools (HSS and LSS hereafter) is evident in the case of only two practices:[8]

- Participating in their own professional development (six HSS versus four LSS)
- Supporting community involvement in student learning (two HSS versus four LSS)

Relatively large differences appeared between teachers in instructionally high- and low-scoring schools for the following practices:

- Providing backup for teachers for student discipline and with parents (18 percent HSS versus 38 percent LSS)
- Helping to ensure consistent approaches to student discipline (18 percent HSS versus 38 percent LSS)
- Providing teachers with instructional resources and materials (6 percent HSS versus 25 percent LSS)
- Supporting teacher collaboration for purposes of instructional improvement (85 percent HSS versus 56 percent LSS)
- Supporting parental involvement in student learning (88 percent HSS versus 72 percent LSS)

These results may reflect a more challenging work context for teachers in low-performing as compared with higher-performing schools. But the results also suggest that teachers with less ambitious instructional practices are more likely to externalize their needs for instructional support (for example, resources, backup for classroom management decisions) than to value support focused more directly on developing their instructional expertise and other sources of student learning (for example, supporting teacher collaboration and parental involvement).

Principals' and Teachers' Judgments and the Core Leadership Practices

Although the results reported to this point have been based on a "grounded" analysis (one not influenced by a prior framework), we end the chapter by comparing these grounded results with our initial perspective on successful leadership, the core leadership practices. How do leadership practices identified as helpful by teachers and principals in this study compare with those practices associated with successful leadership in prior research?

TABLE 5.1 CORE LEADERSHIP PRACTICES AND PRACTICES DEEMED HELPFUL BY TEACHERS AND PRINCIPALS

Core Leadership Practices	Practices Identified as Instructionally Helpful
1. Setting Directions	
1.1 Building a shared vision	Focusing the school on goals for student achievement
1.2 Fostering the acceptance of group goals	Focusing teachers' attention on goals for student achievement
1.3 Creating high performance expectations	Focusing teachers' attention on expectations for student achievement
1.4 Communicating the direction	Staying current
2. Developing People	
2.1 Providing individualized support and consideration	Keeping track of teachers' PD needs Providing general support/open door Being easily accessible Providing backup for teachers for student discipline and with parents
2.2 Offering intellectual stimulation	Providing mentoring opportunities for new teachers
2.3 Modeling appropriate values and practices	
3. Redesigning the Organization	
3.1 Building collaborative cultures	
3.2 Modifying organizational structures to nurture collaboration	Creating structures and opportunities for teachers to collaborate
3.3 Building productive relations with families and communities	
3.4 Connecting the school to the wider community	
4. Improving the Instructional Program	
4.1 Staffing the instructional program	
4.2 Monitoring progress of students, teachers, and the school	Monitoring teachers' work in the classroom
4.3 Providing instructional support	Providing instructional resources and materials
4.4 Aligning resources	
4.5 Buffering staff from distractions to their work	

To answer this question we used, on one side of the comparison, only those practices identified by a sizeable number of respondents (the practices just discussed). Table 5.1 lists those practices in the right-hand column. The four sets of core leadership practices are listed in the left-hand column.

Two sets of practices identified through our grounded analysis are closely aligned with core practices related to *setting directions*: *focusing the school and its teachers on goals* and *focusing the school and its teachers on expectations for student achievement.* These are part of *building a shared vision, fostering acceptance of group goals,* and *creating high performance expectations.* Four identified practices from our grounded analysis align themselves with the *providing individualized support* component of *developing people*: *keeping track of teachers' professional development needs, being easily accessible, providing backup for teachers for student discipline and with parents,* and *providing mentoring opportunities for new teachers.*

Only one set of identified practices was aligned with *redesigning the organization*: *creating structures and opportunities for teachers to collaborate.* Similarly, only one set of identified practices, *monitoring teachers' work,* aligned itself with *improving the instructional program.*

From these comparisons, it is evident that seven of the sixteen core leadership practices were not enacted or experienced as instructionally helpful by our respondents. We cannot know exactly why this is the case, but we can speculate. One possibility is that principals might have enacted some leadership practices not visible to teachers. Another possibility is that only some of the core leadership practices have much influence on teachers' classroom practice. Still another is that the principals in our study worked with a relatively narrow repertoire of leadership practices. Nevertheless, of the leadership practices frequently identified as helpful, one or more are associated with each of the four categories of core leadership practices.

What We Might Conclude? (And One Implication for Policy and Practice)

Evidence described in this chapter indicates that the four categories of core leadership practices provide a comprehensive account of what successful school leaders do: they may be more than what such leaders do, but they are not less. Policy makers and practitioners would be wise, furthermore, to avoid promoting, endorsing, or being unduly influenced by conceptions of *instructional leadership* that adopt an excessively narrow focus on classroom instruction alone. Teachers and principals providing the evidence for this chapter identified as instructionally helpful many leadership practices concerned with the wider organizational context of the school—and very few practices directly concerned with improving the instructional program.

This outcome is consistent with most widely known models of instructional leadership, which actually give considerable weight to noninstructional elements of the school. Hallinger and Heck (1999), for example, conceptualize *instructional leadership* to include attention to "purposes," "people," and "structures and social systems." This conceptualization underscores the point that classroom practices occur within larger organizational systems that can vary enormously in the extent to which they support, reward, and nurture good instruction. School leaders who ignore or neglect the state of this larger context can easily find their direct efforts to improve instruction substantially frustrated. Successful principal leadership includes careful attention to classroom instructional practices, but it also includes careful attention to many other issues that are critical to the ongoing health and welfare of school organizations.

Reflections

1. Think of someone who, in your mind, is clearly providing leadership for his or her school or district. What is this person actually doing that prompts that attribution? How well do the core practices described in this chapter capture what this person is actually doing?
2. How likely is it that the teachers you work with would identify as particularly important the leadership practices identified by teachers in this study? Would they identify any additional practices as critical?
3. Do the core leadership practices leave out any practices that you have experienced as being quite useful for school improvement purposes? If so, what are they?
4. Which practices would you indentify as most helpful to improve teachers' instruction? Why?

CHAPTER SIX

AN UP-CLOSE VIEW OF INSTRUCTIONAL LEADERSHIP

A Grounded Analysis

Kyla Wahlstrom

Claims Supported by Evidence in This Chapter

- Principals engage in two complementary behaviors to influence instruction. One behavior aims to set a tone or culture in the building that supports continual professional learning (*instructional ethos*). The second behavior involves taking explicit steps to engage with individual teachers about their own growth (*instructional actions*).
- Principals whose teachers rate them high on instructional ethos emphasize the value of research-based strategies and are able to apply them in the local setting.
- Instructional actions include principals' direct observations and conversations with teachers, in their classrooms and in team meetings.
- Setting a tone and developing a vision for student achievement and teacher growth (instructional ethos) is present in higher-performing schools of all grade levels, K–12.
- Secondary school teachers rarely report that school-level leaders engage in instructional action. This is the case for their principals, department heads, and other teacher leaders. However, elementary school teachers working with highly rated principals report high levels of both instructional ethos and instructional actions.

As in Chapter Five, this chapter focuses on evidence about practices for successful instructional leadership as judged by principals and teachers. Chapter Five relied on evidence from schools selected for the high quality of the instruction their teachers provided. This chapter examines evidence from schools in which principals received high effectiveness ratings from their teachers. Five of the twenty schools providing qualitative evidence for this chapter were also included in the sample of schools used for Chapter Five.

Starting Point: The Changing Role of the Principal from Manager to Leader

Historically, principals have been responsible for a well-run school. Managing staff, developing rules and procedures, and attending to the general operation of a building have always been part of the job. However, the conception of school management began to shift in the late 1970s. Highly influential school effectiveness studies[1] asserted that effective schools are characterized by elements such as these:

- An ethos or culture oriented toward learning, as expressed in high achievement standards and expectations of students
- An emphasis on basic skills
- A high level of involvement in decision making and professionalism among teachers
- Cohesiveness
- Clear policies on matters such as homework and student behaviors[2]

All this implied changes in the principal's role.

A further shift in the principal's role, beginning in the mid-1990s, involved the expectation that principals would provide instructional leadership. Theorists accepting this expectation contended that the principal's role had changed from management to instructional leadership.[3] What the concept of instructional leadership means, however, remains vague. For example, studies of how teachers use their time during instruction have not focused on actions principals take to monitor or set expectations for the delivery of high-quality instruction.[4] Much has been written about the importance of the principal as an instructional leader.[5] Often, however, this scholarship fails to reflect the messiness of what principals do on a day-to-day basis. Current research about instructional leadership is also focused on distributed leadership[6] or on the leader's content knowledge.[7] Meanwhile, questions about how and when the principal might best engage with a teacher to address specific practices used by effective teachers have been under researched.

A recent example of research about the link between the principal and teachers' professional development is provided by the study of the Institute for Learning (IFL) implementation strategies in three urban school districts.[8] That study found that teachers reported varying amounts of instructional support provided by their principals. Principals whose teachers rated them higher on an instructional leadership scale had participated in more professional development focused on instructional leadership than had lower-rated principals. However, teachers' self-reports of their use of certain instructional strategies were not confirmed in classroom observations by researchers. Furthermore, principals who were described by their teachers as providing instructional leadership were not seen to be providing direct feedback or frequent observations of classroom instruction during the researchers' site visits.

The theory of action shaping the analysis here is based on the belief that high-quality instructional leadership and high-quality classroom instruction are linked, and together they impact students' learning. Thus, when either high-quality instructional leadership or high-quality instruction does *not* occur, student achievement suffers. The main purpose for the analysis reported in this chapter is to clarify the meaning of instructional leadership in order to better understand how it contributes to learning.

New Evidence

This analysis of instructional leadership is guided by three questions:

- What does instructional leadership look like to teachers?
- Are teachers' reports of instructional leadership similar in substance to what principals have to say about instructional leadership?
- Does instructional leadership look different at the elementary and secondary levels?

Both quantitative and qualitative data from our larger study were used to answer these questions. Quantitative data included teacher responses to seventeen items from the second teacher survey administered as part of our larger study. These items asked about principal leadership behaviors deemed likely, in previous research, to influence teachers' instructional behavior. Qualitative data were provided by interviews with principals (twenty) and teachers (eighty-six) in a total of twenty schools. These schools were selected from the total of 127 for which survey data were available. Of the 127 for which site-visit data were also available, the ten highest- and lowest-rated schools were chosen.

Ratings were teachers' perceptions of the leadership provided by principals, as reflected in the seventeen survey items.

Survey Evidence. A factor analysis of responses to the seventeen items resulted in two factors. All 17 items loaded on one of two factors, and no question loaded on both. Ten survey items loaded on the first factor and seven on the second factor.

The ten items (measured on a six-point scale) that were included in Factor 1 ask teachers the extent to which their principals create a productive ethos in the school. Items in Factor 1 are about setting a tone of continual professional growth in the school, where the work culture embraces inclusive decision making and the belief that we can always do better. We call this the *instructional ethos* factor. As Table 6.1 shows, there are significant differences between those schools who scored in the top 20 percent on the composite scale and those who scored in the bottom 20 percent.

TABLE 6.1 TOP VS. BOTTOM 20%* MEAN TEACHER RATINGS PER BUILDING ON FACTOR 1

| | Factor 1 | | | |
| | Top 20% (25 bldgs) | Bottom 20% (25 bldgs) | | |
	Mean	Mean	*t*-value	*p*-value
Overall Mean on Factor 1	5.38	3.68	85.68	<.001
4–1 My school administrator develops an atmosphere of caring and trust.	5.52	3.5	93.42	<.001
4–3 My school administrator creates consensus around purposes of our district mission.	5.35	3.63	76.16	<.001
4–6 My school administrator is effective in building community support for the school's improvement efforts.	5.48	3.64	77.72	<.001

(continued)

TABLE 6.1 (*continued*)

	Factor 1			
	Top 20% (25 bldgs)	Bottom 20% (25 bldgs)		
	Mean	Mean	*t*-value	*p*-value
4–7 My school administrator promotes leadership development among teachers.	5.32	3.65	70.9	<.001
4–8 My school administrator models a high level of professional practice.	5.58	3.74	85.64	<.001
4–9 My school administrator ensures wide participation in decisions about school improvement.	5.19	3.41	78.09	<.001
4–10 My school administrator clearly defines standards for instructional practices.	5.31	3.77	62.11	<.001
4–24 When teachers are struggling, our principal provides support for them.	5.07	3.33	81.46	<.001
4–25 Our principal ensures that all students get high-quality teachers.	5.16	3.70	55.09	<.001
4–27 In general, I believe my principal's motives and intentions are good.	5.77	4.48	84.34	<.001

Scale: 1 = Strongly disagree, 2 = Moderately disagree, 3 = Slightly disagree, 4 = Slightly agree, 5 = Moderately agree, 6 = Strongly agree

*Using Factor 1, we created a ranking of all 127 principals in whose buildings their teachers completed the survey. There were twenty-five buildings in the top 20 percent and twenty-five buildings in the bottom 20 percent of the continuum.

The seven survey items loading on Factor 2 measure the frequency with which specific actions with a direct focus on instructional improvement were enacted by the principal with individual teachers.[9] These questions measure the frequency with which the principal and the teacher have regular, ongoing dialogue about best practices. They ask about the principal being in the classroom, observing instruction, and providing specific feedback. Factor 2 is the *instructional actions* factor—it concerns making manifest the ethos identified by Factor 1. Again, as Table 6.2 shows, the differences between the top and bottom 20 percent of the schools were significant in all cases.

TABLE 6.2 TOP VS. BOTTOM 20%* MEAN TEACHER RATINGS PER BUILDING ON FACTOR 2

	Factor 2			
	Top 20% (25 bldgs)	Bottom 20% (25 bldgs)		
	Mean	Mean	t-value	p-value
Overall Mean on Factor 2	3.73	2.46	132.01	<.001
4–13 How often in this school year has your school administrator discussed instructional issues with you?	3.86	2.69	76.4	<.001
4–14 How often in this school year has your school administrator encouraged collaborative work among staff?	4.27	3.12	70.43	<.001
4–15 How often in this school year has your school administrator provided or located resources to help staff improve their teaching?	3.87	2.65	68.82	<.001
4–16 How often in this school year has your school administrator observed your classroom instruction?	3.44	2.27	63.04	<.001

(continued)

TABLE 6.2 *(continued)*

	Factor 2			
	Top 20% (25 bldgs)	Bottom 20% (25 bldgs)		
	Mean	Mean	*t*-value	*p*-value
4–17 How often in this school year has your school administrator encouraged data use in planning for individual student needs?	3.97	2.37	119.47	<.001
4–18 How often in this school year has your school administrator attended teacher planning meetings?	4.06	2.31	97.35	<.001
4–21 How often in this school year has your school administrator given you specific ideas for how to improve your instruction?	2.69	1.79	54.71	<.001

Scale: 1 = never; 2 = 1–2 times; 3 = 3–5 times; 4 = 6–9 times; 5 = 10 or more times
*Using Factor 2, we created a ranking of all 127 principals in whose buildings their teachers completed the survey. There were 29 buildings in the top 20% and 30 buildings in the bottom 20% of the continuum.

Principals whose teachers' ratings placed them in the top 20 percent on either or both of the two factors were labeled high-scoring principals; principals whose teachers rated them low on either or both of the factors were labeled low-scoring principals.

Student achievement data (mathematics proficiency in 2005–06 on state tests) were used as an independent variable to stratify the population of principals so that we could see whether high- versus low-scoring principals' schools cluster differently, based on their students' mathematics proficiency scores.[10] Finally, we stratified the data further by using building grade level (elementary versus secondary) as the last independent variable. For purposes of our analyses, elementary schools are grades K–6, and secondary schools are grades 7–12. Middle schools with grades 5–8 are included in the group of secondary schools. High- or low-scoring principals, high or low math achievement, and elementary or secondary level provided a sorting mechanism to identify the specific schools where we could begin an exploratory analysis of the interview data.

Interview Results. Responses to three questions from the interview protocol for the teachers provided the qualitative data for this analysis:

- What role does your principal play in guiding and supporting your work in the classroom?
- How often does the principal observe or visit in your classroom?
- What kinds of feedback or suggestions does the principal give to help you improve your instruction?

Data from the interview protocol for the principals were provided by responses to the following questions:

- Tell me about the last time you visited a classroom. What was the purpose of the visit? Describe what you were looking for.
- What communication did you have with the teacher before, during, and after the visit?
- How do you know that changes are being made in instruction?
- How often do you visit classrooms?

Responses to the interview questions were aggregated for each question and the responses were analyzed thematically.

Principals' and Teachers' Views of What Instructional Leadership Looks Like

Initial analysis of the teacher survey data pointed to a clear distinction between principals' efforts to create a vision for learning on the one hand, and what they do to enact that vision on the other. Setting a tone or culture of high standards for quality instruction appears to be different from what the principal does in order to be certain that high-quality instruction actually occurs. Given that these two characteristics of instructional leadership emerged as unrelated factors, we examined them separately in order to better understand possible reasons for why they were revealed as different from one another. The second research question—"Are teachers' reports of instructional leadership similar to what principals have to say about it?"—is answered as the analysis of the teachers' and principals' interviews unfolds. The teachers and the principals were telling somewhat different stories.

Factor 1: Instructional Ethos Instructional ethos encompasses some of the practices associated in Chapter Five with *setting directions*. It is about influencing the context in which instruction takes place. Clearly, what gets the highly rated principals out of bed each morning is what keeps them awake at night. They have a vision and believe that all students can achieve at high levels. They are focused on providing high-quality programs. One characteristic that clearly differentiates high-scoring principals from low-scoring principals is that high-scoring principals want to stay in their current schools until, as one principal put it, the "mission is accomplished."

How do high-scoring principals establish a vision for the school that is centered on high student achievement? For one thing, they emphasize the value of research-based strategies. They speak about the amount of time invested in developing the school's vision, gathering research information, and then applying it to the local setting. An elementary principal passionately stated: "I've researched and researched and done all I can to meet the needs [of my teachers] because they are very bright." Analysis of the teacher interviews in that school reveals the research-based approach as being real and respected by the teaching staff. One teacher said of her high-scoring principal: "My principal is very firm in what she believes." In a separate interview, her principal expressed the vision as being nonnegotiable: "My expectations are high, and [the teachers] know that." The principal went on to emphasize the importance of having an open dialogue about the vision for the school: "I simply put it out there. We've got to kick it up a notch."

The vision for high academic achievement among the principals who score high on Factor 1 also includes a personal vision. As one principal stated: "Our ultimate goal is that our economically disadvantaged children will break the cycle of generational poverty. [We seek] to challenge the status quo and create conditions in which our children have the opportunity to be more academically successful." His focus stands in contrast to that of a low-scoring principal from a different school who emphasized "the standards" without making any effort to connect the standards to a school-level vision. The emerging sense from the analysis of the principal interviews is that low-scoring principals care more about doing their job than about affecting lives.

The differences in ratings on items loading on Factor 1 between high- and low-scoring principals are statistically significant in all cases. This difference is at least one scale step, and more often one-and-a-half or more steps. The largest difference was on item 4–1, which asked teachers about the extent to which their principal develops an atmosphere of caring and trust. And the largest mean rating was on item 4–27 with teachers' agreement that, in general, the principal's motives and intentions are good (see Table 6.1).

Factor 2: Instructional Actions To turn their visions of high student achievement into reality, high-scoring principals are actively engaged in providing direct instructional support to teachers. Instructional actions are how the principal carries out that task. Many of these practices are included in the category of core leadership practices described in Chapter Five as *improving the instructional program*.

Principals guide and support teaching and learning with the goal of enhancing teachers' practices. Responses from the teacher survey indicate that, in particular schools, teachers saw the principal as frequently providing direct instructional support.

Differences were significant between high- and low-scoring principals on all items loading on Factor 2. In every case, the difference between top versus bottom 20 percent mean teacher ratings of principals is the difference of at least one scale step (see Table 6.2). The largest difference among the items in Factor 2 for the top and bottom 20 percent of buildings for perceived principal leadership is on item 4–18, asking how often the principal attended teacher planning meetings. The highest mean rating is on item 4–14, asking how often the principal encouraged collaborative work among staff.

It is particularly noteworthy that the smallest difference, and the lowest-rated item is 4–21, which asked how often the principal has given teachers specific ideas for how to improve instruction. Teachers working with low-scoring principals indicated that somewhere between "Never" and one or two times per year is the frequency with which that happens. Even for high-scoring principals, teachers reported that the principal gave teachers specific ideas about how to improve instruction less than three times per year, on average. Nonetheless, as high-scoring principals implement their mission, their actions are very intentional and focused on high student achievement. For students to learn and grow continually, high-scoring principals claimed, teachers need to learn and grow at the same time.

Thematic analysis of the teacher interviews revealed three kinds of ongoing activities or behaviors that clearly distinguished high-scoring principals from low-scoring principals.

1. High-scoring principals have an acute awareness of teaching and learning in their schools.

One means by which high-scoring principles gain awareness is collecting and examining lesson plans. As one principal noted: "I look at lesson plans and I attend team meetings." A teacher in that building independently concurred: "She makes sure my lessons are in line with the standard course of study." Another teacher explained: "If there are any questions on the lesson plans I turn in, she asks me, 'Why are you doing this? Is this relevant to what you are doing to meet this objective?'" Low-scoring principals described a "hands-off" approach to instructional leadership. One low-scoring principal indicated that she delegates all instructional leadership to an instructional "coach." However, this coach has no role in teacher evaluation and is discouraged from providing any negative feedback to teachers.

2. High-scoring principals have direct and frequent involvement with teachers, providing them with formative assessment of teaching and learning.

Both high- and low-scoring principals said that they frequently visit class-rooms and are "very visible." However, differences between principals in the two groups come into sharp focus as they describe their reasons for making classroom visits. High-scoring principals frequently observed classroom instruc-tion for short periods of time, making twenty to sixty observations a week, and most of the observations were spontaneous. Their visits enabled them to make formative observations that were clearly about learning and professional growth, coupled with direct and immediate feedback. High-scoring principals believed that every teacher, whether a first-year teacher or a veteran, can learn and grow. High-scoring principals described how they "meet each teacher where they are, by finding something good in what they are doing, and then providing feedback in an area that needs growth."

In contrast, low-scoring principals described a very different approach to observations. Their informal visits or observation in classrooms were usually not for instructional purposes. Even informal observations were often planned in advance so that teachers knew when the principal would be stopping by. The most damaging finding became clear in reports from teachers in buildings with low-scoring principals who said they received little or no feedback after informal observations. One of these teachers stated: "I haven't had any feedback or sug-gestions to date." Another teacher considered the lack of feedback as a signal that "my principal has been in [my room] enough to know I am on top of things."

Often, the frequency of informal classroom observations by low-scoring principals decreases as the year progresses. Low-scoring principals focus more on formal, summative observations, providing limited, nonthreatening feedback, pri-marily to nontenured teachers. As to why the principals did not link their obser-vations to any discussion about instructional practice or any attempt at broader efforts to unite teachers around a vision for the school, teachers said, for example, "He is supportive of my teaching philosophy." Insofar as low-scoring principals do not regard the improvement of teaching and learning as an ongoing, long-term process, a culture for continual learning is compromised in their schools.

3. High-scoring principals have the ability and interpersonal skills to empower teachers to learn and grow according to the vision established for the school.

These principals seek out and provide differentiated opportunities for their teachers to learn and grow—one approach to what was described in Chapter Five as *developing people*. For example, one high-scoring principal led Saturday workshops for new teachers in order to catch them up to the rest of the staff. Another high-scoring principal got teaching assistants involved in a workshop designed to help staff members implement a new reading strategy. In contrast, teachers reported, low-scoring principals seldom suggested or supported professional growth opportunities.

Differences in Instructional Leadership Between Elementary and Secondary Schools

Do principals in elementary and secondary schools differ in their enactments of the instructional leadership role? There were some clear differences and some similarities between the two levels evident in the results. Elementary and secondary school teachers' perceptions were similar, as reflected in their responses to the instructional ethos items (Factor 1). All teachers indicated the degree to which their principals were able to create a culture of professional growth and an emphasis on high student and teacher performance. However, elementary and secondary teachers' responses to the instructional actions items (Factor 2) were quite different, as the evidence in Table 6.3 indicates.

For Factors 1 and 2, the percentage of high- or low-scoring principals differs by building level. A higher percentage of elementary school principals scored

TABLE 6.3 TEACHERS' RATINGS OF PRINCIPALS IN THE TOP 20% VS. BOTTOM 20% BY BUILDING LEVEL

Leadership		Building Level	
		Elementary	Secondary
Instructional Ethos (Factor 1)	High (top 20%)	16 64%	9 36%
	Low (bottom 20%)	7 28%	18 72%
Instructional Actions (Factor 2)*	High	19 66%	10 34%
	Low	11 37%	19 63%

*Chi-Square $(1, N = 59) = 4.91, p = .03$.

in the top 20 percent on instructional leadership on both factors. The reverse is true for the bottom 20 percent on instructional leadership, with secondary schools in significantly greater numbers at the low end.

These data confirm our qualitative results. According to interview data, elementary school teachers and principals characterize high-scoring principals who are effective instructional leaders as having a hands-on, direct role in instructional operations. They confirm that instructional ethos Factor 1 is reinforced daily or continually. Teachers in elementary schools whose principals score in the top 20 percent on Factor 1 say, "[New initiatives] will be supported because they are related to a greater vision." This point is consistent with findings from many studies of leadership that have focused on the importance of setting a vision.

Elementary school principals who scored high in both instructional ethos and instructional actions also led schools in which student achievement was relatively high. An elementary school teacher vividly describes the way in which Factor 1 and Factor 2 interact:

> His [the principal's] role and the benefit that I see for me is really two-fold. One is that he is a strong instructional leader. He knows his stuff. It would not surprise me if he were walking in one day and could take over my classroom without skipping a beat. I think that he knows what he's talking about . . . when I sit down and talk with him about an observation that he has made, the questions that he asks, the suggestions that he gives, I know [that these] are from experience and I can trust them. They are the ones that are going to help move me along the path of instructional excellence. So he is not just a principal in name, but he knows what he is talking about. But then on the flip side, he also allows me to be the professional that I have been trained to be. He is not going to mandate that I teach a particular way. He is not going to tell me I have to be on this page on this particular day doing this particular grade-level expectation or this has got to be my learning target. I don't have to be in lock step. When you are as old as I am, you've been around a lot of different people and many times that is the expectation. That is one of the neat things I like about working at this school. [He gives the message that] "I'm going to force you in a positive way to become better, but I'm going to allow you to bring your own personality into the classroom and make that happen." So he is two-pronged on that way [that we are supported].

This combination of instructional ethos and action blends ongoing professional learning with a hands-on, direct role in instructional operations. High-scoring elementary school principals do both effectively.

A different story emerges from evidence about secondary schools. In the interviews, secondary school principals repeatedly said that there was not enough time in the day to complete all their responsibilities, and they told us directly that instructional leadership "gets placed on the back burner." Instructional leadership or planning for it takes place, instead, outside the school day. Secondary school principals assert that they provide instructional leadership through a structural framework of teacher leaders, wherein responsibility is delegated to department heads. In this way, many secondary school principals believe, they act as instructional leaders even though they are one step removed from the process.

Data from the teacher interviews reveals, however, that instructional leadership actions at the secondary school level are generally rare: "Administrators in general observe my classroom one or two times per year," one teacher reported. Another stated: "I've never gotten any feedback that has affected my teaching or that has changed the way I teach besides broad initiatives that the school wants you to do, that everyone wants to see happen." From our analysis of the teacher survey we found that instructional actions, Factor 2, require a direct role in instructional operations. As one teacher noted, "The only time that I was observed was by an assistant principal. It was the second year I taught. She was here five minutes . . . five minutes! And one of the things that she observed about me was that I start on the left-hand side of the room. Do you call that feedback?"

While principals pointed out that they frequently delegated instructional leadership to department chairs, teachers did not regard that sort of delegation as a source of instructional leadership. Most teachers described their department chairs as being in charge of the departmental budget. They also said that teacher leaders have a responsibility to attend team-leadership meetings called by the principal. We did not find any evidence in our interviews with secondary teachers that their department chairs or content-area colleagues were providing instructional leadership in the form of ongoing classroom visits and dialogues about instructional practices. This was true whether the principal scored high or low on instructional ethos, Factor 1.

Even more surprising is the fact that secondary schools dominate the lowest achievement cell in our matrix of high- and low-scoring principals. Of the 31 schools in the bottom 20 percent in the ranking for all principals on instructional actions, Factor 2, 20 schools were middle schools and high schools. Put differently, out of a total of 127 schools returning surveys, with 67 of those being secondary and 60 elementary, nearly 66 percent of all schools with principals scoring in the lowest 20 percent for taking direct action to support teachers' instructional practices were middle and high schools.

The link to student achievement emerged from our quantitative analysis, with apparent differences between elementary and secondary levels emerging as a topic needing further investigation. From the initial sorting of all principals whose teachers rated them as either high- or low-scoring, there were five elementary schools and five secondary schools in the top 20 percent of all schools whose principals were rated high on Factor 1 and who also had high mathematics achievement. Low-rated principals on Factor 1 whose schools also had low mathematics achievement numbered three at the elementary level and eight at the secondary level.

For Factor 2, there were four elementary schools but no secondary schools whose principals were rated high (that is, in the top 20 percent of all schools) and who also had high mathematics achievement. Principals who rated low on Factor 2 and whose schools were lowest in mathematics achievement numbered two at the elementary level and seven at the secondary level (Table 6.4).

When mathematics proficiency for school year 2005–06 is used as a final sorting mechanism (independent variable) for the high-versus low-scoring

TABLE 6.4 RELATIONSHIPS BETWEEN INSTRUCTIONAL LEADERSHIP, SCHOOL LEVEL, AND STUDENT ACHIEVEMENT

Leadership	Math proficiency	Elementary	Secondary
Factor 1 High (top 20%)	High (top 30%)	5 8%	5 7%
	Low (bottom 30%)	7 12%	1 2%
Factor 1 Low (bottom 20%)	High	1 2%	0
	Low	3 5%	8 12%
Factor 2 High	High	4 7%	0
	Low	7 12%	3 5%
Factor 2 Low	High	8 13%	6 9%
	Low	2 3%	7 10%

Note: The number in each elementary or secondary cell is the total number of buildings satisfying the characteristics of each respective cell. The percent is the number of buildings in each cell divided by the sixty elementary or the sixty-seven secondary buildings in the total Round Two survey sample.

principals, the greatest differences appear, once again, at the secondary level. Factor 1 emerges as a significant positive feature of higher-performing secondary schools, and the absence of Factor 1, or instructional ethos, is strikingly evident in secondary schools with low mathematics performance.

Findings for Factor 2 (instructional actions) are equally clear. There were no secondary school principals who scored high on Factor 2 whose schools also had high mathematics achievement. At the other end of the scale, there were seven secondary schools whose principals ranked the lowest on instructional actions and who also had low mathematics achievement.

What Might We Conclude?

Our data revealed a clear distinction about the concept of instructional leadership, suggesting a missing nuance in much of the existing scholarship. It is a distinction between principals who provided support to teachers by "popping in" and "being visible" as compared with principals who were very intentional about each classroom visit and conversation, with the explicit purpose of engaging with teachers about well-defined instructional ideas and issues.

We did find that high-scoring principals emphasized the establishment of a vision for their schools. In many schools, however, the principal's engagement with individual teachers to ensure that the vision would be realized appeared to be either very limited or missing, especially in middle schools and high schools. Some of these principals, mostly at the secondary level, wrongly assumed that if a vision of high-quality instruction was well articulated, then high-quality instruction would happen without much further action on their part or through the delegation of necessary actions to department heads and other teacher leaders.

Indeed, one major finding is that department heads provide little to no instructional leadership. Organizationally, they appear to be particularly well-situated to offer leadership to their colleagues, but that potential for leadership appears to be a squandered resource. Relegating department heads exclusively to a managerial role is a great waste of a potential resource for instructional improvement. A radical redefinition of the role would help school districts solve the historical problem of inertia in secondary schools. Department heads may need to work under revised contractual language, in which their role to provide instructional feedback and support to colleagues is clearly spelled out. For example, Teacher on Special Assignment (TOSA) is a way in which school districts and teacher unions allow for teachers to take on additional supervisory responsibilities that are permissible within the general teacher contract. Mentor teacher and master teacher contracts are common examples of differentiated staffing.

Unsurprisingly, our evidence also points to the continuing preference of many teachers to be "left alone." These teachers typically view the presence of a principal in their classrooms as unnecessary and sometimes bothersome. Said one teacher: "I haven't been observed in 17 years, and that's OK with me." Another teacher noted that her principal had previously been a school psychologist, not a classroom teacher, and for that reason the teacher believed that her principal had an insufficient grasp of the stresses of teaching and could not "really give me any realistic suggestions of how to be a better instructor."

Maintenance of the status quo—which for most secondary school teachers meant not having direct and frequent contact with the principal or anyone else, for that matter, about ways to improve instruction—was preferred. In light of evidence reported in other chapters of this book about the critical contribution to school improvement of well-functioning professional communities in schools, this preference stands as a huge obstacle to secondary school reform.

Evidence in this chapter did not provide a strong test of the impact of instructional leadership on student performance. Nevertheless, those schools that were ranked at the bottom of the instructional leadership continuum for Factor 1 or Factor 2, with student achievement scores in the lowest 30 percent, were predominantly secondary schools. It is even more notable that the raw number and relative percent of secondary schools with low ranking and low achievement were significantly higher than for elementary schools.

Overall, secondary schools appear to suffer from a "double whammy." Low professional growth ethos and few actions taken to support classroom instruction appear to be indicators of lower student performance. Academic achievement in elementary schools, however, appears to be more sensitive to principals who score low on either Factor 1 or Factor 2.

Implications for Policy and Practice

Three implications for policy and practice emerged from this chapter.

1. Principals need to be held accountable for taking actions that are known to have direct effects on the quality of teaching and learning in their schools.

When principals serve effectively as instructional leaders, student achievement is likely to increase. It is not enough to create a vision for instructional improvement. If principals are to act effectively as instructional leaders, instructional actions must complement their instructional vision. Districts should expect principals to take targeted actions aimed at implementing instructional leadership within each school. Most districts will need to have honest and in-depth discussions with their principals about how to practically do this. Districts and principals then, should work together to develop procedures for systematically monitoring such implementation. The needs and circumstances of elementary and secondary school principals may need to be differentially addressed, however the bottom line would have each principal expected to take specific steps to enact instructional leadership in his or her school.

2. District leaders should acknowledge, and begin to reduce, ways in which secondary school principals are limited in their capacity to exercise instructional leadership by the work required of them in their role as it is currently structured.

Findings reported in this chapter indicate that discussions about teaching and learning occur informally between colleagues and peers, but they occur less frequently in the context of structured team meetings, content-area meetings, or formal team leader-follower channels. Infrequent provision of instructional leadership by principals, especially at the secondary school level, leaves little room for dialogue about teaching and learning between leaders and followers. Consistent with Supovitz's (2006) findings, this research indicates that under current secondary school structures, authority relationships tend to discourage candor about problems that secondary school teachers may be having.

District administrators are normally aware of the managerial effectiveness of their principals in addressing immediate tasks and problems. They may also be aware of principals' efforts to create an instructional vision in which student achievement is an explicit priority. Still, a troublesome pattern apparently persists: secondary school principals do not, according to our data, interact with teachers frequently and directly about instructional practice.

3. The role of department head should be radically redefined. Department heads should be regarded, institutionally, as a central resource for improving instruction in secondary schools.

Theoretically, department heads already possess much of the content knowledge that some argue is a significant contribution to the impact of instructional leadership on schools and students. Although acquiring such content knowledge is an especially unrealistic expectation for secondary principals, it is a very realistic expectation for department heads to use both their knowledge of content and best practices for teaching it to take on a larger role for instructional leadership with their peers. Principals and department heads, together, will need to figure out how this can be accomplished.

Reflections

1. In school settings with which you are familiar, how balanced is principals' attention to instructional ethos and instructional action?
2. Does one of these dimensions predominate? If it does, what are the consequences?
3. Think about one principal you know well. Describe how she or he goes about creating instructional ethos. Does this reflect what is reported in this chapter?
4. With the same principal in mind, to what extent do this individual's instructional actions align with those reported in this chapter?

PART TWO

THE BROAD AND UNIQUE ROLE OF DISTRICTS IN THE SCHOOL IMPROVEMENT BUSINESS

CHAPTER SEVEN

HOW TO HARNESS FAMILY AND COMMUNITY ENERGY

The District's Role

Molly F. Gordon and Karen Seashore Louis

Claims Supported by Evidence in This Chapter

- District policies that promote community engagement in schools increase the participation of a wider array of people and groups at the school level.
- District engagement policies can have long-lasting effects on principals. The more principals get used to interacting with the community, the more open they become to involving outside stakeholders in school improvement efforts.
- The role of the principal in interpreting district engagement policies and in creating and communicating school-level expectations for parent engagement is critical.
- In schools with more democratic collective leadership practices that include parents in influential positions, student achievement is higher.

In this chapter, we examine district efforts to engage families and the broader community in school improvement work. Family and community engagement has been a topic of active investigation for many years. There is consensus that family characteristics are linked to student achievement. Our interest, however, is focused on the consequences of school initiatives intended to involve parents and community members as partners in the educational enterprise. In light of this background, we examine these three questions:

- Which district policies and practices foster family and community engagement?
- How do districts influence the level of community engagement in schools?
- How are participatory and collective leadership structures related to student learning?

What Do We Know from Prior Research?

Three areas of prior evidence informed our work in this chapter: (1) studies of recent efforts to create more democratic structures in schools, (2) studies about district and school characteristics that may support or inhibit family and community participation, and (3) evidence linking family engagement with student learning.

Creating Democratic Structures

In the last two decades, educators and community members have shown an interest in creating more democratic educational structures by establishing and using various advisory councils, for example. This movement challenged those who viewed parents and community members as outsiders and not as true members of the school community. Some researchers interpreted the devolution of power from the state to local schools as democracy in action.[1] Reforms such as site-based management, community control of schools, community schools, and school choice were all based on democratic and communitarian theories.[2] In contrast, some researchers and policy makers influenced by economic theory viewed the relationship between schools and communities differently, and defined families and community members as clients or customers. From this perspective, schools should be held accountable to their clients.[3] However, many educators and researchers remain suspicious of the community-as-client view and espouse, instead, an assumption that is more aligned with a professional model, in which educators are the experts whose responsibility is to elicit cooperation from the less-expert patient in carrying out the doctor's prescriptions. In this chapter, we argue that none of these models alone is appropriate for understanding the complex relationships among parents, a community, and schools. A school that is accountable to the community is one that reflects local values and customs, has indicators of success that are visible and well-communicated to the public, and allows parents to choose other schools if they are not satisfied with the service, but that also acknowledges the special role of educational professionals and community members working together to support student development.[4]

The success of current participatory democratic structures in schools has been mixed, and there is often a wide gap between rhetoric and practice. For example, researchers have found that site-based management initiatives rarely challenged existing power structures or altered decision-making patterns in schools.[5] Also, research on formal site councils found that establishing governance structures alone did not bring about shared power and decision making.[6] Instead, these initiatives worked to incorporate outsiders into the school's frame of reference.[7] Even where family and community involvement programs have been mandated, observers have questioned the fidelity of implementation. Because it is easier for traditional power structures to remain in place when environmental factors are "stable and congenial,"[8] giving parents and teachers authority to make some school decisions may in some respects reinforce the status quo.[9]

Cognizant of the gap between practice and rhetoric, several scholars have investigated factors that actually make a difference in these efforts. For example, school principals who are committed to facilitative or distributed forms of governance tend to have stronger, more influential school councils.[10] In addition, fostering communication between teachers and families can help to create a democratic community and support school improvement. Although some teachers and parents desire interaction within a democratic community, they may lack the language necessary to articulate that interest or the knowledge, expertise, or experience needed to make it happen.[11]

In examining the contested nature of schools in a pluralistic society, researchers found that when school members tried to change long-established policies and practices around parental engagement, among the results were conflict and the emergence of competing issues and concerns about education.[12] Researchers suggest, however, that schools can bring competing groups together by developing collaborative structures and involving families in shared decision making. Also, research on community organizing groups showed that educational organizing helped schools expand their capacity to create greater equity in resources, respond to imposed reforms, and generate more meaningful community, parent, and youth engagement aimed at increasing student learning.[13]

District and School Characteristics That Support or Inhibit Family and Community Participation

At the district level, research has shown that school superintendents have a large influence on the relationship between the school board and the surrounding community.[14] In addition to strong support and direction from district leaders, other researchers found that "the bridger role" or "boundary spanner" was central to the process of creating successful partnership structures that promoted democratic interorganizational relationships.[15]

At the school level, research on the principal's role in fostering parent-community involvement found that the notion of ownership in the successful education of students was central. Principals who see parents as equal partners were able not only to foster a greater sense of accountability toward the community, but also to engage parents and community members in the ownership of the educational process.[16] Although principals play a crucial role in engagement policies related to school-improvement initiatives, the school culture or climate is also crucial. Important characteristics of school culture related to engagement include a caring atmosphere, significant family volunteering, and a supportive environment for teachers' work.[17] Widespread trust among participants also promotes collaboration within schools and communities.[18] All of these are important because while parental involvement benefits students in particular, it also benefits families, enhancing their attitudes about themselves, their children's schools, and school staff members.[19]

Some principals and teachers, however, assume that low levels of parental involvement reflect low levels of interest in the education of the children in question. The evidence does not support this view. Parents generally—inner-city and low-income parents as well as others—care deeply about their children's education.[20] Their level of interest is not always readily apparent to educational professionals. Some parents may not know how to be involved helpfully in their children's education.[21] Others may feel constrained by reticence arising from an inhibiting sense of class differences. For reasons like these, educators face a special challenge in seeking to foster increased family involvement. The policies and programs currently targeted to that task are, in many districts, inadequate.[22]

Family Engagement and Student Learning

Research has shown that students who have involved parents are more likely to

- Earn higher grades and test scores, and enroll in higher-level classes
- Be promoted to the next grade level, pass their classes, and earn more credits
- Attend school regularly
- Have better behavior and social skills
- Graduate and go on to some type of postsecondary education[23]

Research has also shown that parents' expectations of or aspirations for their children and the parents' own academic success in school were central factors positively associated with academic growth.[24] In addition, other factors that influence student learning include parents enforcing standards and behaviors that are connected to learning, including monitoring homework, hiring tutors in areas where students struggle, keeping distractions to a minimum during homework time, and actively engaging in educational choices.[25]

Significant findings from two meta-analyses[26] also add credibility to the case that family involvement leads to increased student achievement. The first concluded that family involvement affected student academic achievement, but in different ways for different ethnic groups. For example, for African Americans, there was a strong positive relationship between (1) parenting style and family attendance at various school events and (2) student achievement, but those variables were not statistically significant for other groups. The second meta-analysis, focused exclusively on studies of urban secondary school students, showed that family involvement had a significant effect on student achievement for minority and white students.

Less visible aspects of family involvement—parenting style and parental expectations, for example—may have a greater impact on student achievement than more overt forms such as attendance at school conferences or enforcing rules at home regarding homework.[27] An argument can be made that the less visible forms of family involvement are not easily influenced by schools.[28] However, the value of creating participatory structures in schools lies in its potential for increasing family and community members' sense of engagement and ownership in children's education, which can augment and reinforce the less obvious behaviors responsible for improved outcomes.[29]

New Evidence for This Chapter

This chapter draws heavily on Gordon and Louis (2009), and the vignettes are portions of larger case studies found in Gordon (2010).

Method

In this chapter, we used survey and interview data, along with state mandated measures of student mathematics achievement, to answer our research questions. (For a more detailed description of the methods used in this chapter and the regression tables, please see Appendix B.) We analyzed items from the principal survey that assessed how open principals are to involving outside stakeholders in planning and setting school improvement goals (*principal openness to community involvement*), how supportive the principals think their district is in helping aid school efforts to engage parents and community members (*district support for community involvement*), and how influential parents are in school-level decision making (*principal perceptions of parent influence*). In addition, we analyzed the extent to which outside community stakeholders are represented on school governance structures such as site councils or building leadership teams (*diversity of membership on site councils*).

For the teacher survey, we analyzed items that assessed the degree to which principals encourage and involve teachers and parents in school improvement efforts (*parent/teacher collective leadership*), the level of influence of principals and teachers in school decision making (*principal-teacher shared leadership*), and how teachers perceive the level of direct parental influence in school decision making (*parent involvement*).

In analyzing the surveys, we used regression and path analysis to try and determine which factors influence (1) the diversity of membership on site councils, (2) principals' openness to community involvement, (3) principals' perceptions of parent influence, and (4) parent involvement. Finally, we analyzed how all of these factors link to (5) student math achievement. Results of our quantitative analysis draw on and augment an earlier investigation we did of the relationship between the above variables.[30] We also included poverty and building level in our analysis because several studies examining parent involvement found that poverty and grade level of child were significant factors in the level of parent involvement in schools and because socioeconomic status is also a significant factor in predicting student achievement.[31]

Vignettes based on our interview data were used to illustrate and further explore our quantitative findings. In constructing our vignettes, we analyzed interviews conducted with district and school staff members and a variety of community stakeholders. Interview topics included questions about leadership roles, practices, and behaviors, school and district improvement efforts, district and school policies and practices, and relationships with internal and external stakeholders. More specifically for this chapter, we analyzed interviews to assess the level of influence of outside stakeholders in school improvement efforts and to understand engagement practices and policies.

Which District Policies and Practices Foster or Hinder Family and Community Engagement at the District and School Levels?

Results of our interview and survey analysis reveal that district and school leadership is vital to creating an environment of openness for fostering meaningful community engagement. The following vignette illustrates how one new superintendent connected with and involved community members in school improvement efforts after a long tenure of district disengagement with the community.

Atlas School District

New District Leadership and a Renewed Commitment to Community Engagement

She's much more visible in the community. She's much more involved with communication with the community; personally involved [than the previous superintendent]. Because of that visibility, I think that has strengthened the perception of the school district with our constituents, with our community.

—District staff member

Prior to the tenure of the current Atlas superintendent, Michelle Sorenson, who came into office in 2005, the previous superintendent held the job for more than ten years. That superintendent was not skilled in engaging with the community. Because there were complaints from community groups about the old superintendent, the school board engaged the community in helping to pick the new superintendent. Board members said that they looked for and hired an "avid communicator." When Superintendent Sorenson came on board, she made it a priority to get out into the community, repair relationships with stakeholders, build trust, and restore the reputation of the district.

An executive vice president of a local children's foundation stated that the district has improved since Superintendent Sorenson came on board—in openness and in soliciting community input for discussions of how the district operates and in school improvement efforts. For example, the superintendent focused on being visible by giving approximately 80 presentations to community organizations in the first year she took office. Increased visibility has led to increased trust between the district and various community groups and parents, according to district representatives and community stakeholders. In order to build relationships, gain trust, and communicate the needs of the district, the superintendent engaged as many stakeholders as possible. For example, the district recruited approximately 60 people from various community groups and parents to lobby for a bond measure. The bond measure passed because of the district's renewed commitment to the community.

Superintendent Sorenson says it is important for her leadership to maintain transparency in proceedings at the district level and to communicate continually with the public. The district also brings people in on important district-level initiatives so that stakeholders feel part of the process. The district's mission and goals are well known inside the organization and within the community. Annually, the district prepares and distributes a report to all Atlas residents that includes information such as test scores, results of follow-up studies from graduates, assessment results about the learning climate, financial information, and school demographic characteristics.

In the preceding example, the superintendent communicated regularly with community stakeholders about district and school progress, and was described as open and accessible. As the vignette illustrates, when there is leadership turnover at the district level, especially in districts with weak or negative relationships with external groups, the new superintendent may have to take on the bridger or boundary spanner role and spend a lot of time out in the community creating new partnerships and rebuilding trust in the organization.

This next vignette illustrates how stable district leadership, regular communication, and a commitment by district leaders to reach out to the community for input can create broad based community ownership in the educational process.

North White Pine County

Stable District Leadership and a Culture of Soliciting Community Input

We don't sit on this little island and make the decisions. We seek and value our stakeholder input.

—District staff member

Leadership in the North White Pine County District has been unusually stable compared to other districts in the state, and around the country. Superintendent Samuelson served the district for 16 years, and the superintendent before him served for 19 years. When Superintendent Samuelson retired, a new superintendent, Sheila Wauters—who had been a district staff member for several years—took over the district. She said that because the previous administration did such an excellent job working and communicating with families and the community, she wanted to make sure that she continued their policies and practices.

The district has a long history of gaining stakeholder buy-in prior to launching new programs, thus mitigating pressure of the sort that often arises in other districts. For example, before a redistricting decision, the superintendent and other district leaders took their ideas "on the road" to every neighborhood that would be affected, asking the public for input. Going out to talk about a controversial topic is, in the words of one district staff member, "not always fun," but he adds that people appreciate the chance to give input; they feel that they are valued by the district leaders. North White Pine County district leaders say that regular communication is vital in order to maintain trust and support in the district.

At least annually, district leaders ask for input and feedback on school and district programs and practices from students, parents, colleges, businesses, and community partners, including faith-based groups and the local military base. When asked what contributed to maintaining positive relationships with the community, a district staff member said that it came down to the leadership, both at the district and school levels. In North White Pine County District, he said reaching out and valuing the input of outside stakeholders was "second nature" and "just the culture that we have."

In the preceding vignette, the superintendent of North White Pine County District solicited input from community members prior to implementing new policies and initiatives, which resulted in buy-in from schools and the public and created a communal sense of ownership in the student learning process.

Based on our interview analysis, we identified several leadership and organizational characteristics that can foster greater levels of community engagement at the district level:

- A visible and accessible superintendent who is open to engaging community members in innovative ways
- Organizational transparency, so that community members understand what is happening in the district
- Frequent public communication of the district's mission and goals
- Multiple avenues for community members to give their input on district policies and practices

In these examples, organizational conditions such as collaborative and open cultures along with visible and highly communicative district leadership fostered greater outside stakeholder involvement. These vignettes show that leadership at the district level is critical for creating and sustaining a district culture that fosters parent and community engagement. Other organizational conditions that generally hindered community and parent engagement included unapproachable leadership, vaguely worded and weakly monitored policies, and cultures and structures that kept parents and community members on the periphery.

How Do Districts Influence the Level of Community Engagement in Schools?

Next, we investigated how district policies, support, and practices influence school level engagement practices. In both our survey and interview analysis, we found that many districts mandate governance structures that include external stakeholder representatives. Our survey analysis showed that formal district policies promoting broad community involvement are significantly associated with the diversity of membership on school site councils. The following vignette illustrates how one district used mandated governance structures as a way to foster democratic participation.

Glenhurst School District

Promoting Democracy Through Mandated Formal Governance Structures

You have to maintain a democratic public education system; you have to have the public involved.

—Glenhurst School District leader

District leaders in Glenhurst promote participatory democracy through mandated governance structures. The district has three formal ways for parents and community members to get involved: elected site councils, elected local school committees (LSCs), and parent teacher organizations (PTOs). Every school in the district has an elected site council (50 percent teachers and 50 percent community members) to set the direction for school improvement and to plan staff development. According to district-level staff, both the state and the district put a lot of time and effort into giving the site councils credibility and making sure they have community representation. Superintendent Cameron, along with other district leaders, meets quarterly with all site council members to get updates on the school improvement plan process and address any concerns.

In addition to site councils, every school in the district has an elected local school committee. Every two years, three community members are elected to the LSC through county government elections. The superintendent describes the LSCs as "mini school boards" that help run the school. The superintendent meets with members of the LSCs every two months to talk about their work. Although the primary role of the LSC is to review applications for and manage the use of district facilities, their influence extends beyond facilities management. For example, members of each LSC provide input into urgent district issues, including construction bonds and boundary changes for schools with capacity problems. Even though members of the LSC do not have formal authority to determine policies, members often use their position and power to influence critical district decisions. For instance, LSC members of all of the schools banded together to complain about a district math adoption. Because of their vocal complaints, district leaders invited them, along with other influential parent groups, into the district office to help frame program evaluation and select interventions for students struggling with the new math curriculum. According to the school board vice chair, the democratic process of allowing all voices to be heard is valued by the district, even though it sometimes slows down the process of making decisions.

Aside from the LSCs and site councils, every school is mandated to have a parent teacher organization (PTO) designed to include parents in the operation of schools. The influence of the PTOs, however, varies tremendously by school and is dependent on the preferences of the principal. Although the district does not try and control the level of influence parents have in schools, district leaders talked about the importance of involving parents in school improvement efforts and in helping to increase student learning.

The preceding vignette illustrates how one district used mandates to get the public involved in school-level decisions. As a result, community members and parents did have more formal influence and decision making power, as evidenced by the district response to community protests of the newly adopted curriculum.

Although districts have a significant and direct influence on outside stakeholder engagement at the school level through the creation of more democratic structures, the level of power and influence of parents and community members who serve on those governance structures varies from school to school within the same district. Even though district leaders in the preceding vignettes modeled community engagement—through their partnering, their willingness to listen to public concerns, and their efforts to include families and communities in district level committees—the actual engagement with parents and other external groups at the school level was mixed. For example, Glenhurst's assistant superintendent said that the district relied on their principals to set the tone for engagement and communication, but admitted that she was not sure whether they actually engaged them or not. This is not surprising, in that other research has shown that creating or mandating democratic structures alone will not always lead to shared power and decision making. These findings are also consistent with our quantitative analysis, in which we found that although there was a correlation between district support for more community involvement and diversity of membership on site councils, districts did not have a significantly strong impact on the level of the principals' preferences for widespread parent and community engagement. Therefore the role of the principal is vital both in interpreting unclear district expectations and in creating and communicating school-level expectations for parent engagement.

The following additional vignette from North White Pine County shows how the level of parent and community engagement in schools is primarily dependent upon the principal.

North White Pine County

Limited District Influence on Schools Level Engagement Practices

Even though North White Pine County district leaders encourage principals and teachers to reach out to the community, participation levels vary from school to school. The district is committed to site-based management policies, and as a result each principal sets the school tone for community engagement. The district gets involved in school operations only when there is a problem. The district did intervene in one case, in which an influential group of parents complained that a new administrative team was less responsive to them than previous administrators had been. The district worked with the new administration and parents to make sure that a strong relationship was built. At most schools in the district, however, district leaders emphasized the importance of community engagement and encouraged principals to be open, but stopped short of recommending individual school engagement practices. The degree of influence the district had on principal openness to engagement was therefore low. The following school-level examples illustrate the vastly different engagement practices occurring in different schools in the district:

At the elementary school, the principal mimicked the long-standing district practice of going out to the community to gain buy-in and support prior to changing policies or practices. For example, she and a team of teachers lobbied for their school to become a magnet school by going out into the neighborhoods to talk about how the change to a magnet program would affect the school and families. She explained that even after the decision was made to become a magnet school, she and other school staff did "road shows" to recruit families. The principal said that district leaders valued the amount of research and community outreach that she and her staff did to sell the magnet program.

At a middle school in the district, on the other hand, the principal blamed the community for "allowing" the school to let athletics overshadow academic progress. The principal agreed that part of the problem was that some parents might feel unwelcome at the school, and that it was "going to take me and my teachers knocking on doors and calling and actually going out to the community" to change the culture. There was no evidence that this kind of work occurred, however, and the professionals continued to report that most of the parents in the community just "didn't get it." Low parental involvement led the principal to conclude that it was the school's responsibility to educate and "parent" the children while they were at school. Engaging with families was not part of her equation.

As the preceding vignette illustrates, the elementary school principal was influenced by the long-standing district practice of going out into the community to gain buy-in prior to making major changes. On the other hand, the middle school principal came to believe that family engagement was not a priority in a school whose efforts were focused on increasing achievement. These examples show that when districts are not explicit about the locus of responsibility for community involvement, engagement practices at the school level become dependent on whether it is high or low on a principal's priority list. These data also suggest that district and school leaders who want to meaningfully engage parents and community groups need to move past simply viewing external stakeholders as "clients" who deserve information about what the district or school is doing and to actually start viewing parents and community stakeholders as vital partners in the learning process.

Despite finding weak links between district-level policies and practices and school-level policies and practices in our vignettes, both our survey and interview findings suggest that districts *can* support schools by not only creating formal structures for involvement, but also by actively supporting and encouraging community and parent involvement. Figure 7.1 shows the relationship between *district support for community involvement* and school-level engagement, as measured by principal's perceptions of *parent influence.* (Figures 7.1 and 7.2 summarize the results of a structural equation model using the AMOS program in SPSS. The relevant statistics for all models [RMSEA, NFI, CFI] indicate that the models are a good fit with the data.)

The model in Figure 7.1 shows that district support for community involvement is linked to the level of influence parents have in schools in two ways. The strongest link is through policies that districts create to include outside stakeholders on school site councils or other building leadership teams. Diversity of membership on site councils, in turn, has a strong and significant impact on how open a principal is to community involvement—a factor that is statistically related to the level of parental influence. The model also shows that district support for community involvement affects how open a principal is to engagement, which increases the argument for a prominent district role.

This result supplements our findings from a survey analysis showing that district support alone (encouragement rather than clear formal policies for engagement) had a positive, but not statistically significant influence on a principal's openness

FIGURE 7.1 RELATIONSHIP BETWEEN DISTRICT SUPPORT FOR COMMUNITY INVOLVEMENT AND SCHOOL-LEVEL ENGAGEMENT, AS MEASURED BY PRINCIPAL'S PERCEPTIONS OF PARENT INFLUENCE

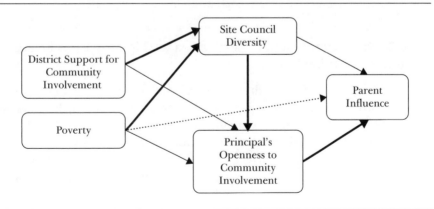

Solid line = a positive relationship
Bold line = a strong positive relationship
Dotted line = a negative relationship

to community involvement. Figure 7.1 suggests that formal district policies have a much greater impact on school engagement practices. Combined with the case study analyses, the results also suggest that as principals become used to interacting with their community (because of district mandates to engage, for example), they become more open to engagement. The more principals get used to interacting with the community, the more open they become to involving outside stakeholders in school improvement efforts. Conversely, as in the case of the middle school principal in North White Pine County, limited interaction with community members may increase the principal's sense of a conflict of interests and concerns.

Another important finding is that in higher-poverty schools there is more diversity of membership on site councils or building leadership teams. In other words, principals and teachers in less affluent communities tend to include more diverse voices in formal governance structures. Community engagement is, overall, lower in high-poverty communities, where principals report significantly more limited parent influence. However, that is not the case where district policies, diversity of membership on site councils, and principal openness to community involvement are aligned. In settings with those characteristics, parent influence is, according to principals, high. Having a diverse site council does not equal a culture of collective or shared leadership. It is up to individual school leaders to go beyond simple district support in order to develop meaningful parent engagement practices.

Figure 7.1 showed how district support was related to parental influence. In our next inquiry, we used regression and path analysis to understand how participatory and collective leadership practices and principals' perceptions of parental influence were related to student achievement.

How Do Participatory and Collective Leadership Structures Relate to Student Learning?

We used data from both the principal and teacher surveys to investigate which participatory and leadership structures are related to student learning. Specifically, we were interested in extending the results of Chapter Three, which suggested that collective leadership, defined as more influence from more different partners, could affect student learning. More specifically, we investigated whether collective leadership at the school would affect parents' involvement as partners in their children's educational success. Figure 7.2 illustrates our results.

Our analysis presented in Figure 7.2 shows that collective leadership as measured by *parent teacher / shared leadership* and *principal / teacher shared leadership*, in addition to principals' perceptions of *parent influence*, has an influence on the level of *parent*

FIGURE 7.2 SHARED LEADERSHIP AND STUDENT ACHIEVEMENT

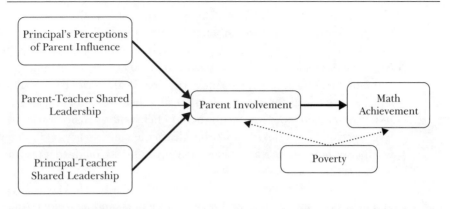

Solid line = a positive relationship
Bold line = a strong positive relationship
Dotted line = a negative relationship

involvement, which is a factor significantly related to *student achievement*. These results show that in schools where parents are influential and where principals share leadership with teachers and parents, there is more parent involvement and thus higher student math achievement. In other words, in schools with democratic collective leadership practices that include parents in influential positions, student achievement is higher. Because parental involvement is linked to student achievement, we assert that principals, as well as teachers, can impact student learning by creating a culture of shared leadership and responsibility and by instituting more democratic processes in schools—not merely among school staff members, but also collectively within the wider community. We also examined whether site council diversity, another indicator of school-based collective leadership, would have the same positive effect on parent involvement and student achievement, with similar results.

At the same time, the figure also shows that family poverty levels have a significantly negative relationship with parent involvement and student math achievement, a finding that is consistent with other research. This and other analyses suggest that although efforts to engage families and the community do mitigate the effects of poverty, they do not erase it. What is more important is that schools make a difference. Where districts and schools welcome and encourage genuine community and parent participation in decision making, irrespective of their family income, parents will be more involved with their children's education, and children will do better.

What Might We Conclude?

The results of our analyses show that districts can play a role in promoting participatory democratic structures in schools by creating policies and expectations for participation by a wide array of peoples and groups. For example, districts can help schools create more diverse school-site councils, especially in more affluent communities. Outside of the formal structures, districts can try informal ways to engage outside stakeholders, such as seeking their input on district policies and practices, and collaborating with them to help with specific district- or school-level needs. Our research shows that district leadership is vital in determining whether or not outside stakeholders had any influence on district priority setting, programs, and/or policies.

There was a disconnection, however, between district-level policies, practices, and behaviors, and school-level policies, practices, and behaviors. All three districts in the preceding vignettes modeled community engagement, partnering, and a willingness to listen to public concerns, and all made efforts to include families and communities in district-level committees. In all three cases, however, the district stopped short of making sure that principals modeled these same behaviors. One reason may be that the districts are committed to local control and a hands-off approach to day-to-day operations within schools. Another explanation for the disconnect may be that districts had vague and noncommittal parent/community involvement policies (besides mandated involvement on building leadership teams), which resulted in varied school-level engagement practices. In each case, district leaders acknowledged that engagement with communities varies from school to school, depending on the leadership style of the principals. Leaders in all three districts were aware of research linking family involvement with increased student learning, but they did not believe it was their role to mandate engagement among schools, parents, and other community members. This finding suggests that districts are not doing enough to create a climate or expectations for schools to be open to community and parental involvement. If districts want schools to engage with parents and community members in productive and meaningful ways, then they need to not only create clearer policies and strategies for schools to follow but also do a better job of monitoring engagement practices and holding school leaders accountable to engaging with outside stakeholder groups. Vaguely written policies, encouragement, and even expectations alone will not work, unless districts specify clear strategies, actually monitor the level of implementation, and hold school leaders accountable.

Reflecting on our findings, we note that district-level policies and structures are necessary to maintain communication and provide opportunities for engagement with parents and other community members. At the same time, we observe that establishing policies and providing structures alone will not ensure widespread, genuine participation. To gain the benefits of widespread participation, district leaders will need to do more. They will need to focus more sharply and energetically on collective leadership by engaging teachers, administrators, parents, and community members in ongoing, reflective discussions of what each party can and should contribute to students' learning.

Implications for Policy and Practice

Four implications for policy and practice emerged from this component of our study.

1. District leaders need to engage in dialogues with principals about what openness to community and parental involvement means in practice, beyond merely establishing policies and structures. Pertinent topics for such discussions include the value of partnering with parents and community members in school-improvement efforts, parents as vital partners in the learning process, the importance of shared leadership, and the critical role that the community plays in every child's life.

2. Principals need to engage teachers and other staff members in similar discussions, focused especially on ways to involve parents in roles beyond the superficial tasks often allocated to them (for example, coordinating social events, fundraising through bake sales). Many parents feel marginalized because they are given tasks that do not reflect the crucial role they could otherwise play in support of their children's education. Parent participation as tutors or mentors, or in other forms of classroom support, are as vital as the roles they take on in site council activities.

3. Districts should take an active role in teaching parents and other community members how to be involved in education. This effort should include providing informational and instructional sessions about shared governance. These discussions could help to create a sense of ownership among all staff parents, parents, and other community members, helping to increase student learning.

4. Similar to other countries, states should consider using measures of genuine community and parent engagement as part of their school accountability systems.

Questions for Reflection

1. All of the district leaders in the Glenhurst, North White Pine, and Atlas districts tried several ways to engage parents and community members and were committed to involving a wide array of outside stakeholders in decisions. Despite this, we saw very different engagement practices from school

to school. How can districts stay committed to a more hands-off, site-based management approach for school management but also ensure that principals and teachers actively engage with parents and community members?

2. Shared and collaborative leadership, involving principals, parents, and teachers, appears to be a sturdy three-legged stool that supports student success. In your experience, what conditions are required to make this combination of factors work well? Why are they relatively rare in many districts and schools? How can schools overcome the tendency to see low-income parents as uninterested or unable to become engaged?

CHAPTER EIGHT

CONFIDENCE FOR SCHOOL IMPROVEMENT

A Priority for Principals

Kenneth Leithwood, Blair Mascall, and Doris Jantzi

Claims Supported by Evidence in This Chapter

- Districts that help their school leaders feel more efficacious or confident about their school improvement work have positive effects on important school conditions, as well as on student learning.
- School leaders who believe they are working collaboratively toward clear and common goals with district personnel, other principals, and teachers in their schools, are more confident about their leadership.
- District size is a significant moderator of district contributions to school leaders' efficacy. School leaders in larger districts need more direct and explicit support from their central office colleagues for building their sense of efficacy for accomplishing agreed-on goals.
- School level is a significant moderator of district contributions to school leaders' efficacy. As compared with their elementary school counterparts, secondary school leaders are likely to need more direct and explicit support from their central office colleagues in building their sense of efficacy for accomplishing agreed-on goals.

One of the most powerful ways in which districts influence teaching and learning is through the contribution they make to principals' feelings of professional efficacy; in particular, their efficacy for school improvement. This chapter uses quantitative evidence from our larger study to demonstrate how principal efficacy provides the crucial link between district initiatives, school conditions, and student learning. Evidence summarized in this chapter describes:

- The extent to which district leadership and district conditions influence principals' sense of efficacy for school improvement
- The influence of principal efficacy on: (a) principals' leadership practices, (b) learning conditions in their schools, and (c) student learning
- The extent to which personal and organizational characteristics moderate the influence of principals' efficacy on student learning

The next chapter (Nine) extends our analysis of principal efficacy to examine the positive and negative influences of district actions.

Starting Points

Our starting points were (1) evidence about the nature of leader efficacy and (2) both leadership practices and district conditions that seem to be consequential for student learning.

Leader Efficacy

Efficacy is a belief about one's own ability (self-efficacy) or the ability of one's colleagues collectively (collective efficacy) to perform a task or achieve a goal. It is a *belief* about ability, not actual ability. Albert Bandura (1997a), self-efficacy's most prominent theorist, claims:

> People make causal contributions to their own functioning through mechanisms of personal agency. Among the mechanisms of agency, none is more central or pervasive than peoples' beliefs about their capabilities to exercise control over their own level of functioning and over events that affect their lives. [p. 118]

Most leader-efficacy studies have been influenced by Bandura's sociopsychological theory of self-efficacy.[1] In addition to defining the meaning of self-efficacy and its several dimensions, this body of work identifies the effects of self-efficacy feelings on a leader's behavior, and the consequences of that behavior for others. This line of theory also specifies the direct antecedents of self-efficacy beliefs and the mechanisms through which such beliefs develop.

Efficacy beliefs, according to this theory, have directional effects on one's choice of activities and settings, and they can affect coping efforts once those activities are begun. Such beliefs determine how much effort people will expend and how long they will persist in the face of failure or difficulty. The stronger the feelings of efficacy are, the longer the persistence. People who persist at activities that they subjectively perceive to be threatening—but that are not actually threatening—gain corrective experiences that further enhance their sense of efficacy. In sum, "Given appropriate skills and adequate incentives . . . efficacy expectations are a major determinant of peoples' choice of activities, how much effort they will expend and how long they will sustain effort in dealing with stressful situations."[2]

Efficacy beliefs, according to Bandura, develop in response to cognitive and affective processes. Among the cognitive mechanisms, and potentially relevant to our research, are perceptions about how controllable or alterable one's working environment is. These are perceptions about one's ability to influence, through effort and persistence, what goes on in the environment, as well as the malleability of the environment itself. Bandura reports evidence suggesting that those with low levels of belief in how controllable their environment is produce little change, even in highly malleable environments.[3] Those with firm beliefs of this sort, through persistence and ingenuity, figure out ways of exercising some control, even in environments that pose challenges to change. This set of efficacy-influencing mechanisms may help to explain some results of our research on district conditions and initiatives that foster principal efficacy.

Self-efficacy beliefs also evolve in response to motivational and affective processes. These beliefs influence motivation in several ways: by determining (1) the goals that people set for themselves,[4] (2) how much effort they expend and how long they persevere in the face of obstacles, and (3) their resilience in the face of failure. Also, motivation relies on discrepancy reduction as well as discrepancy production. That is, people are motivated both to reduce the gap between perceived and desired performance and to set themselves challenging goals that they then work hard to accomplish. They mobilize their skills and effort to accomplish what they seek.[5] Such beliefs, we surmise, also are likely to be influenced by some of the conditions that principals experience in their districts.

Pointing to the similarity of efficacy and self-confidence, McCormick (2001) claims that leadership self-efficacy or confidence is likely the key cognitive variable regulating leader functioning in a dynamic environment. "Every major review of the leadership literature lists self-confidence as an essential characteristic for effective leadership" (p. 23). That said, we know very little about the efficacy beliefs of leaders,[6] and even less about the antecedents of those beliefs. Most organizational research has focused on the outcomes of efficacy beliefs, with much less attention to their antecedents.[7] Furthermore, the antecedents of leaders' self-efficacy (LSE) and leaders' collective efficacy (LCE) may well differ.[8] For example, district leadership practices and organizational conditions may predict collective efficacy more immediately than they predict self-efficacy, because leadership practices relate only indirectly to the more proximal antecedents of individual efficacy, such as role clarity and psychological states.[9]

Prior evidence about the antecedents of both self- and collective-leader efficacy warrants several conclusions. First, no single antecedent has attracted much attention from researchers. Second, the most frequently studied antecedents—leader gender, leaders' years of experience, level of schooling, and compliance with policy or procedures—have not found much evidentiary support, by any conventional social science standard. Third, what evidence there is about the impact of various antecedents on leader efficacy suggests that results are either mixed or not significant. Finally, as far as we could determine, there has been very little effort to understand district influences on school-level leader efficacy.

Leadership Practices and District Conditions

Underlying the measure of leadership providing evidence for this chapter was an account of successful leadership practices described in some detail in Chapter Five. In brief, these practices were of four types, aimed at: setting directions for the organization, developing the capacities of organizational members to pursue those directions, redesigning the organization to align with and support members' work, and improving the instructional program (see Chapter Five for a fuller description).

The measure of district conditions providing evidence for this study was based on reviews of research about the characteristics of higher-performing districts.[10] These conditions, described more fully in the next chapter, include, for example,

- A widely shared vision
- A focus on the quality of curriculum and instruction
- District culture
- Targeted and phased focus for school improvement
- Relations with schools and other stakeholders
- Emphasis on teamwork
- Use of data for decision making
- Job-embedded professional development for staff
- Investment in instructional leadership at the district and school levels

New Evidence

Evidence used for this chapter was provided by the first principal and teacher surveys collected in our study, along with student achievement data. Survey data included responses from 96 administrators (an 83-percent response rate) and 2,764 teachers (a 66-percent response rate). Principal survey items measured LCE (four items), LSE, district conditions, and district leadership. We measured three additional variables with the teacher survey: school leadership, classroom conditions, and school conditions.

Because leaders' influence on student learning was a focus of our larger study, the principal survey included six items measuring feelings of self-efficacy for school improvement, each beginning with the stem *To what extent do you feel able to* . . .

1. Motivate teachers?
2. Generate enthusiasm for a shared vision of the school?
3. Manage change in your school?
4. Create a positive learning environment in your school?
5. Facilitate student learning in your school?
6. Raise achievement on standardized tests?

A new scale was developed for the principal survey to measure leaders' collective efficacy beliefs about school improvement. These items began with the stem *To what extent do you agree that* . . .

1. School staffs in our district have the knowledge and skill they need to improve student learning?
2. In our district, continuous improvement is viewed by most staff as a necessary part of every job?
3. In our district, problems are viewed as issues to be solved, not as barriers to action?
4. District staff members communicate a belief in the capacity of teachers to teach even the most difficult students?

Previous studies of school-leader efficacy have measured the effects of various demographic variables, but have not made much effort to explain why such variables might influence sense of efficacy. Few demographic variables have been shown to have a significant influence on leader efficacy. Personal characteristics measured in our study include leader race or ethnicity, gender, years of experience as a school administrator, and years of experience in one's current school. Also measured was a handful of organizational characteristics plausibly related to leader efficacy including school and district size, school level, and the number of different principals in the school over the past ten years. Results described in the following section are based on a series of correlations and regressions followed by a path analysis. Technical information about these analyses can be found in the final report of our study for the Wallace Foundation (Louis, Leithwood, Wahlstrom, & Anderson, 2010) elsewhere.[11]

District Leadership and School Leader Efficacy

As Table 8.1 indicates, our aggregate district leadership measure was strongly related (.63) to leaders' collective efficacy (LCE) and significantly but moderately related (.33) to leaders' self-efficacy (LSE). Among the four dimensions included in our conception of district leadership, the strongest relationship with LCE was *redesigning the organization* (.63) followed by *developing people* (.55), *improving the instructional program* (.55), and *setting directions* (.49). For LSE, the strongest relationship was with *improving the instructional program* (.36) followed by *redesigning the organization* (.28), *developing people* (.28) and *setting directions* (.22).

Additional analysis[12] showed that our aggregate measure of district leadership explains 11 percent of the variation in LSE—5 percent of which is accounted for

TABLE 8.1 DISTRICT ANTECEDENTS OF SCHOOL LEADER EFFICACY: CORRELATION COEFFICIENTS

	LCE	LSE	Combined
District Leadership	.63**	.33**	.59**
Setting directions	.49**	.22*	.44**
Developing people	.55**	.28**	.51**
Redesigning the organization	.63**	.28**	.56**
Managing instructional program	.55**	.36**	.55**
District Conditions	.70**	.39**	.67**
Focus on quality/achievement	.65**	.33**	.60**
Use of data	.54**	.27**	.49**
Targeted improvement	.63**	.30**	.57**
Investment in instructional leadership	.55**	.28**	.51**
Job-embedded professional development	.43**	.32**	.46**
Emphasis on teamwork	.57**	.37**	.58**
New school relations	.59**	.30**	.55**
District culture	.61**	.35**	.59**

(N = 134 schools)

*p < .05

**p < .01

by *improving the instructional program*—and it also explains 42 percent of the variation in LCE, of which significant contributions are made by *redesigning the organization* (9 percent) and *improving the instructional program* (3 percent).

District Conditions and School Leader Efficacy

All eight sets of district conditions are significantly related to leader efficacy, strongly so with LCE. The strongest relationship with LCE is the district's expressed concern for student achievement and the quality of instruction (.65), followed, in order, by targeted and phased focus of improvement (.63); district culture (.61); new approaches to board-community and district-school relations (.59); emphasis on teamwork and professional community (.57); investment in instructional leadership at the district and school levels (.55); district-wide use of data (.54); and district-sponsored, job-embedded professional development focus for teachers (.43).

Relationships between district conditions and LSE are generally weaker, although still statistically significant. The strongest of these relations is with the emphasis on teamwork (.37) and district culture (.35), followed by a focus on achievement and the quality of instruction (.33), job-embedded professional development for teachers (.32), new district-school relations (.31), targeted and phased focus of school improvement (.30), investment in instructional leadership (.28), and district-wide use of data (.27).

Our analyses also indicate that the aggregate measure of district conditions explains 15 percent of the variation in LSE and a much larger 49 percent of the variation in LCE. Among the eight sets of specific conditions included in our district variable, significant contributions to explained variation in LSE were made by: teamwork (13 percent of variation); district culture (12 percent); focus on achievement and instructional quality (10 percent); professional development for teachers (10 percent); district-school relationships (9 percent); targeted and phased improvement (8 percent); instructional leadership (7 percent); and data use (6 percent). For LCE, contributions to overall explained variation were: focus (42 percent); phased improvement (39 percent); district culture (37 percent); relationships (34 percent); teamwork (32 percent); instructional leadership (30 percent); data use (28 percent); and professional development (18 percent).

Effects of Leader Efficacy on Leader Behavior and School and Classroom Conditions

Table 8.2 reports correlations between (1) LSE, LCE, and an aggregated measure of efficacy, and (2) leader behavior, school conditions, and classroom conditions,

TABLE 8.2 LEADER EFFICACY RELATIONSHIPS WITH SCHOOL LEADER PRACTICES AND SCHOOL AND CLASSROOM CONDITIONS

	LCE	LSE	Combined
School leadership	.27	.30	.34
Setting directions	.26	.34	.36
Developing people	.26	.23	.29
Redesigning the organization	.27	.30	.34
Managing instructional Program	.23	.28	.30
School conditions	.41	.33	.45
Classroom conditions	.39	.27	.40

(N = 134 schools)

Note: For all measures, $p < .01$.

using standard regression equations. The strongest relationships are between school conditions and our combined efficacy measure (.41) followed closely by the relationship between classroom conditions and aggregated efficacy (.39). Correlations between school leader practices and both aggregated efficacy and LSE are comparable (.27 and .30). Correlations between LSE and the four separate dimensions of leader behavior included in our study are roughly similar, ranging from a low of .23 (developing people) to a high of .34 (setting directions); for LCE, the range is between .23 (improving instruction) and .27 (redesigning the organization).

Our analysis[13] indicated that the aggregate efficacy measure explained 11 percent of the variation in school leader behavior, LSE explained 8 percent, and LCE explained 6 percent. The two forms of efficacy, examined together, explained more variation in school (20 percent) and classroom (15 percent) conditions than did either separately. When examined separately, LCE explained slightly more of the variation in school conditions (17 percent versus 10 percent) and twice as much of the variation in classroom conditions (15 percent and 7 percent) as was explained by LSE.

Effects of Leader Efficacy on Student Achievement

Table 8.3 reports correlations between alternative estimates of student achievement and our three leader efficacy measures. Leaders' self-efficacy (LSE), by itself, is not significantly related to any of the estimates of student achievement. However, there are consistent and significant relationships with each year's annual achievement scores (percent of students achieving at or

TABLE 8.3 LEADER EFFICACY RELATIONSHIPS WITH MEAN ACHIEVEMENT GAIN AND PERCENTAGE OF STUDENTS AT STATE PROFICIENCY LEVEL

	LCE	LSE	Combined
Mean Achievement Gain (N = 99)	−.08	.05	−.02
Proficiency 2003 (N = 99)	.33**	.10	.26*
Proficiency 2004 (N = 124)	.26**	.10	.22*
Proficiency 2005	.28**	.13	.26**

*p < .05

**p < .01

above the "proficient" level) for both LCE and our combined efficacy measure. Two of the three annual achievement scores are significantly related to LCE (.33 and .29). All three annual achievement scores are significantly related to our aggregate efficacy measure (.28, .24 and .25).

Leader efficacy explains significant variation in annual achievement scores. The aggregate efficacy measure and LCE explain comparable amounts of variation in achievement scores for 2003 (6 percent and 10 percent), 2004 (4 percent and 6 percent), and 2005 (6 percent and 7 percent). LSE alone had no significant explanatory power.

Moderating Variables

The variables we designated as "moderators" have possible potential effects on the relationship between district leadership, district conditions, and leader efficacy. Potentially, they may also influence the relationship between leader efficacy and conditions in the school and classroom, as well as student achievement. Our results indicated that some of these moderators had no influence on either set of relationships. Because this was the case for leader's gender, experience, and race or ethnicity, we do not consider them further.

School level and district size, our analysis suggests, contributed unique variation to many of these relationships and should be considered the most powerful of the moderators included in this study. Both of these moderators depressed the strength of the relationships in which they were significant. In other words, the contribution of both LSE and LCE to most of the relationships with which they were associated were muted by increased district size and in secondary schools as compared with elementary schools.

The Causes and Consequences of School Leaders' Efficacy Beliefs: Testing a Model

Our final analysis of these data entailed the testing a model of the causes and consequences of leader efficacy beliefs, using path modeling techniques similar to those reported in some other chapters of this book. Results of this test, in brief, found that:

- The most direct "effects" of district leadership are on the creation of those district conditions believed to be effective in producing student learning (.85).
- District leadership effects account for 72 percent of the variation in district conditions.
- District conditions influence LCE (.69) but not LSE (.19); 47 percent of the variation in LCE is explained by the effects of district conditions, but only 17 percent of the variation in LSE is explained by the combined effects of district conditions and LCE.
- LCE is moderately associated with school conditions (.24), but LSE has no such association.
- LSE and LCE explain 13 percent of the variation in leader behavior. Together, LCE and leader behavior explain 52 percent of the variation in school conditions.
- The model as a whole explains 10 percent of the variation in student achievement.

Most of these results seem reasonable, the exception being the behavior of classroom conditions. Our analysis produced a statistically nonsignificant and negative direct relationship between class conditions and student learning. We have no firm explanation for this surprising result, but the marginal reliability of the scale used to measure classroom conditions (alpha = .60) may be part of the answer.

Conclusion

Evidence described in this chapter indicates that the effects of district leadership on principals, schools, and students are largely indirect, operating through district conditions.

District leaders help to create conditions that are viewed by school leaders as enhancing and supporting their work. All four dimensions of district leadership were moderately to strongly related to principal efficacy, arguing for district leaders' adoption of a holistic approach to their own practice. The greatest effect of district leaders will be the outcome of engaging in all four sets of practices in a skillful manner.

District conditions had substantially greater effects on principals' collective efficacy than on their individual efficacy, which provides some confirmation for the expectation that such differences would likely exist.[14] This expectation is based on the relatively direct influence of organizational conditions on collective efficacy, with less direct influence on individual efficacy. Common to both types of efficacy, however, is the strong influence of the district's focus on student learning and the quality of instruction, as well as district culture and targeted approaches to school improvement. These mutually reinforcing district conditions seem likely to attract the collective attention of school leaders to the district's central mission.

The extent of principal-efficacy effects on schools and students is significantly moderated by a handful of organizational characteristics (school size, district size, school level, frequency of principal succession), but by none of the personal variables included in our study (namely, leaders' gender, experience, race, or ethnicity). The moderating effects of organizational characteristics are to be expected, as district size and school size almost always "make a difference," no matter what the focus of the research is.[15] Elementary schools are typically more sensitive than secondary schools to leadership influence, although previous leader-efficacy research has reported mostly nonsignificant effects.[16] And the rapid turnover of principals has been widely decried as anathema to school improvement efforts,[17] an issue we explore in more depth in Chapter Ten. Now we have some evidence that the positive effects of leader efficacy are also moderated by school and district size (the larger the organization, the lower the level of principals' sense of efficacy for school improvement).

These results recommend that school leaders seek out the kinds of experiences that will build their own confidence for school improvement, and that district leaders consider school leaders' collective sense of efficacy for school improvement to be among the most important resources available to them for increasing student achievement.

Implications for Policy and Practice

Three implications for policy and practice emerged from this section of our study.

1. District leaders should consider school leaders' collective sense of efficacy for school improvement to be among the most important resources available to them for increasing student achievement.

2. District improvement efforts should include, as foci for immediate attention, those eight sets of conditions that the best available evidence now suggests have a significant influence on principals' sense of efficacy for school improvement.
3. Principals who believe themselves to be working collaboratively toward clear, common goals with district personnel, other principals, and teachers in their schools are more confident in their leadership.

Questions for Reflection

1. To what extent do your own principal colleagues seem confident about successfully improving student achievement in their schools or districts? What explains their levels of confidence or efficacy, as far as you can determine?
2. In your experience, what is it about larger district and school sizes that erodes principals' sense of efficacy for school improvement? How might principal efficacy be protected and enhanced in larger schools and districts?
3. What could your own district start and stop doing that would enhance the collective efficacy of its principals?

CHAPTER NINE

PRINCIPAL EFFICACY

District-Led Professional Development

Kenneth Leithwood, Stephen E. Anderson, and Karen
Seashore Louis

Claims Supported by Evidence in This Chapter

1. Districts contribute most to school leaders' sense of efficacy by:
   - Unambiguously assigning priority to the improvement of student achievement and instruction
   - Making significant investments in the development of instructional leadership
   - Ensuring that personnel policies support the selection and maintenance of the best people for each school
   - Emphasizing teamwork and professional community
2. Districts also contribute to principals' efficacy through worthwhile programs of professional development, aimed at strengthening their capacities to achieve shared purposes.

   The efforts that districts make to build principals' sense of efficacy can have positive or negative consequences, depending on the manner in which the initiatives are implemented. Much depends on the frequency, nature, and quality of experiences provided in the course of implementation.

Chapter Eight outlined evidence strongly suggesting that a key focus for district leaders should be the further development of their principals' collective sense of efficacy for school improvement. Evidence in that chapter suggested that few other district initiatives are likely to have comparable payoffs for schools, classrooms, and students. Assuming reader familiarity with the efficacy concepts described in Chapter Eight, this chapter extends our understanding of how central office staff develop school leaders' efficacy, and what school leaders should expect from their districts as part of the leadership development they experience.

There are two main sections to this chapter. Using a sample of our qualitative data, the first section describes in some detail how districts build principal efficacy. The second section, drawing on our quantitative data, explores the role of district professional development in fostering the efficacy of school leaders. The background theory and evidence about efficacy on which this chapter builds was described at the front end of the previous chapter.

Insights from the Qualitative Evidence: Nine Efficacy-Producing District Conditions

The 31 principals providing evidence for this analysis were 19 females and 12 males from 13 elementary, seven secondary, nine intermediate, one combined elementary/middle school, and one junior/senior high school. These principals had been leading their schools for an average of 4.67 years (ranging from 1 to 22 years), and had been working in their present districts for an average of 7.83 years (ranging from 1 to 27 years).

Our sixty-minute interviews were guided by semistructured questions asking principals about their views on state and district initiatives, principals' leadership practices, the distribution of leadership in their schools, professional development needs of teachers and principals, and relationships between their schools and their communities. Interview transcripts were examined for evidence of district conditions that would influence principals' efficacy.[1]

District Conditions Associated with Principals' Efficacy for School Improvement

Questions motivating the analysis in this chapter's substudy are about the extent to which conditions associated in previous research with district effectiveness are also influences on principals' sense of efficacy, and whether additional district conditions also have such influence.

Table 9.1 summarizes evidence about the number of respondents who identified each of the original district conditions, along with two more suggested by our data (number 4 and number 9) as having a bearing on their own sense of professional efficacy. The first column of Table 9.1 shows the relative rankings of the nine conditions and the efficacy-influencing enactments related to each condition (also ranked). The second and third columns show positive and negative effects on efficacy, and the fourth column shows the total number of respondents who made positive or negative comments. (Several respondents identified both positive and negative features of some conditions.)

TABLE 9.1 DISTRICT CONDITIONS ASSOCIATED WITH PRINCIPAL EFFICACY

District Conditions	Respondents N = 31 (Rank) Positive	Respondents N = 31 (Rank) Negative	Totals
1. District-wide focus on student achievement and instruction	28 (3)	16 (1)	44
Provides clear sense of direction through establishment of achievement standards and provision of district-wide curriculum and/or programs**	23	8	
Provides human and financial resources to assist schools in achieving district-established directions	15	11	
Communicates high expectations for the work of teachers and principals in accomplishing district directions and implementing effective instruction	14	2	
Allows schools sufficient flexibility in pursuing district directions	11		
Engages in ongoing or periodic review of directions and plans	5		
2. Job-embedded professional development (PD) for teachers	29 (2)	10 (2)	39
Provides evidence to assist in the planning of teacher PD	4		
Holds principals accountable for implementing and following up on what is learned during district-sponsored PD	19	2	

(continued)

TABLE 9.1 (*continued*)

District Conditions	Respondents N = 31 (Rank) *Positive*	Respondents N = 31 (Rank) *Negative*	Totals
Encourages the use of school staff meetings for purposes of PD	11	1	
Approves of a wide variety of types of PD but insists they be meaningful for teachers and aligned with district goals and priorities	17		
Provides adequate funds to support significant PD	13	6	
May mandate participation in PD considered critical to the achievement of district priorities.	17	5	
3. Investment in both school- and district-level instructional leadership	30 (1)	3 (7)	33
Establishes teachers' work as the main focus of attention for school leaders	28		
Provides a wide range of professional development opportunities to help build the instructional leadership capacities of principals	20	3	
Holds principals directly responsible for student achievement in their schools	23		
4. District personnel policies*	22 (5)	10 (3)	32
Stability in district leader roles	10	3	
District hiring policies ensure principals can select outstanding teachers	9	4	
District leaders assume school leadership roles when needed	4		
Competent principals are hired from within the district and their capabilities matched with school needs	9		
Principal succession is planned and minimized	4	2	
5. Emphasis on team work and professional community	26 (4)	2 (8)	28
Support and encouragement are provided for teacher and principal collaboration	6		

District Conditions	Respondents N = 31 (Rank) *Positive*	Respondents N = 31 (Rank) *Negative*	Totals
Principals and teachers participate in district-wide decisions that directly impact on their work	12	1	
Structures are established that allow for sharing of information and collaborative problem solving within and across schools	10		
District ensures that schools are kept informed about both state and district initiatives	13		
6. District-wide use of data	18 (7)	5 (5)	23
Insists on data-based decision making in schools	12	5	
Provides schools with much of the data they need to exercise data-based decision making	4		
Assists schools in the interpretation and use of data for decision making	4		
Creates structures that foster the sharing of information across schools and between schools and the district	3		
Uses data to determine the goals for principal and teacher professional development	6		
7. Targeted and phased focuses for improvement	20 (6)	1 (9)	21
Requires the development of improvement plans in all schools (either district- or school-developed)	9		
School improvement goals are clear and aligned with state and district standards	7		
School improvement plans are aligned with district improvement plans	7		
In cases of school-developed improvement plans, district provides a procedure for the development of the plan	6		
8. Relations with schools and stakeholders (district, board, union, school)	16 (8)	4 (6)	20

(continued)

TABLE 9.1   (*continued*)

District Conditions	Respondents N = 31 (Rank) Positive	Respondents N = 31 (Rank) Negative	Totals
Provides significant opportunities for principals and teachers to be involved in decisions at the district level	4		
District staff keep well informed about school programs, priorities, initiatives, and programs	6	1	
Encourages communication across schools by principals and provides opportunities for this to occur	10	1	
Permits flexibility for schools in the enactment of district initiatives	9	4	
9. District policy governing school choice*	0	8 (4)	8
District protects schools from rapid and dramatic changes in curriculum and student population		8	

Note: Two district conditions added to the original eight are identified by *.

**All statements related to conditions are stated in the positive.

Table 9.1 indicates that principals viewed the enactments of the conditions of interest in their own districts with a largely positive bias. The conditions making the greatest positive contribution to principals' sense of efficacy were, in order:

- District-wide focus on student achievement and instruction
- Job-embedded professional development for teachers
- Investment in both school- and district-level instructional leadership
- District personnel policies

Principals mentioned *district policies governing school choice* as the only negative influences on their sense of efficacy.

The conditions cited most frequently (by a third or more of the sample) as negative influences on efficacy were

- District-wide focus on student achievement and instruction
- Job-embedded professional development
- District personnel policies

These three conditions account for a disproportionate number of both positive and negative influences on efficacy—very sharp double-edged swords.

Our findings regarding the nine district conditions and the related efficacy-producing enactments are described in the following section. The numbers in parentheses following efficacy-producing enactments indicate how many principals made comments that reflected a positive influence on their efficacy (for example, 9+), or a negative influence on their efficacy (for example, 3–). Excerpts from principals' transcripts illustrate positive influences.

1. District-wide focus on student achievement and the quality of instruction. This condition elicited positive responses from 28 principals and negative responses from 16. The enactments of this condition that are positively associated with principal efficacy include the following:

- District-provided curriculum and performance standards, with flexibility for implementation
- Clear policies, with a procedure for ongoing review and revisions
- Assignment of subject-area facilitators to schools
- Support for differentiated instruction.

Enactments negatively associated with principal efficacy include the following:

- District enforcement of common standards, with no credit given for large gains that schools have made in cases where standards have not yet been reached
- Adoption of initiatives based on conflicting assumptions or ideologies
- Adoption of a focus for student learning that narrows the curriculum and minimizes the value of important fields of study
- Excessive prescriptions about how principals and teachers must pursue the district's curriculum standards and achievement goals

In sum, according to our evidence, principal efficacy is enhanced when enactments of this condition include the following:

- Districts provide a clear sense of direction through the establishment of achievement standards and district-wide curriculum and/or programs. (23+, 8–)
  Excerpt: The fact that we have a more central focus and central direction, I think, has improved student instruction and improved student learning, and forced us to take a hard look at what we're doing with students.
- Districts provide human and financial resources to assist schools in achieving district-established directions. (15+, 11–)

Excerpt: I think in general it's really a privilege to work in a district like this. There's a great deal of support, you know, budgetarily, which helps us to move things in a direction that we feel is positive, that's gonna help the students, so we have a lot advantages.

- Districts communicate high expectations for the work teachers, and principals do accomplish district directions and implement effective instruction. (14+, 2–)

  Excerpt: I would say the accountability at all campuses. The superintendents that we've had have put a lot of pressure on the principals, to make sure that the teachers feel more accountable for the students that they have.

- Districts allow schools sufficient flexibility in pursuing district directions. (11+, 1–)

  Excerpt: The impetus to tailor it to the school site has been very clearly indicated. But the initiatives have come out of the district office.

- Districts engage in ongoing or periodic review of directions and plans and make revisions as appropriate. (5+)

  Excerpt: Our district curriculum now has been rewritten to mirror the state curriculum, but also all of that ties into our state testing. So the state testing now is more in alignment with what is actually being taught.

2. Job-embedded teacher professional development. Professional development is an important element in the enactment of most of the conditions we are investigating. It elicited positive responses from twenty-nine of the thirty-one principals in our sample. Ten principals, however, identified some aspect of district-sponsored professional development as having a negative influence on their efficacy.

Enactments of this condition positively associated with principal efficacy include the following:

- Districts providing data and guidelines to help principals and teachers to deliver better instructional programs
- District support for attendance at professional development conferences
- Encouragement to use school staff meetings for professional development purposes
- Alignment of professional development programs with the district's curriculum
- District provision for flexibility, such that schools may design their own professional development programs
- Provision of adequate funding for various approaches to professional development

Enactments of this condition viewed less favorably by principals include the following:

- Requiring excessive professional development for teachers and principals
- Allowing in-school professional development to crowd out time for teacher collaboration
- Setting limits on the use of substitute teachers
- Setting restrictive limits on authorized absences from the school building for professional development
- Providing inadequate funding for professional development
- Focusing on professional development for one initiative in such a way that other important initiatives are left unsupported

In sum, according to our evidence, principal efficacy is enhanced when enactments of this condition include the following:

- Districts hold principals accountable for implementing and following up on what is learned during district-sponsored professional development. (19+, 2–)
  Excerpt: I think fundamentally my role is to help hold people accountable that the professional development initiatives and activities . . . are then reflected in practice so that it's not just simply, "Here's a good idea somebody thinks we should be talking about."
- Districts approve many types of professional development but insist they be meaningful for teachers and aligned with district goals and priorities. (17+)
  Excerpt: I think we do have some direction from our central office and from our curriculum director about where we should go, but we also have flexibility about how we are going to do that.
- Districts mandate participation in professional development considered critical to the achievement of district priorities. (17+, 5–)
  Excerpt: With that the district said how we were to do it. It provided professional development for the teachers, for myself, so that we could go and be trained in it. And then as a result we are expected to follow that curriculum.
- Districts provide adequate funds to support significant professional development. (13+, 6–)
  Excerpt: [Districts] encourage [teachers] to attend professional development that's offered by the district. Encourage and/or financially support them to attend outside professional development.
- Districts encourage the use of school staff meetings for professional development. (11+, 1–)

Excerpt: Because part of what we do is if the district office offers in-service kinds of things or professional development, either the department chairs go, or they send stronger teachers to go and bring it back to the department.

- Districts provide evidence to assist in the planning of professional development for teachers. (4+)

  Excerpt: Definitely a push towards using data . . . to create teacher leaders, recognizing that that's where the staff development needs to happen.

3. Investment in both School- and District-Level Instructional Leadership. This condition elicited positive responses from all but one of the 31 principals and elicited negative responses from three. Enactments of this condition positively associated with principal efficacy include these district actions:

- Providing support for principals' professional development
- Providing individualized support for principals depending upon the challenges they face in their schools
- Holding principals accountable for student achievement and teacher contributions to student achievement
- Giving principals responsibility for responding to student data
- Providing district staff to oversee subject-matter teaching in all elementary schools
- Providing a curriculum with supporting professional development for principals and teachers

Enactments of this condition associated with negative consequences for principal efficacy include these district actions:

- Not supporting principals' professional development
- Not providing enough professional development
- Requiring teachers and principals to participate in excessive amounts of professional development

As these examples illustrate, enhancing efficacy through professional development requires something of a balancing act. Principal efficacy is fostered in a positive way by the right amount of professional development and in a negative way by either too much or too little.

In sum, according to our evidence, principal efficacy is enhanced when enactments of this condition include the following:

- Districts make teachers' work the main focus of attention for school leaders. (28+)
  Excerpt: We have to participate, we have to help rather than manage. Although a lot of the job is still managing because there is still the paperwork. . . . We also have to relate more to the teachers and the students. To actually know what they are doing in the classrooms.
- Districts hold principals responsible for student achievement. (23+)
  Excerpt: Frankly, my communication is very simplistic. I tell people, I tell our staff constantly that my goal, and I expect it to be theirs, is that we help improve the student achievement and that we do so in a caring and nurturing environment.
- Districts provide a wide range of professional development opportunities to help build principals' capacity for instructional leadership. (20+, 3–)
  Excerpt: We have principal meetings two times a month and then . . . because I am a new principal this year, I get a third one. . . . About every year I go to either a state or national conference and attend courses there . . . and occasional workshops.

4. District Personnel Policies. This condition elicited positive responses from 22 principals and negative responses from ten. Enactments of this condition positively associated with principal efficacy include encouraging promotion of principals from within the district and giving principals a significant role in selecting teachers.

Respondents mentioned the importance of "matching" teachers and principals to the mission or culture of the school, and allocating especially effective principals to especially challenging schools. Hiring district office staff into school leadership roles was typically viewed as adding strength to the collective capacity of schools in the district. Stable and consistent district leadership, which we included as a feature of district personnel policies, also contributed to principals' sense of efficacy. Principals' commitment to directions established by the district, and confidence in being able to pursue them successfully, were significantly eroded by frequent superintendent turnover. Principals' efficacy was especially challenged when principals were appointed to schools that had been experiencing frequent turnover of leaders in recent years.

In sum, according to our evidence, principal efficacy is enhanced when enactments of this condition include the following:

- Districts provide stability in district leader roles. (10+, 3–)
  Excerpt: There have been a lot of changes in the district in the last couple of years. Some probably stem from the fact that there was a large turnover in leadership in the last couple of years. But education is constantly evolving. It's not a static thing.

- Districts hire competent principals from within, and principals' capabilities are matched with school needs. (9+)

    Excerpt: When I first took this building in 1989, I didn't want to come back because the morale was terrible here. But I took the challenge, I had been asked to come back and so I did. I have not been sorry. It has turned out to be everything I wanted it to be. Now I can kind of sit back and enjoy it.

- District hiring policies ensure that principals can select and retain outstanding teachers. (9+, 4–)

    Excerpt: Well, the principals do almost all the hiring in the district. As a matter of fact, I will be hiring a new teacher. . . . So we control over what our staff looks like. . . . It is about hiring good people but it is not always a guarantee. It is about keeping good people.

- District leaders assume school leadership roles when needed. (4+)

    Excerpt: When I was weighing whether to leave Central Office or stay or leave to go to the building level, it was . . . [this school]. I was interviewing prospective candidates for the principal here. No one knew anything about small schools. What they were going to do with this building was distressing me, you know?

- Principal succession is planned and minimized. (4+, 2–)

    Excerpt: Cultivating our own leaders is very important . . . which I really appreciate and admire about the school district. So that when you step into that [principal] position you kind of know the district's way of doing things and you are able to just pick up and go.

5. Emphasis on Teamwork and Professional Community. This condition elicited positive responses from twenty-six principals and negative responses from two. Enactments of this condition positively associated with principal efficacy include the following:

- Keeping schools informed about state and district initiatives
- Providing support and encouragement for principal-and-teacher collaborative relationships
- Following through on state requirements in ways that led to greater collaboration within schools
- Ensuring that district leaders meet with principals frequently to work through decisions together

Efficacy was influenced in a negatively at one small school where involvement in the district meant the principal had to allocate fifteen curricular liaison positions among eleven staff members without overwhelming anyone.

In sum, according to our evidence, principal efficacy is enhanced when enactments of this condition include the following:

- Principals and teachers participate in district-wide decisions that have a direct impact on their work. (14+, 1–)
  Excerpt: The superintendent's office, the curriculum department really was working with a group of teachers and supervisors, administrators to come up with a new form that would make it easier for you to observe 40 teachers but really pinpoint some areas that we wanted to work on.
- Schools are kept informed about state and district initiatives. (13+)
  Excerpt: That is my work. . . . The district translates what the state expects from us. . . . We need to translate for our students, teachers, support staff, parents, what that means.
- Districts provide structures that allow for sharing of information and collaborative problem solving within and across schools. (13+)
  Excerpt: During the summer, the superintendent housed all the top administrators, the principals and assistant principals for a whole week, and they had to learn to work together, not just within their campus, but within the district.
- Districts support and encourage teacher and principal collaboration. (8+, 1–)
  Excerpt: One thing that our superintendent has presented us with is he wants [principals and teachers] to be more collaborative.

6. District-wide Use of Data. This condition elicited positive responses from 18 principals and negative responses from five. Enactments of this condition positively associated with principal efficacy include the following:

- District provision of data useful to schools in planning for professional development
- Involvement of schools in decision making related to the data
- Engagement of an external person to conduct a curriculum audit, thus encouraging improved alignment within the district
- Detailed guidance and support by the district for schools trying to interpret and use their data

Of the five respondents who claimed negative effects on efficacy for this condition, one said that his or her district required more information about student achievement than he or she could collect. Another was unnerved by having sole responsibility for explaining state requirements to students, parents, and teachers. In these and other cases, resistance and negative feelings were focused largely on state requirements over which the principals had no control.

In sum, according to our evidence, principal efficacy is enhanced when enactments of this condition include the following:

- Districts insist on data-based decision making in schools. (12+, 5–)
  Excerpt: But the good news about all of that [district direction] is that we make very data-driven decisions now. We do a lot of assessments. Those are both local assessments and state assessments. We use that information obviously to plan for our children.
- Districts use data to set goals for principal and teacher professional development. (6+)
  Excerpt: One of them is the data part and the district calls it data sources. Everybody has a data source. Then with the data source . . . each teacher created a goal for him or herself in professional development.
- Districts provide schools with much of the data they need to practice data-based decision making. (4+)
  Excerpt: [The district provides] an amazing amount of data. And the people to help us interpret that data.
- Districts assist schools in the interpretation and use of data for decision making. (4+)
  Excerpt: We have had . . . extensive training from our central office on understanding and utilizing test data.
- Districts create structures that foster the sharing of information across schools and between schools and the district. (3+)
  Excerpt: As an entire district we have our hand on every kid's test data. I don't care if it's elementary or high school. We have weekly administrative meetings and you know those issues will come up and communication is really strong.

7. Targeted and Phased Focus for Improvement. Enactments of this condition elicited positive responses from twenty school leaders and a negative response from one. Enactments positively associated with principal efficacy include the following:

- District requirements for improved goal setting
- Establishment of detailed school-improvement plans
- Requirements that community people participate in formulating school-improvement plans
- Clear articulation of expectations for student outcomes, derived from state policy

- Support for collaboration between high schools and middle schools
- Support for teachers engaged in using new instructional programs

Overall, principals associate positive feelings of efficacy with a significant level of prescription by the district about the nature of school improvement plans and the process for creating those plans.

In sum, according to our evidence, principal efficacy is enhanced when enactment of this condition includes the following:

- Requiring the development of improvement plans in all schools (either district- or school-developed). (9+)
  Excerpt: The school improvement plan is a requirement that we all have to do, which lays out staff development and the plan for school improvement.
- Clear school-improvement goals aligned with state and district standards. (7+)
  Excerpt: But . . . [the school-improvement plan] is campus-based. . . . We have to align it with the district's improvement plan.
- School improvement plans aligned with district improvement plans. (7+, 1–)
  Excerpt: The district and the school board have sent down a five-year goal for us. It's to improve academic achievement for each and every child, especially in the area of literacy and math.
- In cases of school-developed improvement plans, district provision of a procedure for the development of the plan. (6+)
  Excerpt: We're in a five-year cycle. We involve teachers, administrators, business people, parents, community people, and we set forth a plan of how we can improve our schools. The process begins with parent surveys.

8. Relations with Schools and Stakeholders (district, board, union, school). This condition elicited positive responses from sixteen principals and negative responses from four. Enactments of this condition positively associated with principal efficacy emphasized district sharing of key decisions with administrative staff members. In particular, principals emphasized the importance of listening to staff members, staying in touch with them, involving principals and teachers in the writing of school plans, budgeting for implementation of those plans, and field-testing new programs. A number of principals also pointed to the small size of their districts as an important contributor to positive district-school relations. In smaller districts, they noted, district leaders were more likely to be in touch with the challenges that principals and teachers face.

Principal efficacy is undermined, principals said, when districts neglect to provide adequate information for schools and parents about expectations from the state level. Insufficient information leaves them in the difficult position of having to explain requirements over which they have no control. Almost all comments from principals focused on district-school relations. Not surprisingly, principals had little to say about board-district relations.

In sum, principal efficacy is enhanced when enactments of this condition include the following:

- Encouragement for communication among principals across schools, and provision of opportunities for this to occur. (10+, 1–)
  Excerpt: Monthly meetings really looking at our school-improvement plan and having the opportunity to visit with other schools and talk with them, to share ideas and find out what's worked in one school that we might be able to look at as a possible intervention.
- Flexibility for schools in the implementation of district initiatives. (9+, 4–)
  Excerpt: I have a lot of autonomy as far as what kind of staff development I do for my own teachers on my campus . . . and I make a lot of decisions with my team.
- District staff keeping themselves well informed about school programs, priorities, initiatives, and programs. (6+, 1–)
  Excerpt: [The district listened] . . . to the concerns of the teams. . . . We felt that there was a need to kind of look at some parts of the instructional parts of things. . . . So they came out and helped make that happen.
- Significant opportunities for principals and teachers to be involved in decisions at the district level. (4+)
  Excerpt: That is certainly a team that works at the district level and then that framework of curriculum comes back to our level and then our individual teams and departments work on it as well.

9. District Policy Governing School Choice. This condition was mentioned by eight principals who identified instances in which a change in district policies had affected their efficacy negatively. School-choice policies, these principals suggested, can create significant challenges and have adverse effects on principal efficacy. Creating an open choice policy, one principal recounted, meant that his school—which was serving a relatively stable group of local students, quite well by all accounts—suddenly found itself serving students from a radius of about fourteen miles. Another principal described how his school had changed "overnight" from serving a fairly stable student population to a highly diverse group of students from the entire district, including members of more than thirty gangs. Principal efficacy is enhanced, in sum, when the district helps schools respond to rapid and dramatic changes in curriculum and student population. (8–)

Insights from the Quantitative Evidence: District Investments in Instructional Leadership Development

Albert Bandura, undoubtedly self-efficacy's premier theorist and researcher, has identified a small handful of underlying sources of efficacy development; each of the nine district conditions just described are manifestations of at least one of those sources.[2] The most powerful underlying source of efficacy is having "mastery experiences." Not surprisingly, when people have opportunities to develop the capacities needed to grapple productively with the challenges they face, their sense of confidence or efficacy grows significantly.

Among the most direct avenues districts have to provide principals with mastery experiences is the professional development they provide for their school leaders and other staff. The qualitative evidence reviewed in the previous section of this chapter supports this claim. Principals claimed *Investments in both school- and district-level instructional leadership* were among the most powerful influences on their own sense of self-efficacy.

Many districts consider development of their principals' capacity for instructional leadership to be a cornerstone of their improvement efforts. In light of this, we used quantitative evidence from our second principal surveys to understand in greater depth how district efforts to bolster principals' capacity for instructional leadership influenced schools and students. More specifically, we asked:

1. How do principals assess the professional development and support their districts provide?
2. How does principals' experience of professional development affect their collective sense of efficacy?
3. To what extent is principals' professional development associated with student learning?

How Do Principals Assess the Professional Development and Support Their Districts Provide?

The second principal survey included a number of items reflecting principals' beliefs about the efforts district staff members were making to develop their skills. We framed these items generically in an effort to tap the respondents' belief that professional development and support were being provided by the district. Sample items follow. Although in many cases we have chosen to look at only principals, rather than including assistant or associate principals, in this case we chose to include all respondents (211), as there is no reason to assume that assistant or associate principals can or do receive fewer professional development opportunities, and our preliminary analysis suggested that there are no significant differences between the two groups.

What becomes immediately apparent is that principals have a generally positive view of the districts' professional development efforts. The mean responses to the survey items are in all cases above the midpoint. This means that most principals agree—either slightly, moderately, or strongly—that their district provides the type of professional development indicated. In addition, in no case did we find principals strongly disagreeing that their district provides them with a particular type of support.

Principals do, however, differentiate among the different categories of support and professional development examined by the survey. The most positive view of district support occurs on three items. Most principals agree, either moderately or strongly, that district leaders:

- Encourage administrators and teachers to act on what they have learned in their professional development
- Encourage school administrators to work together to improve their instructional leadership
- Work with school administrators who are struggling to improve their instructional leadership

Principals appear to be somewhat less positive about three other indicators. Many indicate they strongly disagree, disagree, or are uncertain that district leaders *take a personal interest in my professional development.* Many also indicate that district leaders *provide quality staff development focused on priority areas* only occasionally, rarely, or very rarely. They also give weak ratings to the frequency with which the district *provides opportunities to work productively with colleagues from other schools.*

How Does Principals' Experience of Professional Development Affect Their Collective Efficacy?

To explore this question, we examined professional development in the context of several other factors that might affect principals' sense of collective efficacy. In particular, we wished to explore the general issue of whether professional development, which we view as *targeted support* for leadership, is more or less important than *pressure to increase achievement,* which is a major component of state policy. We assumed that effective leadership may require a combination of external support and pressure. In order to address this question we developed several new scales, using the second principal survey:

○ **Professional Development Measures**. The six example items shown in Figure 9.1) were highly correlated with two additional items:

- How frequently do your district leaders provide feedback to school administrators about the nature and quality of their leadership?
- How frequently do district leaders encourage administrators and teachers to act on what they have learned in their professional development?

FIGURE 9.1 PRINCIPALS' VIEWS OF DISTRICT ACTIONS TO SUPPORT PROFESSIONAL GROWTH

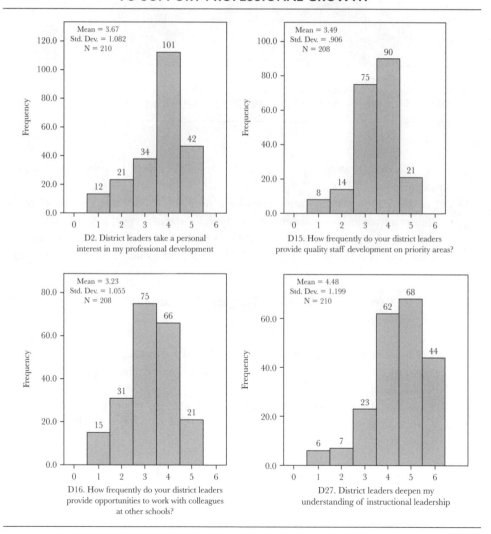

FIGURE 9.1 (*continued*)

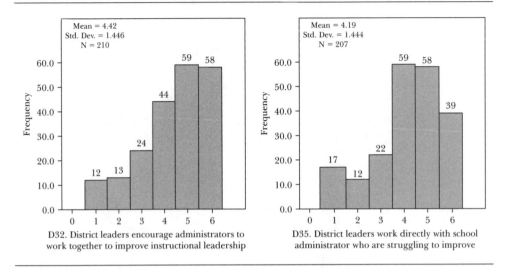

D32. District leaders encourage administrators to work together to improve instructional leadership

D35. District leaders work directly with school administrator who are struggling to improve

Therefore we computed a composite scale using the eight standardized items.

We conducted factor analyses for a number of additional items related to district initiatives for improvement. Of these, we selected one that seems particularly pertinent to elaborating on the findings presented earlier in this section, as it emphasizes the district's accountability and pressure focus. To examine the relative importance of targets and accountability, we computed a new scale:

○ **District Data Use and Targets Measures**. This factor loaded highly on items such as these:

- Our district has explicit targets beyond NCLB targets.
- Our district incorporates student and school performance data in district-level decisions.
- Our district assists schools with the use of student/school performance data.
- The district uses student achievement data to determine PD needs and resources.

Two other scales were also included in this analysis:

○ **Principals' Collective Sense of Efficacy**. Our measure of collective efficacy varied from the first survey, but it still emphasized the ability of leaders in the district to solve problems and improve student learning. Three items composed the scale for the sense of collective efficacy:

- School staffs in our district have the knowledge and skill they need to improve student learning.
- In our district, continuous improvement is viewed by most staff as a necessary part of the job.
- In our district, problems are viewed as issues to be solved, not as barriers to action.

◦ **Principals' Individual Sense of Efficacy Scale**. This measure differed somewhat from the measure used in the first survey. A longer battery of leadership competencies was used. These were items on which the principal self-rated on a four-point scale ranging from "basic" to "highly-developed." This scale included ten items, including expertise in instructional strategies, coaching, managing student behavior, developing unity and teamwork among teachers, and motivating others.

The effects of these variables on collective sense of efficacy were examined, also taking into account such school variables as school size, school level (elementary/secondary), percentage of non-white students, percentage of students in poverty, and the individual's position (principal or assistant principal). Results indicated that district professional development and district targets both have a strong association with collective sense of efficacy (with pressure through targeted and data-focused expectations contributing more to collective efficacy). The individual's sense of self-efficacy also makes a significant contribution, but school characteristics do not. Pressure and support, we conclude from this analysis, are important predictors of collective sense of efficacy, but pressure may be more important than support, at least in the form of professional development for school leaders.

To What Extent Is Principals' Professional Development Associated with Student Learning?

The bottom line for judging investments by districts working to develop instructional leadership is whether such investments are linked to student achievement. We examined this issue using causal modeling techniques,[3] which assumed that *professional development of school leaders (Support)* and *targets and data (Pressure)* are both associated, directly and indirectly, with student achievement.[4]

This analysis explained approximately 7 percent of the variance in achievement, largely through the direct relationship assumed between collective efficacy and students' test scores. *Professional development of school leaders* had an insignificant direct path coefficient with student achievement, while *Targets and Data* had a significant negative relationship. This unexpected finding suggests that pressure arising from targets, and an emphasis on data use, may backfire in the classroom unless it is balanced with support (in this case, through professional development), so that it works by building a strong collective leadership base in the district.

Conclusion

Taken as a whole, the qualitative evidence described in the first section of this chapter suggests that if principal efficacy is a key link in the chain joining successful district leadership with student learning, as Chapter Eight indicated, then creating the most positive enactments of those district conditions described in some detail in the first section should be considered well worth the attention of district leaders. Such attention would produce higher levels of principal efficacy, with other positive consequences for districts, schools, and students.

Analysis of the quantitative data in the second section of the chapter indicates that one of the most popular strategies for district improvement—and an important source of principal efficacy—*investment in the professional development of school leaders* will have limited effects on efficacy and student achievement unless districts also develop clear goals for improvement. On the other hand, setting targets and emphasizing responsibility for achieving them is not likely to produce a payoff for students unless those initiatives are accompanied by leadership development practices that principals perceive as helping them to improve their personal competencies.

These findings about the importance of targets and data use, in combination with district professional development, are quite strong when moderated by principal efficacy. However, an analysis of data-use effects reported in Chapter Eleven, which did not use principal efficacy as a moderating variable, reported significant data-use effects on students as well, although only in elementary schools. Together, these analyses suggest that district data use matters, but further research is needed before we fully understand the nature of that influence.

Implications for Policy and Practice

1. Many things that districts typically do can make positive contributions to the collective efficacy of principals. But how those things are enacted will

determine whether the effects on principal efficacy are positive or negative. District leaders should reexamine how their strategies are being enacted, in order to ensure positive consequences for principal efficacy.

2. Districts should approach their efforts to build principals' collective efficacy as one element of a more comprehensive improvement strategy that includes some form of pressure for principals to learn and improve. Efficacy-building initiatives alone may not motivate the type of intentional school improvement efforts needed to increase student achievement.

Reflections

1. Select two of the nine district conditions associated with principal efficacy in Table 9.1 that are evident in your own district. Are the enactments of these two conditions likely to generate positive or negative collective principal efficacy? Explain why you believe this.

2. In your own district, how are targets for student achievement and policies about data use in schools perceived by principals and other school staff members? Do they encourage or discourage principals from further developing their instructional leadership abilities? Why is that the case?

CHAPTER TEN

SUCCESSION

A Coordinated Approach to Leadership Distribution

Blair Mascall and Kenneth Leithwood

Claims Supported by Evidence in This Chapter

- Schools experience fairly rapid principal turnover: on average, about one new principal every three to four years.
- Principal turnover is not significantly related to a school's average student socio-economic status.
- Rapid principal turnover has moderately negative effects on both school culture and student achievement.
- Rapid principal turnover seems not to have much direct effect on teachers' general perceptions of their classroom conditions.
- Coordinated forms of leadership distribution have the potential to mitigate at least some of the negative consequences of rapid principal turnover.
- Newly assigned principals who initially work within the existing culture of their schools rather than attempting to quickly and substantially change it are more likely to avoid negative turnover effects.

Principal turnover is currently a hot topic.[1] Large numbers of baby boomer principals approaching retirement age, increasing accountability, and reform agendas that intensify the work of principals, and the narrowing of the job definition to make it more managerial all have made the job less attractive for many[2] at the same time that there is a reduced supply of people to fill the position.[3] The demand for new principals is expected to increase substantially over the next decade, and the frequency of principal turnover also seems likely to increase.

This chapter examines the impact of principal turnover on schools and considers how schools might mitigate the negative effects of such turnover through greater leadership distribution. Results of the qualitative and quantitative data analyses described in this chapter show that rapid principal turnover does indeed have a negative effect on a school—primarily on its culture, and most significantly on the achievement of its students. However, taking a coordinated approach to leadership distribution has the potential to mitigate at least some of these negative consequences.

Principal turnover is fostered in part by district policies. Some districts, for example, still have policies requiring regular principal rotation.[4] It is typically the district's responsibility to find replacements for departing principals, whatever the reasons for departure. Principal turnover is a problem that districts help to create and so must help to resolve.

Although principal turnover is inevitable in every school, an excessively rapid pace of turnover or succession is widely thought to present significant challenges to districts and schools. Many districts, for example, struggle to find suitably skilled and experienced principals, partly because of the above-average replacement rates required by a bulge in the proportion of incumbents currently becoming eligible for retirement. It is far from a trivial problem. For example, schools experiencing exceptionally rapid principal turnover are often reported to suffer from lack of shared purpose, cynicism among staff about principal commitment, and an inability to maintain a school improvement focus long enough to actually accomplish any meaningful change.[5] Our efforts to learn more about the nature and consequences of rapid principal turnover have been guided by five questions:

- How frequently does principal turnover occur in the average school?
- Does principal turnover significantly affect conditions across the school and in classrooms?
- Does principal turnover significantly affect student achievement?
- Do coordinated forms of distributed leadership have the potential, as some evidence suggests, to reduce negative influences arising from frequent principal turnover?
- What, if anything, can incoming principals do to minimize the negative effects of rapid principal turnover?

Starting Points

The starting points for this part of our study concerned with leadership succession were the results of previous research on school and classroom conditions influenced by rapid turnover and the effects and frequency of such turnover, as well as how distributed leadership might serve as an antidote to some of the more negative outcomes of rapid principal succession.

School and Classroom Conditions Influenced by Rapid Turnover

For the most part, school leaders influence students indirectly. Efforts to increase leaders' influence on students will therefore depend on identification of factors that mediate what leaders do. Rowan's (1996) framework identifies one promising set of mediators. This framework suggests that the performance of teachers—clearly the most powerful mediator of leaders' influence on students[6]—is a function of their abilities, their motivation, and the nature of the settings (or conditions) in which they work. The strength of leaders' influence on students will depend on their success in improving these three building blocks of teachers' performance. In this chapter we focus on teachers' school and classroom working conditions, exploring the degree to which variations in the rapidity of principal turnover influence, more specifically, school culture and classroom conditions, including curriculum and instruction.

Prior research indicates that the impact of school leadership on student achievement is mediated by school cultures (shared values, norms, and contexts), and that healthy school cultures are strongly related to increased student achievement and motivation.[7] School leaders who build productive "cultures of change" enhance teacher motivation, build teacher capacity, promote teacher efficacy, and create the professional unity and cohesion required for effective instruction and student success.[8] In sum, principals can have a strong effect on school culture and on curriculum and instruction, which, in turn, affects student success.[9]

Principal Turnover Effects

Principal turnover is often associated with negative consequences.[10] Changing principals, it is argued, disrupts staff members' focus on improving student achievement when a leader who supports a project leaves and is replaced by a leader with different priorities.[11] Disruption is also likely when a charismatic principal who had radically transformed the school in four or five years departs, or when there is a poor fit between the leader and school[12] (the notion of "fit" between leader and school is central to district administrators' decision making concerning principal placement).

Some caution is in order, however, when describing the link between principal turnover and student achievement. Although there certainly is research concluding that frequent principal turnover leads to lower student achievement, the current accountability climate in the United States also leads to the opposite possibility: low student achievement leading to frequent principal turnover, as leaders of "failing" schools are replaced.

Although principal turnover often has negative consequences, the outcome is not consistently negative. For example, student achievement may operate independently of changes in school leadership.[13] Miskel and Owens' (1983) study of 89 schools in the U.S. Midwest found that principal succession had no significant effects on staff members' job satisfaction, communication, instruction, school discipline, or school climate. But there is considerable evidence to the contrary.

Leadership turnover does not have to occur every year or two to be problematic. Even in cases in which a principal's tenure extends over a period of several years, teachers may remain alienated when principal turnover is the result of a district leadership rotation policy.[14] Teachers may become cynical and resistant to change because of the "revolving door syndrome" (the uncertainty and instability that turnover causes) and the perception of the new leader as a "servant to the system."[15]

Some teachers develop a deep mistrust of the new leader's loyalty, suspecting that he or she is committed more to career advancement than to the long-term welfare of the school and community. Under conditions of regular principal turnover, teachers learn to "wait them out."[16] That is, teachers maintain barriers between themselves and new leaders, ensuring that their school's culture becomes self-sustaining, "immunized," and impervious to change instigated by those in formal leadership positions.[17]

Working with research on principal turnover is challenging because results are seldom linked to measures of the *quality of leadership* being provided. Where the research cites frequent principal turnover as the cause of low teacher morale, for instance, there is an assumption that these were all good principals. If one considered the possibility that any of the principals involved had not been an effective leader, it would change the dynamic considerably—and perhaps lead to different conclusions about how well a school had done under poor management.

Frequency of Principal Turnover

Because some principal turnover is inevitable in all schools, it is important to ask about optimum frequency: How frequent is too frequent? How long is too long for a principal to stay in one school? Two theoretical perspectives—stage theory and change theory—have guided our efforts to answer these questions.

Stage theory conceptualizes *leadership succession* as a process with distinct phases and demands, rather than a singular event.[18] Patterns in the process have been identified, and the ways in which each phase of the succession process shapes and influences the outcome of subsequent phases have been described.[19] Most stage models predict that it takes at least five to seven years to build relationships of trust that can serve as a foundation for movement to later stages of the succession process—"consolidation and refinement," in Gabarro's (1987) terms. According to this view, principals need to be in their schools for about five years in order to have a positive impact. After five years, the principal's work may continue, but such work is not often associated with demonstrable improvement in the organization.

Change theory conceptualizes change as a process of initiation or adoption, implementation, and institutionalization or continuation. According to Fullan (1991), all successful schools experience an "implementation dip," a drop in performance and confidence that occurs when people are faced with innovations that demand new knowledge, skills, strategies, and relationships. People who are experiencing fear and anxiety about their capacity to manage change need leaders they can trust, as well as leaders who are empathetic and socially skilled.

Fullan (1991) asserts that although there is no standard formula for changing the culture of an organization, sustainable improvement requires several years of effort to work through complex cultural issues such as resistance to change and acculturation of the new leader. Turnover that occurs every two or three years makes it unlikely that a principal will get beyond the stages of initiation and early implementation. Like stage theory, then, change theory also argues that leader tenure beyond three years is typically necessary for significant improvements to occur in response to a principal's initiatives.

But what about the upper limit of a principal's tenure in a school? Does change theory suggest a "best by" date for principals, beyond which they should move on—or be moved on? There is little hard evidence bearing on this question, but that fact has not prevented some districts from creating policies reflecting the professional experiences of their staffs. District superintendents, for example, often justify their principal rotation policies as a means of reinvigorating school administrators, who seem to reach their peak effectiveness after five to seven years.[20] Realistically, there is bound to be enormous variation among individual principals, suggesting that districts should avoid a one-size-fits-all approach to principal succession.

Although it seems appropriate to focus on factors within the school at play in the changes of principals, we should not ignore the context in which such changes are taking place. The socioeconomic status of the community is strongly related to the success of students of schools in that community. "Study after study suggests that socioeconomic status (SES) of families explains more than half of the difference in student achievement across schools; it is also highly related to violence, dropping out of school, entry to postsecondary education and levels of both adult employment and income" (Leithwood, Louis, Anderson, & Wahlstrom 2004, 46–47). A context of low student achievement, plagued by dropouts and violence, may lead to a low sense of principal efficacy (that is, a belief that there is not much a leader can do to improve low SES schools). This would lead to two effects: first, it is likely to be difficult to keep principals, so the rate of turnover is often higher in low SES communities; and second, such a context would make it very difficult to attract new principals. White, Cooper, and Brayman (2006) cite concerns, in schools they studied, about areas where the local economy was in decline. In such areas it was increasingly difficult to find applicants for new positions as principals. Although SES is seen to have a range of effects on students and schools, the impact is felt particularly on the turnover of the principal.

Leadership Distribution

Evidence about the effects of principal turnover assumes that a considerable proportion of the leadership in schools is provided by the principal. But supposing school leadership was more dispersed or distributed: Would more leadership distribution within a school moderate the effects of rapid principal turnover, as some are now suggesting?[21] Among the many different conceptions of leadership distribution in the literature,[22] we use a conception developed by Leithwood, Mascall, and Strauss (2009), which includes four distinct patterns of leadership distribution:

- *Planful Alignment.* In this pattern, leaders' tasks and functions result from prior, planful thought by organizational members, and functions are rationally distributed in ways comparable to Gronn's (2009) holistic notion of "institutionalized practice."
- *Spontaneous Alignment.* In this pattern, leadership tasks and functions are distributed with little or no planning, and tacit or intuitive decisions determine who should perform which leadership functions. Fortuitous, positive, short-term working alliances evolve.
- *Spontaneous Misalignment.* Here there are disjunctions among leadership functions, causing unpredictable outcomes and negative effects on short- and long-term organizational effectiveness and productivity.
- *Anarchic Misalignment.* This pattern is similar to the condition Hargreaves and Fink (2006) describe as anarchy: members of the organization reject or compete with one another in making claims of leadership regarding decisions, priorities, and activities.

Recent scholarship suggests that leadership distribution may moderate the effects of principal turnover on school culture. Hargreaves and Fink (2006) conclude that the post-succession process is best managed when the departing leader leaves a legacy of distributed leadership marked by shared vision, investment, and capacity that ensures the sustainability of school improvement initiatives. This leads us to expect that in times of frequent principal turnover (leader changes every one, two, or three years), involving leaders shaped by different experiences, priorities, and leadership styles, teachers are prompted (or forced) to take leadership into their own hands, and to create some stability in their schools by means of a self-sustaining professional culture that operates independently of the principal. The result then will be distributed leadership, in one form or another.

Where teacher leadership evolves strategically (planned and aligned with school goals), a self-sustaining culture can become both collaborative and productive. Copland (2003) found that schools with a history of leadership distribution pushed teachers to find new roles in the school and to broaden their perspectives beyond their own classrooms. Indeed, Copland's research has identified schools where teams of teachers are providing extensive leadership in schools and providing bridges during times of principal succession.

When leadership distribution is neither planned nor aligned, however, the self-sustaining culture drifts, gradually loses its collective sense of vision and purpose, and becomes increasingly balkanized; each teacher focuses on his or her classroom, works in relative isolation from colleagues, and takes responsibility only for his or her own work. The result is an ineffective organization of neglect and anarchy, where student achievement may remain unchanged or even deteriorate.

New Evidence for This Chapter

Beginning with a brief summary of the methods used to collect and analyze evidence for this part of our study, this section of the chapter reports both quantitative and case study results in response to our questions about leader succession.

Method

We used quantitative and qualitative evidence to answer the five questions presented in the introduction to this chapter. Quantitative data were provided by 3,793 teachers and 130 principals (from the 130 schools in which at least seven teachers responded) to questions about average principal turnover rates, as well as effects on school culture, curriculum, instruction, and student achievement.

Using a six-point scale, school culture was measured with seven items, each of which began with the stem: *To what extent do you agree or disagree with the following statements?*

- Disruptions of instructional time are minimized.
- Most teachers in our school share a similar set of values, beliefs, and attitudes related to teaching and learning.
- Students feel safe in our schools.
- In our school, we have well-defined learning expectations for all students.
- Students in our school meet or exceed clearly defined expectations.
- We provide opportunities for students to discuss the effects of intolerance on their lives.
- Our student assessment practices reflect our curriculum standards.

Classroom conditions were measured with a five-item scale using the same stem and the following statements:

- I have sufficient written curricula on which to base my lessons.
- My instructional strategies enable students to construct their own knowledge.
- I maintain a rapid pace of instruction in my classes.
- I feel adequately equipped to handle student behavior in my class.
- Our school/district provides a rigorous core curriculum for most of our students.

Responses to the survey questions were linked to student achievement results in all 130 schools.[23]

Interview data were collected from four schools in response to questions about the potential for some patterns of distributed leadership to mitigate the negative effects of rapid principal turnover, and what, if anything, incoming principals might do to minimize negative turnover effects. The four schools used in this chapter had the highest principal turnover rates among all forty schools included in the first round of site visits for our larger project.

Principal Turnover: Frequency and Effects on Schools, Classrooms, and Students

Table 10.1 reports the means, standard deviations, and scale reliabilities (Cronbach's alpha) of the measures used in this chapter. As the first row in this table indicates, the average number of principals in the school over the past ten years was 3.08, for an average length of tenure of 3.2 years per principal.

TABLE 10.1 SUMMARY OF SURVEY RESULTS

Variables	Mean	SD	Reliability
Principal Turnover	3.08	1.74	
School Culture	4.43	.49	.91
Classroom Conditions	4.87	.28	.76
SES (percentage of students receiving free or reduced-price lunch)	46.84	.27	
Student Achievement (percentage at proficiency)	67.20	23.40	

(N = 130 schools)

TABLE 10.2 RELATIONSHIPS AMONG THE VARIABLES

	SES	Principal Turnover	School Culture	Classroom Conditions	Student Achievement
SES	1.00	.03	−.34**	−.21*	−.44**
Principal Turnover	.03	1.00	−.24**	−.20*	−.11
School Culture	−.34**	−.24**	1.00	.74**	.47**
Classroom Conditions	−.21*	−.20*	.74**	1.00	.26**
Student Achievement	−.44**	−.11	.47**	.26**	1.00

(N = 130 schools)

**Correlation is significant at the 0.01 level (2-tailed).

*Correlation is significant at the 0.05 level (2-tailed).

The standard deviation for this measure is a relatively large (1.74), with some schools experiencing little turnover while many experience quite a bit.

Correlation coefficients between all of the variables of interest in this chapter appear in Table 10.2. Relationships among principal turnover and measures of school and classroom conditions are negative. There is a high level of correlation among our school variables and student achievement, and a moderate but still significant correlation between the school variables and the number of principals over the past ten years. Principal turnover is moderately and negatively correlated with school culture, classroom curriculum, and instruction; it has a weak negative relationship with student achievement.

SES has a significant negative relationship with our school variables and with student achievement. Surprisingly, the relationship between SES and principal turnover was not significant in these schools, which differs from findings in other research about principal turnover.

FIGURE 10.1 TESTING THE MEDIATED EFFECTS OF PRINCIPAL TURNOVER ON STUDENT ACHIEVEMENT

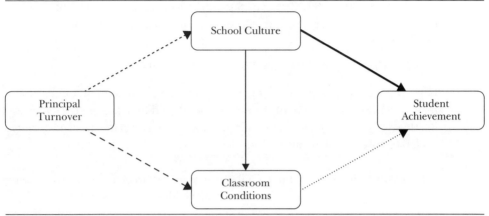

Solid line = positive effect
Bold line = significant positive effect
Dotted line = negative effect
Light dotted line = not significant negative effect
Dashes = not significant effect

Figure 10.1 summarizes the Results of a Path Model[24] we used to explore the relationships among these variables more precisely

This model as a whole is a good fit with the data, and it explains 24 percent of the variation in student achievement. The total effect of principal turnover on student achievement was small but significant and negative (–.11). This effect, however, is indirect, through school culture. Principal turnover has significant and moderately negative effects on school culture (–.24), and school culture has moderately strong, significant, and positive effects on student achievement (.61). The effects of turnover on classroom conditions are not significant, and the measure of classroom conditions is negatively though nonsignificantly related to student achievement.

In the next step we examined the extent to which adding the socioeconomic status of schools as an independent variable (along with principal turnover) would alter our findings. This expanded analysis increased the overall explanatory power of the model as a whole, although SES was not related to principal turnover. And principal turnover retained its modest but significant indirect effect on student achievement.

In sum, our quantitative results suggest that principal turnover has negative effects on student achievement. These effects are mediated more by school-level than by classroom-level conditions. The weaker impact of principal turnover on classroom variables might suggest that teacher classroom practice is in some way buffered from direct effects of changes in principal leadership. We speculate that teachers may continue to feel secure in their classrooms, regardless of the school culture around them. Although buffering of this sort limits the negative effects of principal turnover, it may also limit positive effects of a principal's improvement efforts.

Leadership Distribution and Leader Turnover Illustrated

Given the significant influence of principal turnover on student achievement mediated primarily by school culture, we developed four case studies to examine this dynamic in greater detail and to learn what part patterns of distributed leadership play in the relationships.

Culbertson Elementary School Culbertson is an urban elementary school with an enrollment of just over 600 students, almost all of whom meet state achievement expectations on the grades 3–5 standardized tests in reading, science, and mathematics. At the time of our study, the school had had three principals in the last three years, and the current principal had been promoted to the post from a district intern position. High principal turnover had become a challenge for the district, in part because a new state retirement policy had induced 20 percent of the district's principals to retire in the year that a new option was announced. To deal with the challenges of principal succession, district leaders established a number of support mechanisms to help new principals acclimatize themselves in their new jobs, including monthly meetings and a mentoring program with retired principals.

Principal turnover in Culbertson had no measurable impact on student performance, positively or negatively. From 2003 through 2006, the percentage of students meeting or exceeding state norms held consistently to a range in the high nineties across all grades and subjects.

The principal three years earlier had explicitly encouraged teachers to assume leadership roles in the school in accordance with district policies that supported the designation and implementation of formal teacher-leader positions. The principal also saw to it that this leadership distribution was both planful and well aligned with the school's goals. By the time of our study, leadership had become distributed to a considerable extent, and teacher-leaders were able to help introduce incoming principals to the school culture. Because student achievement was not a source of concern in the school, there was little pressure to bring about any radical changes in teaching and learning. Consequently, new principals did not feel compelled to innovate either rapidly or radically.

A *planful alignment* pattern of leadership distribution had stood the staff in good stead through two succeeding principals. The teachers had been able to work together, share the leadership for that work, and sustain the learning of their students despite changes in principals. The current principal seemed to be in tune with this approach to distributed leadership.

Molina Elementary School Molina is a small elementary school in an urban community. At the time of our study, 31 percent of the students in the district qualified for free and reduced-price lunches, and the school had a 35 percent nonwhite (mostly Hispanic) population. Student achievement scores were uneven across grades and subjects: strong in grade 3, but weak in grade 4; strong in reading but not in writing. In the three years for which we had data, however, overall levels of achievement had been improving.

State policy on principal retirement was in flux at the time of our study. This situation was encouraging some principals who were facing an uncertain future to get out "while the getting was good." Over the five years prior to our study there had been a high level of retirements across the district, and Molina had not been immune to this trend, having had four principals in that period of time. District office staff remarked on early retirement as an ongoing problem and a significant source of stress on the system's capacity to train and replace its district and school leaders. The pressures of early retirement—as many as 20 percent of the total number of principals in the district changing in any one year—had spawned district initiatives to address the turnover problem. As a result of a District Literacy Initiative, there had been a structural shift to create teacher-leader Literacy Coaches in each school. Molina had five of these Literacy Coaches, with an additional Literacy Coach position scheduled to be added in the next year.

Cultural and emotional turmoil was apparent at Molina because principal turnover had been accompanied by fundamental changes in philosophy and leadership style. The four principals in five years at Molina had had different personalities and insufficient time to establish trust and rapport. Long-serving support-staff members, who were familiar to teachers, parents, and students, were able to take on certain leadership roles in light of the annual change of principals. This case provides, accordingly, some evidence for our expectation that greater distribution of leadership would ameliorate some negative effects of rapid principal turnover. But life in schools is not shaped by a single variable. In the case of Molina, a high rate of teacher turnover exacerbated the effects of rapid principal turnover, thereby muting the potentially stabilizing benefit associated with more teacher leadership.

Molina's pattern of distributed leadership could best be described as *spontaneous misalignment*. There was no planned effort to share leadership, nor was there a sense that leadership as it evolved was being aligned with school goals. Despite the teachers' best efforts to provide leadership for their school, along with the district's initiatives to establish formal teacher-leadership positions, the combined effects of frequent principal turnover and frequent teacher turnover made it impossible for this school to sustain any momentum in its improvement efforts.

Blake Elementary School Blake is a small elementary school in an inner-city district. At the time of our study, a high proportion of its student population was black, and a significant proportion of the community lived below the poverty line. Student achievement was not high. Achievement levels in grades 3 and 4 communication arts and grade 3 math tests were at or above state averages, but results for grades 4 and 5 math and grade 5 communication arts remained below state averages. The number of children achieving at the state standard in literacy, however, had been increasing steadily over the past three years.

Three administrators had been appointed to Blake in seven years. There had also been a significant number of new senior administrators in the district in the preceding two years: a new superintendent and three new directors at the district level, and three new administrators at the school level, across a total of seven schools.

Blake's story has much to do with a charismatic principal whose vision for a professional learning community (PLC) had shaped the school's identity, structure, and culture. Although the principal in position at the time of our study had not initiated the PLC concept, she had chosen to carry on with it as the central feature of the school's shared vision. Thus the PLC provided the foundation for cultural and structural continuity from the previous principal to the current principal.

Principal turnover did not result in cultural chaos or teacher alienation at Blake, because there was a clear and planned focus for school culture and instruction. This school-wide focus survived rapid principal turnover, partly because collaborative structures were well established and accepted, and partly because the new principal's philosophy and practices supported the existing school culture. Blake therefore provides another case of *planful alignment* in the distribution of leadership. Teachers at Blake had developed a shared vision for the school and were able to sustain it despite the change in leadership. Indeed, the new principal's support for the existing vision became a key element in further developing a positive culture in this school.

Rhodes Middle School Rhodes Middle School is located in a low-income community. At the time of our study, 13 percent of the population fell below the poverty line, and 60 percent of the Rhodes students qualified for free or reduced-price lunch. Four different principals had served at Rhodes in four years, and the student and teacher populations were highly transient. The first of the four principals believed strongly in site-based management and fostered a culture in which teachers learned to rely on their own leadership to get things done. Theirs was an autonomous teacher culture in which each staff member was encouraged to take personal responsibility for her or his own classroom practice, but not much else. Collaboration was not encouraged. Student achievement, however, had been consistently high over the previous three years.

Although many teachers at Rhodes seemed satisfied with their autonomous culture and its contribution to sustaining their efforts through frequent principal turnover, the principal in place at the time of our study saw professional entrenchment and barriers to administrator influence. This new principal set about changing the culture of the school, without going so far as to dismantle its existing decision-making structures. She aimed for a balance of authority between herself and the staff, given the instability caused by frequent principal succession. She set out to establish a collective focus on instructional practice and data-driven decision making.

The school seemed to be poised on the cusp of moving from traditional forms of teacher autonomy to a more planful pattern of leadership distribution. The approach of the new principal was more directive than collaborative. But her intention was to create a more collaborative culture, with teachers exercising more leadership across the school as they learned to work together.

◆ ◆ ◆

In summary, then, all four schools experienced high rates of principal turnover during the period of the study—ranging from a new principal every year for three or four years, to one every two years over a seven-year period. In all four schools there had been some attempt at distributing leadership, but each school approached such distribution differently, since the culture varied from school to school. Although the four schools seem to have little in common beyond rapid principal turnover, two schools found ways to deal productively with changing leadership, whereas the other two did not.

Culbertson took a deliberate approach to the distribution of leadership, driven by a principal and district leaders committed to collaborative work and planfully aligned leadership distribution. Blake built a strong professional community, also producing planfully aligned patterns of leadership distribution capable of surviving changes in leadership. In both cases, leadership was distributed among a number of teachers. Despite frequent changes in principals, the supportive cultures that developed in these schools continued to thrive.

In the other two schools, there was less success with leadership distribution. At Molina, the district's attempts to foster teacher leadership as one response to frequent principal turnover were thwarted by frequent teacher turnover. At Rhodes, the efforts of an earlier principal to foster a high degree of individual teacher autonomy had been sufficiently successful that the principal in place at the time of our study was experiencing considerable difficulty in her efforts to promote collaboration and more leadership distribution. Teachers still remained independent, in a strong culture of individual isolation.

Conclusion

Evidence serving as the basis for this chapter included both large-scale survey data linked to student achievement and interviews with teachers and administrators in four case schools. From the survey evidence we learned that frequent principal turnover was common across schools in our study, occurring on average about every three years. Analysis of the survey evidence also demonstrated negative effects of rapid turnover on both school culture and student achievement. However, qualitative evidence from four schools indicated planfully aligned forms of leadership distribution within schools have the potential to moderate the negative consequences of rapid principal turnover, and principals have significant leverage in the distribution of leadership across their schools.

The challenge of fostering leadership distribution is greatly influenced by the existing culture of the school, as autonomous teacher cultures are strong sources of resistance to leadership distribution efforts. So some individual schools are much more able than others to manage rapid turnover in ways that prevent achievement decline. It seems very unlikely, however, that student achievement will improve under most conditions associated with rapid principal turnover.

Implications for Policy and Practice

Three implications for policy and practice emerged from this section of our study.

1. Districts should aim to keep most principals in their schools for a minimum of four years, and preferably five to seven years.
2. Under conditions of rapid principal turnover, districts need to encourage incoming principals to understand and respect the school-improvement work in which staff members have previously been engaged. Incoming principals will likely have a smoother transition if they see their job as continuing and refining that work. Principals assigned to schools identified as in need of being "turned around" are clearly exempted from this recommendation.

3. Incoming principals should not have the sole responsibility to encourage distributed leadership in schools that have previously experienced rapid principal turnover. Under such conditions, districts need to directly encourage and support planfully aligned forms of leadership distribution, providing training and support to staff members in carrying out shared leadership functions.

Reflections

1. When principal turnover occurs rapidly in schools you are familiar with, what are the usual causes? Are some of these causes alterable? How?
2. How might a principal new to a school ensure a productive entry?
3. What could district leaders do to reduce the negative effects of rapid principal succession?

CHAPTER ELEVEN

DATA USE

An Exploration from the District to the School

Stephen E. Anderson, Kenneth Leithwood, and Karen Seashore Louis

Claims Supported by Evidence in This Chapter

- District priorities and practices concerning data use substantially influence the leadership behavior of principals and teachers.
- District leaders' influence occurs through setting expectations, modeling data use in district decision making, and by providing direct support to schools.
- Data use in schools occurs as a collective activity involving principals with teachers in multiple contexts (for example, school improvement teams, grade team meetings). Principals are more likely to enable data use by teachers than to be the primary data users.
- Leaders in high-data-use schools have clear purposes for analyzing data linked to goals for improvement in student learning. They build internal capacity for this work and use data to solve problems, not just to identify them.
- Principals and teachers have and use considerable amounts of evidence about the status of individual students and their student populations. They report less use of evidence about school and classroom conditions that would need to change for achievement to improve.
- Intensity of data use is significantly associated with student achievement in elementary schools.

Although in the past it was possible for administrators and teachers to pay limited attention to student achievement data and research as they engaged in efforts to improve their schools, the circumstances have changed rapidly over the last twenty-five years. In the United States, the shift is often tied to 1983 report of President Ronald Reagan's National Commission on Excellence in Education, which used data to argue that the United States was caught in a "rising tide of mediocrity" in student performance. Today, it is hard to attend an education conference or read an education magazine without encountering broad claims for data-based decision making. Of course, the admonition for administrators and teachers to be more evidence-based is not simply an admonition to make greater use of data; as Wilson (2004) points out, "assessment information drawn from standardized tests represents no more than a drop in the bucket of all assessment information that is gathered in a typical classroom" (p. 2). Rather, it is an admonition to make greater use of a different type of evidence than administrators and teachers have typically used: formally and systematically collected evidence of student performance and factors affecting student performance. In this chapter, we follow Wayman, Jimerson, and Cho's (2010) caution that use of formal data to inform instructionally related decision making should be integrated with more informal sources of evidence as a basis for exercising professional judgment, not serve as a replacement for that action.

The analysis described in this chapter was stimulated by the pervasive demand that educators make more use of systematically collected data for decisions in combination with the limited body of research about the nature and consequences of such use. Specifically, we addressed four questions:

- Do variations in district approaches to data use affect data use by principals' and teachers?
- What types of data and patterns of data use are found in typical schools, as compared with schools in which evidence-driven decision making has become a priority?
- What organizational conditions influence principals' and teachers' use of data for school improvement and instructional decision making?
- Is there an association between data use by districts and principals, and student achievement?

What Do We Know from Prior Research?

Almost all accountability-driven, large-scale reform efforts assume that greater attention by district and school personnel to systematically collected data is a key lever for improving student performance. Actual evidence in support of this assumption is thin and mixed.[1] As others have noted, much of this research focuses on the uses of data by school district and/or school personnel, and on conditions affecting data use, without directly measuring the impact of data use (and different patterns of use) for teaching and for student outcomes.[2] The brief track record of systematic data use by school systems and school personnel makes it difficult to be confident about the frequency, quality, and effects of data use at both district and school levels, and about the conditions that influence the nature and value of such use.

Another limitation in our understanding of current expectations for data-informed decision making arises from research that focuses primarily on small samples of school districts and/or schools that are known by reputation either to be active data users[3] or to conduct research on the implementation of particular data use systems developed and supported by external organizations.[4] Such research provides insights about what high engagement with data use for decision making looks like in practice, and about factors affecting data use at the school and district levels; however, it does not represent what is happening in the majority of schools and districts. Research on data use in typical schools and districts presents a more sobering picture of the challenges of incorporating effective data use into the ongoing work of school systems, school administrators, and teachers.[5]

Data Use and Support for Data Use at the District Level

Research on data use practices at the school district level, and the difference that such practices make for school improvement activities and outcomes at the school level, varies greatly in scope and depth. Numerous research reviews and case studies of school district policies and strategies associated with district effectiveness and improvement cite the systematic collection and use of data by district leaders, in order to set goals and plans for improvement and to monitor progress, as one of many strategic factors contributing to district effectiveness.[6] This research stops short of analyzing the interaction of district data use practices with other strands of district improvement activity or exploring the relative effects of different strategies on school leadership or on teaching and learning.

Another strand of research focuses uniquely on the role and use of evidence in decision making related to student learning at the board and central office level. Coburn and her colleagues' research, for example, dispels visions of district decision making as a highly rational process "driven" by hard data.[7] It documents the micropolitical nature of how district actors often seek and use evidence to support prior beliefs and commitments to particular directions and actions. Studies that focus uniquely at the district level, however, provide limited insight into the influence of district data use activity on school leadership, teaching practices, and student learning processes and outcomes.

Wohlstetter, Datnow, and Park (2008) investigated what central office agents were doing to develop and support data-driven decision making at the district and school levels in four school systems (two districts, two education management organizations) that had a reputation as leaders in the use of performance data for decision making. Their findings highlight a number of ways in which central office agents can build a foundation and culture for data use as an ongoing dimension of continuous improvement activities in schools, such as these:

- Establishing meaningful goals for improvement in student performance that are aligned with system-wide curriculum and accountability requirements
- Creating explicit norms and expectations for data use for decision making
- Developing structures to enable interchange of information between central office and school about performance and plans for improvement
- Investing in developing the capacity of school and district personnel to use data

Our findings, as presented in the following section, are largely supportive of the findings from this study but draw from a larger and less selective sample of school districts and schools. In addition, unlike in previous studies, we connect the work of districts to teaching and learning.

Data Use and Conditions Affecting Data Use at the School Level

Our particular interest is in data use and conditions affecting data use in a broad sample of schools with varying levels of engagement in data use for instructional decision making and school improvement; our interest is not restricted to intensive users of data or to the implementation of particular data use processes or tools.

Notwithstanding their stated belief in and commitment to enhancing educational data use in schools and school districts, Ingram, Louis, and Schroder (2004) and Wayman, Jimerson, and Cho (2010) provide a rather stark picture of data use in typical schools of varying size. Both of these studies draw attention to multiple practical obstacles to constructive use of standardized tests and other forms of systematically collected data by principals and teachers, such as

- The absence of a shared vision for teaching and learning linked to data use
- Lack of perceived need where students are performing reasonably well
- Low capacity (knowledge, skill) to effectively lead and support data use by school teachers
- Inadequate time and weak structures to promote collaboration in data use among teachers
- Insufficient professional development

Our findings and analysis corroborate many of the factors highlighted by these authors, drawing from a broader sample of typical schools, while highlighting some key differences observed in schools identified as intensive users.

Our school-level analysis builds on Ikemoto and Marsh's (2007) framework of data use patterns and conditions as a lens for the analysis of our qualitative interview data further on in this chapter.

Data Use and Student Learning

Evidence about the impact of data use on student learning remains limited, a point routinely acknowledged by those who have studied data use activity in schools and districts.[8] The most compelling line of research focuses on teachers' use of formative or just-in-time evidence about students' learning to shape their own instruction. Black and Wiliam's (2004) review of more than 250 studies serves as the primary source for the claim that formative assessment, in Popham's (2008) words: "can fundamentally transform the way a teacher teaches" (p. vii). Evidence about the impact of large-scale state and district testing programs on student achievement is mixed at best. Koretz (2005), for example, claims that evidence about the effects of assessment-based accountability is both sparse and discouraging. On the other hand, in a comparison of high- and low-accountability states, Carnoy and Loeb (2002) found significantly greater achievement in eighth-grade mathematics for students in high-accountability states, with no difference in retention or high school completion rates. Research on effective and improving schools and school districts often cites data-informed decision making, with an emphasis on data about student progress and outcomes as characteristic of leadership in these settings.[9]

Although the correlation of systematic data use with positive student achievement results at the school and/or district levels provides some logical support for arguments that data use is a key factor in improving student learning at a larger scale than individual students, causal linkages between data use policies and practices and the quality and improvement of student achievement remain uncertain and unclear. Our analysis does not resolve this gap; however, in our quantitative analysis of principal and teacher survey data, we did explore the possible links between district and school variables associated with data use and our measures of student achievement in the schools we sampled.

New Evidence for This Chapter

Evidence for this analysis comes from the principal and teacher survey data, along with principal interview data collected during the second round of site visits. Evidence also included case studies based on interviews with school administrators and selected teachers from six site-visit elementary and middle schools identified from the survey responses as high users of data for decision making, and interviews with district administrators across the full sample of thirty-six site visit districts.

Results are reported in four subsections of this chapter. The first section uses survey evidence to explore data use and support at the district level. The second section pursues the same issues using interview and case study evidence. The next section outlines findings about patterns of data use in schools, as well as organizational conditions affecting such use; in this section we draw on principal interviews and our case studies. Finally, the chapter reports our analysis of the results of our efforts to clarify relationships between district and school-level data use and student achievement.

Data Use and Support at the District Level: Findings from the Surveys

Data use by teachers and principals is not an isolated activity; rather, data use occurs in the context of other critical activities, such as developing consensus around clear targets for improvement and developing the capacities of the professionals in the school to act on both the data and improvement goals. This is clearly illustrated in findings from our second principal and teacher surveys. The principal survey included a variety of items related to district policy conditions and actions identified from prior research on the characteristics of effective school districts[10] as reported in the analysis of district influences on principal efficacy in Chapter Nine. An exploratory factor analysis of the second principal survey responses revealed that items associated with several of these conditions could be clustered into broader categories. This led us to identify two district factors that might be expected to influence principal and teacher leadership directly, and student achievement indirectly. One we labeled "district use of targets and data," and the other "district focus on professional development" (including principals and teachers). We examined the relationship between these two factors and two measures of school leadership drawn from the "round two" teacher surveys, including teacher ratings of their principals' instructional leadership behaviors and of the strength of professional community in their schools.

Figure 11.1 represents the results of our analysis of the statistical relationships among these variables, as measured in our surveys.[11] This analysis includes only the sixty-eight elementary schools in the study.

The figure suggests several important conclusions. First, the establishment of data-informed targets for improvement at the district level is directly and positively associated with teacher reports of the depth of principal's instructional

FIGURE 11.1 HOW DISTRICT APPROACHES TO DATA USE INFLUENCE STUDENT ACHIEVEMENT

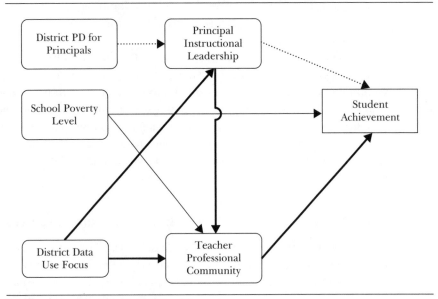

Bold line = significant positive relationship
Solid line = positive relationship
Dotted line = negative relationship

leadership and also with teacher leadership as manifested through the strength of professional community in their schools (see Chapter Three for a more in-depth analysis of the importance of instructional leadership and professional community in schools).

Second, the influence of district professional development initiatives on school leadership (instructional leadership of principals, and teachers' professional community) is negligible—or even negative—*unless those inputs are integrated with district targets and data use.* Professional development alone does not appear to increase principals' ability to exercise and encourage leadership in the school. Our qualitative data suggests one possible reason for this. In many cases district professional development activities for principals are not well aligned with district improvement goals and data use priorities.

The evidence summarized in Figure 11.1 also echoes our finding (reported in Chapter Three) that the effects of principals' instructional leadership behaviors on teaching and learning are mediated by the quality of teachers' professional community in the school. Instructional leadership must be coupled with the principal's work in teacher professional communities in order to have the desired positive effect on student learning. Thus when districts focus their professional development and data use work around shared instructional leadership, data use, and the joint responsibilities of teachers and principals for learning, it results in a strong, albeit indirect, relationship to achievement scores.

One aspect of this analysis is important, but puzzling. We found that there is a strong and significant effect of student poverty levels on achievement among the schools in our study. Even when we look at the hard work of districts and school leaders to develop initiatives designed to close the achievement gap that exists between students from poorer and wealthier backgrounds, this gap persists. However, when bodies of evidence from elementary schools and secondary schools are considered separately (Figure 11.1 includes only elementary schools), there is a surprising difference. The basic relationships among district actions, principal leadership, professional community, and student learning are the same. However, in elementary schools, the association between student poverty levels and student achievement is negligible, whereas in secondary schools it is very strong. In other words, the district's work on using data to drive decisions about school improvement appears to have an impact on the achievement gap in elementary schools, but not in secondary schools.

Although there is no simple explanation for this finding, it is useful to reflect on our earlier observations in Chapters Five and Six about the enactment of instructional leadership in elementary and secondary schools. Although secondary school teachers are as likely as elementary school teachers to indicate that they like and trust their principals, they are much less likely to see them as having much influence on their teaching strategies, and they are also less likely to experience professional community. If we look at these two sets of findings together, we are led to hypothesize that the districts in our study have been better able to organize a support system for elementary school leaders to promote data-driven improvement than for leaders in the more complex and subject matter–driven contexts of secondary schools. Of course, the collection and analysis of data to inform principals' and teachers' instructional decision making is only one dimension of the instructional leadership behavior of principals. We also examined more precisely the extent to which district leader engagement with and support for data use had a direct relationship with the data use practices of principals. Table 11.1 draws upon findings from our initial principal survey and shows a direct correlation between principals' reports of data use at the district level and their own engagement with data use at the school level. Although one cannot necessarily infer causality from this analysis, all relationships between principals' reports of their own and their districts' data use are significantly though modestly correlated. In short, in settings where district leaders exhibit support for principals and engagement

TABLE 11.1   RELATIONSHIP BETWEEN PRINCIPAL AND DISTRICT DATA USE

	Principal Responses to Items about the School		
	I rely frequently on research evidence in my decision making.	I rely frequently on systematically collected evaluation data about my school in my decision making.	I use data about student achievement to help make most decisions in my school.
Principal responses to items about the district			
Our district has the capacity for reliable assessment of student and school performance.	.331	.271	.195
Our district incorporates student and school performance data into district-level decision making.	.402	.384	.317
Our district assists schools with the use of student and school performance data for school improvement planning.	.344	.416	.317
The district uses student achievement data to determine teacher professional development needs and resources.	.426	.397	.355

Note: all correlations are statistically significant (p < .01).

with student performance data for instructionally related decision making, principals are more likely to follow suit.

In sum, the findings from our surveys indicate that district office leaders, acting in response to state/federal accountability requirements and pressures, are indeed key players in the use, and support for the use, of data for instructionally related decision making at the district and school levels, and that principal and teacher use of data is clearly shaped by district action. These findings are corroborated by our interviews at the district and school levels.

Data Use and Support at the District Level: Findings from Interviews and Case Studies

State and federal accountability systems require district and school personnel to pay attention to any evidence of students who are struggling or failing to meet mandated standards and targets for academic performance. Most district leaders we interviewed described this as a positive turn of events, though they were not all equally well-supported by their state education agencies in local efforts to make use of data. Few principals among those we interviewed were deeply and skillfully engaged in data use on their own. Districts were the main source of support for data use in schools; district leaders played key roles in guiding how data were used by principals and teachers to guide their decisions. They did this by taking these actions:

- Setting expectations for and monitoring data use in school improvement activities
- Modeling data use in district decision making and in their engagement with schools
- Mobilizing supplementary tools and resources to facilitate data use (for example, data reports for schools, curriculum-embedded teacher assessment instruments, time and data use teams)
- Providing access to the expertise needed to meaningfully incorporate data use into the school's efforts to improve student learning and school results

Setting Expectations and Monitoring One obvious way that district leaders fostered principals' and teachers' data use was by explicitly insisting on it in various ways. The principal interviews suggest that districts do this by requiring principals to link school improvement goals and progress reports to student performance data, and by insisting that teachers justify their claims about good practice with some type of data beyond informal observation and professional opinion. Simple monitoring often suffices: requiring decisions about the expenditure of money to be justified with evidence, and expecting professional development to be based on areas of needed improvement apparent in the data are as important as formal monitoring schemes.

In schools and districts in which data use appeared to be more deeply embedded into routine practice, district administrators commonly talked about engaging principals individually in data-informed discussions about the school goals and progress during the school year.

Modeling District leaders also foster data use by modeling the use of data relevant to student and school performance by being explicit about what data were used in making decisions about system improvement goals and initiatives or in decisions about how they define and respond to particular school needs. In one district, for example, central administrators established improvement in high school graduation rates as a system priority, jointly studied the academic records of students who failed to graduate on time, shared their findings with principals, and set an expectation that principals and their staffs would take action to address the factors contributing to failure. In another district, the superintendent mobilized a district-led investigation into why the proportion of children reading at grade level had declined between grades 3 and 5.

Developing Supportive Tools In some districts, central office administrators promoted and supported data use in schools by providing school personnel with tools to facilitate data collection and interpretation. At minimum, this included data reports that assemble, present, and perhaps simplify the variety of data on student performance and characteristics required by the state and district for accountability purposes. In addition, some districts had developed local assessment tools (for example, subject benchmark tests for continuous assessment, scoring rubrics aligned with state or district curriculum standards) to enable formative assessment of student progress. In the most elaborate systems, district staff members have created procedures and forms to help principals and teachers link assessment data to specific curriculum standards and to information about instructional strategies and programs that could address identified gaps in student performance. However, the nature and range of school-level data use tools created, accessed, and supported by district office leaders varies from district to district and is not clearly associated with either district size or relative affluence. In other words, the development of additional tools to support school-level data analysis is a matter of district policy choices.

Tools and resources can be more than rubrics or assessment. In some districts we observed district-wide organizational structures and routines created to promote and facilitate data use for improvement in student learning in schools, most notably opportunities to share information across schools. District administrators and principals, for example, frequently referred to times set aside in monthly principal meetings for data sharing and interpretation by principals in consultation with district supervisors and professional staff. Although not as widely in evidence, a few principals mentioned recent district initiatives to establish student learning–focused professional learning community structures (teacher teams) and time in schools in which the use of student performance data was an expected component.

Developing School-Based Capacity As we noted in the survey analysis presented earlier, professional development seems to be effective largely when it is associated with a district focus on data use. When districts develop the professional capacity of school personnel to interpret and incorporate data into decision making for school improvement and student learning, more data-based leadership for learning occurs. Interviewees referred to several aspects of their districts' capacity building assistance—in particular, providing access to district or external experts (for example, regional education service center staff, university faculty) to help with organizing and interpreting data from state tests and/or to deliver professional development for teachers and principals regarding data interpretation and use.

District size was clearly a factor in how this support was provided. Whereas large districts were likely to have assessment and evaluation specialists on staff, smaller districts were more likely to rely on district administrators or curriculum staff who had developed additional expertise in assessment matters, and they were also more likely to seek assistance of curriculum and assessment specialists from regional education service centers.

The most successful districts did not expect data use capacities to mushroom overnight. Some district leaders were committed to the need to develop the capacity of school personnel to use student assessment and other performance data to inform collective decisions about school improvement plans and programming to meet student needs without turning to outside expertise. In a few districts, we observed a developmental progression to capacity development. Over time, an initial emphasis on developing principals' expertise in data use shifted to training use by classroom teachers working in teams.

Overall, our findings about district-level leadership and support for data use in schools are consistent with evidence from other research on the district role in school improvement and from research that specifically addresses district leadership and support for data-driven decision making, as described in the introductory sections of this chapter.[12]

Data Use at the School Level

We adapted Ikemoto and Marsh's (2007) framework to guide our analysis and reporting of findings about in-school data use. This framework focuses attention on who is involved in data use, the sources of data, and the complexity of the data analysis (for example, scope, frequency, depth). Findings about conditions affecting data use builds on conditions identified not only by Ikemoto and Marsh but also by others who have studied this issue.

Who Is Involved in Data Use? Table 11.2, based on evidence from the first principal and teacher surveys, summarizes mean responses and standard deviations (a six-point scale from Strongly Disagree to Strongly Agree) for items related to the incidence of principals' data use and their support for teacher data use. Overall, principals rated the extent of their own data use and encouragement to

TABLE 11.2 EXTENT OF PRINCIPAL DATA USE

Items	N	Mean	Standard Deviation
Principal survey (scale = .866)			
I rely frequently on research evidence in my decision making.	237	4.86	.962
I rely frequently on systematically collected evaluation data about my school in my decision making.	236	4.97	.958
I use data about student achievement to help make most decisions in my school.	237	5.14	.914
I encourage my teachers to make use of data in their decision making.	237	5.32	.802
Teacher survey (scale = .941)			
School's principal(s) encourages you to use data in your work.	4039	4.34	1.427
School's principal(s) encourages data use in planning for individual student needs.	4038	4.40	1.410

Note: Although most of our analyses rely on only the reports of the head principal, we include assistant principals in this table under the assumption that in many cases they have been delegated responsibilities for supporting data use.

teachers as quite high; there was considerable agreement among principals, as the small standard deviations of their responses suggest. As Table 11.2 indicates, teachers' opinions about the encouragement they received from their principals to use data was much more varied (standard deviations were in the 1.4 range for teachers as compared to the .90 range for principals).

In the second teacher survey we asked about the frequency of principals' instructional leadership actions. As reported in Table 6.2 (Chapter Six), there was wide variation in teacher reports of how often their school administrators encouraged data use in planning for individual student needs. In schools where teachers gave high ratings to principals' instructional leadership behaviors (the top 20 percent, twenty-five schools), teachers reported principal encouragement on average four (3.97) times a year, whereas in schools where teachers gave lower ratings to principals' instructional leadership behaviors (the bottom 20 percent, twenty-five schools) they reported principal encouragement on average between two and three (2.37) times a year.

In sum, survey data from principals and teachers indicates that principals use data and provide moderate encouragement for data use by staff, though the extent to which teachers experience principal encouragement and support for data use varies.

We turn to the principal interviews and case study findings for further insight into data use among principals and their staffs. The normative literature on effective data use recommends the engagement of teams or groups of people in the collection, analysis, and interpretation of data. Two-thirds of our principal interviewees provided evidence about collaboration with others in these processes. Collaboration around data happened in grade team meetings, subject-area groupings, professional learning community groups (which often overlapped with grade or subject teams), committees convened to track at-risk students' needs, school leadership or improvement teams, and whole staff events, such as data retreats and faculty meetings. This finding is consistent with evidence reported earlier in this chapter demonstrating significant relationships among the principals' instructional leadership behaviors, teachers' professional community, and district expectations for data use.

Our analysis did not systematically explore the users and uses of data in a specific set of decision-making contexts across all the site visit schools (for example, school improvement goal setting and progress monitoring, and identifying students for special program interventions, such as tutoring or accelerated programs). However, principals and teachers referred to these contexts for decision making and action with sufficient frequency to enable us to highlight some key patterns and variations concerning participation in the uses of data in those contexts.

It would be overstating the role of principals to infer that their participation in these contexts necessarily meant they personally were collecting and interpreting data. In fact, principals typically assumed the role of data use "enablers" rather than direct data users themselves. In these instances, teacher leaders or regular classroom teachers are typically the "street-level" data users. Principals may be giving them access to data, providing tools and time to help collect or interpret the data, accessing external expertise or trying to develop in-school expertise, and holding teachers accountable by requiring them to justify recommendations for school improvement or for student interventions, yet not directly engaging in the processes of data analysis and use themselves.

In a few schools, Ikemoto and Marsh's (2007) inquiry-oriented data use was modeled by the principal, but had not evolved into a more collective activity involving teachers. A principal in one school, for example, did her own investigation of why so many Hispanic students entering the school at grade 3 had not transitioned to English medium classrooms as expected by grade 6, and she presented her findings and plans to her staff. In another school, the principal sought out comparison data on state test results from other sites to help understand why the school's performance had slipped below the state's exemplary rating, and he took action based on his analysis of the finding.

The fact that a principal took the initiative to engage in more complex levels of data analysis, however, did not necessarily mean the school scored as a high-data-use school in the combined data use measure from our principal and teacher surveys. Our qualitative data suggest that more complex patterns of data use—to inform instructional decision making and school improvement—are most likely to arise in schools where this is pursued collectively by the faculty with principal leadership. This finding resonates with our previous discussions of leadership distribution and professional community in Chapters Two through Four.

Expertise considered useful in the prescriptive literature includes proficiency in both data collection and analysis (such as statistical expertise), and/or being knowledgeable in the subject area about which data have been collected (for example, literacy, math problem solving). Among our site visit schools, two-thirds of principals reported that they and their teachers had benefited from expert assistance in the collection and interpretation of data for decisions related to school improvement and instructional programming. Our interview data point to five potential sources of expertise in data use in schools: central office personnel (superintendents, curriculum or assessment specialists), state supported regional education center specialists, principals, key teachers trained to serve as assessment and data experts, and classroom teachers in general.

The sources of expertise varied. This was not just a function of the availability of technical know-how; it was also dependent on the depth of experience within the schools in the use of data to inform school decision making. In lower-data-use settings, there was a tendency to depend on external experts, or to rely on the principal or a key teacher (for example, a counselor or a literacy coach) as the resident data expert. In higher-data-use schools, expertise to guide and support data use was more widely distributed. Principals and teachers reported increasing efforts to develop the capacity of teachers to engage collectively in data analysis for instructional decision making, supported by but not dependent on other experts. This was often the focus of professional learning community initiatives and was assisted by district interventions such as training in the use of curriculum-linked classroom assessments, school-wide data analysis events, coaching of teacher teams (grade or subject teams, professional learning community groups), and the purchase of data software and training in its use.

Sources of Data A significant proportion of the principals reported using several different sources of data—state mandated assessments in almost all cases (26 principals), along with district-sponsored (18), and teacher- or school-developed (15) assessments of student learning. Less commonly, principals talked about the development and systematic use by teachers of diagnostic and formative assessments of student learning aligned with state/district curriculum expectations. Not surprisingly, given federal reporting requirements, principals often mentioned the availability of data about student demographic characteristics, such as ethnic and linguistic background and socio economic status, and other bureaucratically designated indicators of student characteristics, such as mobility rates, attendance, Title I eligibility, special education needs, and English language proficiency. However, both school and district personnel were less likely to report using such background information to help interpret student and school performance data.

Although principals and teachers routinely use data to inform instructional decision making and improvement goals, they draw on a limited range of formally collected data. Our school-based respondents rarely spoke about the collection and use of other kinds of information that might inform their understanding of challenges for student performance (individual or group) and their decisions about how to respond. For example, few principals across the site visit schools mentioned data on teacher performance and needs for professional support, whether gathered formally through teacher appraisal processes, or informally through classroom walk-throughs. Similarly, principals rarely mentioned attempts to systematically gather and use information about parental support for student learning that might contribute to collective understanding and plans for addressing student learning gaps and goals. Similarly, working with information from published research was mentioned by only a handful of teachers and principals in reporting how evidence was used in their schools. Principals in the higher-data-use schools reminded us that the development of teachers' expertise in interpreting student data is of limited use unless teachers also have knowledge of how to respond appropriately to the identified needs and problems.[13] At a few high-data-use schools, principals emphasized the importance of ensuring that teachers had access to appropriate professional knowledge (research) in order to make good decisions about how to respond to findings that emerged from examining student data. This was accomplished through a variety of mechanisms that tended to blend research with other sources of knowledge, such as training by district or external consultants, book study by teachers, and sharing and discussion of results of teaching strategies, including those created by teachers themselves.

Both high- and low-data-use schools have access to abundant externally collected data about student performance. Our findings also suggest that principals and teachers neither have nor use much systematically collected evidence about school or classroom conditions that might need to change in order to improve the status of student learning. In other words, data use and analysis in schools centers more on identifying problems in student learning than on investigating the causes and possible solutions.

Nature and Complexity of Analysis The scope, frequency, and complexity of data use for problem identification varied widely across schools. Principals in most schools, for example, cited state test results as a factor in setting improvement goals. However, the number of schools where principals and teachers were actively using these data to monitor the outcomes of school improvement plans was more limited. Schools differed in the degree to which they identified improvement goals for specific subgroups of students who were not meeting targeted proficiency standards and the ways they linked them to specific tested curriculum expectations. The level and detail of analysis of test results was influenced by the availability of expert assistance from the district or state, suggesting that few schools have the capacity to do this on their own.

In high-data-use settings, districts provided critical support for formative assessment practices of teachers and principals by developing local benchmark assessments that were closely aligned with state and district curriculum expectations. When these were regularly administered by classroom teachers as part of the ongoing assessments of student performance, there were more frequent adjustments in student programming. Local tests provided a basis for individual and collective teacher decision making that had a greater potential for contributing to student performance on state tests than the use of externally developed supplemental assessments whose alignment to state standards was not guaranteed. In sum, district actions simplified the process of linking diagnostic and formative assessments to curriculum standards and increased the likelihood that the data would be used to good effect at the school level.

In schools where most students met minimum state proficiency standards, the use of test data was less prominent in setting school improvement agendas. There were exceptions, of course. In one suburban elementary school where over 95 percent of the students were at or above state proficiency standards, the principal called in a district assessment specialist to help the faculty determine annual goals. They settled on increasing the number of students who would qualify for the highest rating on the state tests (having missed only two or three questions on a test). In most of the higher-performing districts, a test-driven response was not apparent.

Most schools used diagnostic assessment instruments to identify struggling students and to develop plans for remediation, but in higher-data-use schools, personnel were more likely to use formative assessments throughout the year and to regularly adjust additional help for struggling students. The incorporation of student performance data into teachers' ongoing instructional decision making was more evident in settings where district and school leaders had linked data use to specific interventions.

Principals, district administrators, and some teachers described the potential for more complex analysis of student performance in varied student groupings, examining correlations between student characteristics and programming and performance, and studying longitudinal records of student performance for individuals or groups. However, they offered few examples of the actual exploitation of this analytical potential for understanding or responding to student needs, perhaps because their adoption was relatively recent. In higher-data-use schools, teachers were gathering and analyzing additional data to better understand the contributing factors to identify problems, and to monitor the effects of interventions implemented in order to ameliorate those problems. In one elementary school, for example, the principal and teachers identified improvement in children's expository writing as a school goal. The principal mobilized teachers to develop mid-year writing prompts to supplement beginning- and end-of-year assessments developed by the district. She called on district consultants to provide in-service training for teachers, not only on the use and interpretation of assessments based on the district's standards-based writing rubric, but also on teaching methods associated with the goals for improvement in writing. Teacher groups were asked to study student progress and the effects of teacher interventions to improve student writing, including interviewing students about their reactions to teaching strategies. The enabling role of both the principal and the district are apparent in this example.

Patterns of data use in our high-data-use schools, however, were consistent with findings from other case studies. Both our cases and previous studies point to these factors:

- The salience of district and principal leadership in data use
- The significance of using varied data sources for multiple improvement purposes
- A focus on formative assessments of student learning throughout the school year for student programming and tracking progress
- Teacher and principal access to tools for data use that are aligned with expectations for curriculum and learning
- The collective nature of data use activity
- The facilitation of data use processes by local educators who have acquired expertise

What Influences Data Use in Schools? Evidence about influences on data use in schools was provided in principal surveys, principal interviews, and our school and district case study interviews in high-data-use sites. Interview results offer a perspective on the extent to which principals were aware of and attended to conditions that foster data use in schools, and what they believed districts were doing to foster such use, as reported in our discussion of district data use and support.

Table 11.3 profiles site visit principal interview results about attention to data use conditions in schools. The left column lists conditions that influence school data use identified by Ikemoto and Marsh (2007). The number of principals who mentioned each condition is indicated in column two. Column three reports the number of principals who also described actions they had taken concerning that condition.

These results suggest that many of the principals in the typical school sample used for this analysis communicated an awareness of key conditions identified by Ikemoto and Marsh (2007) as influencing the use of data by school personnel, particularly in regard to accessibility and timeliness of data, school staff capacity for data use, and external (district, state) support for data use. Data quality, time to interpret and act on data, and the availability of tools to facilitate data collection and interpretation were also mentioned, albeit less frequently.

Awareness, however, does not necessarily translate into action. The number of principals who talked about actions that they were taking to influence one or more of the conditions in Table 11.3 was much smaller and more unevenly distributed across the conditions. This pattern leads us to surmise that some principals felt more skilled to act on organizational and technical conditions that affect the potential for productive data use for decision making by school staff. The pervasive contextual influence of district and state priorities and expectations is evident

TABLE 11.3 PRINCIPALS' ATTENTION TO CONDITIONS AFFECTING DATA USE

Conditions Affecting Data Use	Mentioned	Mentioned/Actions Described
1. Accessibility and timeliness of data	16	–
2. Perceived quality of data	8	–
3. Staff capacity and support for considering data	15	5
4. Time available to interpret and act on the evidence	6	4
5. Partnerships with external organizations in analyzing and interpreting data	–	–
6. Tools for both data collection and interpretation	4	2
7. Organizational culture support for data use	14	3
8. District and state policy support for data use	17	6

in the frequent comments about district organizational norms and support for data use, as well as policies to that effect.

Data Use and Student Achievement

Although data use may improve student achievement under some conditions, the path linking data use to such achievement is indirect. Figure 11.1 (earlier in this chapter) clearly supports the claim that district targets and data use influence the shared instructional leadership work of principals and teachers. The impact of district leaders flows through their influence on what principals and teachers do.

We were struck by the finding summarized in the discussion of Figure 11.1, which noted that district efforts to support data-driven decision making had a stronger impact on student achievement in elementary schools, and district-led initiatives significantly reduced the effects of the poverty levels in the school. We carried out additional analyses that examined the emphasis that the principal placed on data use (see Table 11.2) as well as district pressure and support. Results confirm that data use initiatives from the district have a greater impact on data use in elementary as compared with secondary schools.

This analysis also suggests that principals' efforts to promote data use are less important than district policies and initiatives.[14] Modest principal influence on data use in schools may be a function of the lack of expertise in data use reported by principals. Local expertise for data use was typically concentrated at the district level.

Conclusions

This analysis of findings was prompted by the encouragement embedded in much current educational policy for district and school leaders, along with teachers, to become more data-informed in their decision making.[15] Underlying this encouragement is the assumption that greater attention to formal student test results, along with systematically collected evidence about related organizational conditions, will lead to more effective school and classroom practices along with improved student learning.[16] (Although this is a dominant feature of much current policy, most notably the No Child Left Behind Act of 2001, there is not actually much empirical research to justify this foundational assumption, and the evidence that does exist reports mixed results).[17] Nor do we know much about what school and district leaders are doing in the name of evidence-informed decision making or the conditions that either foster or inhibit the use of systematically collected data in their decision making.[18] The purpose of this chapter was to better understand the relationship between data use practices at the district and school levels and data use practices of principals and teachers in typical, as compared with high-data-use, schools. We also aimed to better understand the organizational conditions influencing data use in schools and to investigate whether data use had any discernable relationship to students' academic performance. These concluding comments pick up selected themes that we believe warrant the attention of education policy makers, practitioners, and researchers alike.

First, we were impressed by the powerful role of district leaders in shaping data use in schools. They did this by setting the tone, directions and expectations for data use, modeling data use, and addressing some of the key technical and organizational conditions that challenge data use by principals and teachers. Indeed, many organizational conditions affecting school data use identified in prior research—such as accessibility, timeliness, quality of data, plus time and human resource capacity to make good use of data[19]—are more susceptible to influence at the district level than at the school level because of their technical complexity, resource requirements, and policy constraints. In short, the potential for effective data collection to inform school-level decisions related to improvement in student learning is highly dependent on leadership and support at the district level.

Second, we began this analysis in this chapter with an overly narrow focus on data use by principals. But we quickly realized that the focus needs to be on leadership for data use in schools, with direction largely coming from the district office. In the high-data-use schools there was collective activity involving principals working with their teachers. Principals in these schools were data savvy but did not always present themselves as experts. They took strategic action to develop or access expert assistance as needed. In sum, principals played a leadership role in establishing the purposes and expectations for data use, structured opportunities (collegial groups and time), training and assistance, access to expertise, and follow-up actions, but were less often involved in setting clear expectations and providing direct support. Where districts and principals did not make data use a priority, mobilize expertise, or create working conditions to facilitate data use in instructional decision-making contexts, teachers were not doing it on their own. As we have become more sensitive to the emphasis that states, districts, and schools are placing on a relatively narrow band of systematically collected data for decision making, we have a growing concern that a data-driven conception of how to improve schools is in danger of underestimating the improvement challenges that schools actually face. The term "decision making" implies that the improvement challenge for schools is to choose among a set of known solutions for their readily understood improvement problems. Using the term "problem solving" rather than "decision making" invokes a more accurate picture of the improvement challenge faced by most educational leaders and their teacher colleagues. And the systematically collected data that our results suggest are available to, and used by, most principals and their staffs play a potentially important yet limited role in such problem solving. Mostly, these data describe the current status of students' learning and reveal something about students' backgrounds. But problem solving (and school improvement) is about closing the gap between the current status and a more ideal or preferred status.[20] Where do school staffs look to better understand the underlying causes of current states? Where will they find the knowledge they need about how to close the gap? In particular, what types of systematically collected evidence, if it were available, would significantly improve the quality of school staff's improvement efforts?

Finally, we worry that a laser-like focus on systematically collected data might increase the power of "single loop learning" (that is, refining current understandings and practices without changing assumptions) but significantly discourage "double loop learning" (challenging the assumptions on which current understandings and practices are based).[21]

This concern is also reflected in the distinction between information-intensive organizations and knowledge-intensive (or expertise-intensive) firms or organizations (KIFs). The former process large amounts of evidence, much of which often does not actually get used for decision making, whereas the latter typically process very little such information, relying instead on high levels of expertise about the work that needs to be done.[22] Professional organizations are typically KIFs.

Evidence in this study might be interpreted to suggest that many schools are used to behaving as KIFs (whether or not they genuinely have the levels of expertise they need), and this raises an intriguing question for both research and policy: What is the relative benefit to the quality of schooling of spending resources on providing schools with more information as compared with spending the same resources on building the instructional and related expertise of those in schools? It is possible to do both, and that seems to be the path followed in most current reform initiatives. But that means dividing the available resources between the two options, thereby reducing the resources available for either one. We need more and better evidence than is currently available about the consequences of advocating greater use of data for decision making in schools before the tradeoffs between these two options for improvement can be discerned.

Implications for Policy and Practice

At least four implications for policy and practice emerge from the evidence discussed in this chapter:

1. Districts should ensure that professional development opportunities for principals are linked to their data use policies. Additional development to create

more expertise among principals is necessary for them to support teachers in using data to improve student learning.

2. Districts appear to be most effective when they supplement state tests with locally designed assessments that are linked to state standards and tests and are used to provide more frequent and more timely feedback.

3. High-data-use schools and districts approach data use as a collaborative activity. They move beyond using data to identify problems and toward using data to develop strategic interventions.

4. Administrative attention should be turned toward developing models to improve data use in secondary schools.

Reflections

1. What differences between elementary and secondary schools might account for the apparent difference in both the level of data use and its impact on students?

2. What might be done to support data use in middle and high schools?

3. How active a role should principals take in coordinating district, outside expert, and teacher leader work around data use?

4. How important is data use, as a priority, given the workload of a typical school administrator? Why?

CHAPTER TWELVE

THE "DISTRICT DIFFERENCE"

A New Perspective on the Local Challenges for Improvement

Stephen E. Anderson and Karen Seashore Louis

Claims Supported by Evidence in This Chapter

District policies and practices around instruction are sufficiently powerful that teachers may feel them, indirectly, as stronger and more directed leadership behaviors by principals. Higher-performing districts tend to be led by district staff who take these actions:

- Communicate a strong belief in the capacity of teachers and principals to improve the quality of teaching and learning, and in the district's capacity to develop the organizational conditions needed for that to happen (high collective efficacy)
- Build consensus about core expectations for professional practice (curriculum, teaching, leadership)
- Differentiate support to schools in relation to evidence of compliance and skill in implementing the expectations, with flexibility for school-based innovation
- Set clear expectations for school leadership practices, and establish leadership-development systems to select, train, and assist principals and teacher leaders consistent with district expectations

- Provide organized opportunities for teachers and principals to engage in school-to-school communication, focusing on the challenges of improving student learning and program implementation
- Develop and model strategies and norms for local inquiry into challenges related to student learning and program implementation
- Coordinate district support for school improvement across organizational units (for example, supervision, curriculum and instruction, staff development, human resources) in relation to district priorities, expectations for professional practice, and a shared understanding of the goals and needs of specific schools

In Chapter Nine we examined district leader actions and district policy conditions that affect principals' collective and individual efficacy to influence the quality of teaching and learning in schools. Our measure of collective efficacy assessed principals' confidence in the overall capacity for improvement of school district personnel, whereas the measure of individual capacity zeroed in more concretely on principals' confidence in their personal capacity to influence the quality of teaching and learning in their schools. Interestingly, we found that district actions and characteristics influenced principals' sense of collective efficacy more strongly than their personal sense of efficacy. We also found that principals' collective efficacy—as distinguished from individual efficacy—had a greater influence on student achievement. It appears that principals attribute student learning less to their individual leadership than to the combined efforts of their school and district colleagues.

We also observed that although a wide variety of district-level features (policies, leader actions) can be shown statistically to affect both principal efficacy and their instructional leadership behaviors (as perceived by teachers), these features are highly correlated and interact in a synergistic way rather than as independent sources of influence. District professional development, for example, has a greater influence on school leaders when it is focused on explicit, data-informed, system-wide targets for improvement. Well-intentioned district support for leadership development and practice may be for naught without good alignment to clear directions for improvement.

In Chapters Ten and Eleven we explored how some district strategies, such as setting targets and using data, affect principal leadership more directly and powerfully than others, such as district provisions for principals' instructional leadership development. The indirect paths of district influence on principals' leadership, however, remain an important strategic consideration for district leaders. As reported in Chapter Three, for example, we found that the effects of principals' instructional leadership behaviors on teachers' instructional practice (and on student achievement) were strongly connected to the quality of shared leadership and professional community in the school. District leaders striving to improve the effectiveness of principals' instructional leadership should take action to strengthen teachers' professional community, in conjunction with direct efforts to develop principal competence and confidence.

Finally, this chapter will expand on the findings of the previous three by examining principals' explanations of how district-level actions affect their capacity to enact the challenging work of instructional leadership. Using both interview and survey data, we will explore how district actions and policies interact to either increase or interfere with the exercise of leadership within the school. In doing so, we will direct attention to dimensions of leadership support and practice that make a difference, as well as to key relationships and interactions among those factors, providing concrete illustrations to flesh out these claims. This chapter extends our prior analyses of school district pressure and support and its consequences for school leadership, teaching, and learning. We assumed at the outset that (1) successful districts actively focus on and support efforts to improve teaching and learning, and (2) districts are not all alike in the ways in which they embody this focus in policies and actions. Our analysis supports both assumptions. Our findings also suggest that differences between districts regarding efforts to improve teaching and learning cannot be determined merely by asking administrators and specialists to articulate their priorities. Although all district leaders believe that they focus on instruction, we found substantial variation among districts in the skill and understanding with which they address this focus.

To describe and analyze interdistrict differences, it was necessary to examine actual practices related to curriculum and instruction, and the interaction of those practices with other strands of district-level action and influence. Our analysis in this chapter is based on two sets of data:

- Principal and teacher survey data measuring the district's focus on instruction and its relationship to principals' instructional leadership
- Interview findings about key focuses of district support for improvement identified by district leaders and principals (for example, student performance, curriculum implementation, principal leadership, and teacher quality)

Prior Evidence

Throughout the twentieth century, North American school districts were more concerned with school finances, administration, and supervision of compliance with district and government policies than with leadership and technical support for curriculum, teaching, and learning. The pedagogical leadership and support functions of school districts emerged largely in response to state and national government interventions aimed at improving the quality of education from the 1960s onward. That focus of school district activity has taken on increasing significance in the context of accountability policies, which hold schools and school districts publically accountable for student and school performance in accordance with externally prescribed standards. There has been an ongoing debate nationally and internationally, however, as to whether school district–level policies and actions actually make much difference in the quality of teaching and learning.

One strand of research suggests that although school districts may serve a useful intermediary function in governance and management of public education systems, they exert little influence on the nature and quality of teaching and learning.[1] Studies of this sort typically involve the analysis of large-scale surveys and databases that encompass districts in a wide variety of contexts (for example, urban and rural; low- and high-income communities; small and large numbers of students and schools; low and high diversity in student SES or ethnolinguistic characteristics). A careful quantitative analysis of school district effects on student learning across England, for example, found that after controlling for differences in school populations and contexts, district influences on student achievement accounted for only about 1 percent of the variability in outcomes between districts.[2] Generally, when researchers sample "typical" districts (that is, not specifically chosen on the basis of prior evidence of effectiveness), they come up with similarly discouraging results.[3]

There is, however, a second strand of research on school district effectiveness in North America that has persistently highlighted the presence of particular districts whose students achieve beyond expectations for districts serving similar types of students in similar contexts. This research dates at least from mid-1980s investigations of instructionally effective school districts in California[4] and Tennessee.[5] Since the mid-1990s there have been several widely disseminated single and multisite case studies of effective and improving school districts.[6] An obvious implication is that if some districts are able to make a significant positive impact on student learning, then others should be able to as well.

This recent research on the district role in school-improvement activity has focused on the identification of specific district-level policies, actions, and conditions related to improvement in teachers' and students' performance. Findings from this research converge on a common set of policies, actions, and conditions associated with district-wide improvement and effectiveness, as described in detail in Chapters Eight and Nine. The findings are consistent with investigations that have focused more specifically on the actions of superintendents and other senior administrators.[7] Despite the consistency in findings, reviewers caution against making causal claims about district policies and strategies based on outlier studies of small numbers of higher-performing districts without the methodological controls needed to confidently assert what has enabled those districts to achieve success in comparison to others.[8] Furthermore, although providing illuminating accounts of what districts are doing and evidence of effects on student learning, most of these studies fall short of actually demonstrating how district-level actions actually influence the work of principals and teachers that affects student learning. In this and preceding chapters, we address these gaps in our understanding of the district influences on school leadership and teachers' work that contribute to the quality of teaching and learning.

A number of studies in the 1970s and 1980s documented differences in district-level orientations and approaches to educational change. Berman and McLaughlin (1977) distinguished districts in terms of bureaucratic, opportunistic, or problem-solving motivations of district authorities. Not surprisingly, they found that teachers and principals implemented and developed new programs and practices more effectively in districts that approached change with a problem-solving orientation. Rosenholtz (1989) differentiated between "stuck" and "moving" districts in her investigation of teachers' workplace conditions and change. More effective schools were located in districts that give a higher priority to improving teaching and learning.

Louis (1989), drawing from a survey and case-study investigation of initiatives in urban secondary schools, identified four district-level approaches to school improvement: innovation implementation (uniform processes and outcomes); evolutionary planning (uniform processes, variable outcomes); goal-based accountability (variable processes, uniform outcomes); and professional investment (variable processes and outcomes). Louis also emphasized the importance of relationships between schools and districts, as evident in levels of bureaucratic control (rules and regulations) and organizational coupling (for example, shared goals, community, joint planning and coordination). The issue of top-down versus bottom-up approaches to improvement has a long history. Massell and Goertz (2002) described alternative—and reportedly successful—top-down and bottom-up district strategies for change and improvement, with the implication that no best way can be generalized to all settings. Other research has pointed to the possibility that top-down and bottom-up approaches need not be viewed as alternatives, but can be combined.[9] We return to this topic in our discussion of findings concerning differentiation of district support for improvement within a context of centralized expectations for performance.

In a recent commentary on the district role in system-wide improvement, Fullan (2010) argues that the policies and strategies that districts employ to effect district-wide improvement are increasingly alike on the surface. This makes it difficult to distinguish more and less effective districts simply by referring to generic strategies like setting clear goals for improvement, making decisions based on data, embedding professional development in the job, promoting instructional leadership, and building professional community. Differences in district success depend less on such strategies and policies than they do on the skill and continuity of their *enactment*—and on organizational learning that leads to local expertise and sustainability of effective practices.

To date, interest in the district role has focused on overall differences in district effectiveness and on system-wide policies and strategies intended to improve and sustain the quality of teaching and learning. There has been little inquiry and discussion about whether and how district-level actors differentiate support based on individual school needs within their jurisdictions.[10] Historically, school districts have supported schools differentially according to differences in school types (for example, elementary, middle, and high schools) and compliance requirements specified by legislated categorical differences in students and programs (such as Title I and English Language Learners [ELL]). The latter categories of support are rationalized in terms of the perceived challenges that schools face in serving certain categories of students. Contemporary accountability policies have created the added expectation that districts will differentiate support to schools on the basis of achievement results from state testing programs and other accountability measures, with particular attention to be given to schools where large numbers of students are not meeting standards of proficiency. Exactly how that expectation plays out in school districts has not been systematically studied. On the one hand, districts may simply be complying with specified interventions to schools that fail to meet Adequate Yearly Progress targets. On the other hand, school district leaders may be developing and implementing their own strategic responses to various school needs for improvement, in conjunction with NCLB and state-mandated interventions. The qualitative findings from our site visits to eighteen districts provide some new insights into differentiated support for improvement across districts within our sample.

New Evidence

The findings and analysis in this chapter address three questions pertaining to district central office leadership and support for improvements in teaching and learning.

1. How do principals assess the emphasis given to improving teaching and learning by their district administrators?
2. Does the district's emphasis on teaching and learning affect the principal's instructional leadership behavior?

3. How do district leaders conceptualize and address differences in school performance and progress in implementing local improvement efforts?

We used data from the principal and teacher surveys to address questions one and two. A factor analysis of all the district-related items from the second principal survey yielded a cluster of six items that measured principals' perceptions of the district's focus on and support for improvements in teaching and learning (for example, communicate standards for high-priority areas of instruction, actively monitor the quality of instruction). We analyzed the responses to these six items descriptively, and we developed a "district focus on instruction" scale that combined them for purposes of this analysis. The items and scale do not encompass the full spectrum of district improvement activity,[11] some elements of which have been separately analyzed in other chapters (such as district professional development, district data use and target setting). However, the "district focus on instruction" items and scale work well as a measure of variation in district emphasis and support for improvement in teaching and learning as experienced by principals. In order to examine how district policies and practices for instructional improvement (as measured by the focus on instruction scale) are reflected at the building level, we used teacher assessments of their principals' instructional leadership from the second survey. The "principal instructional actions scale" (see details in Chapters Three and Six), assessed the frequency of principal instructional leadership behaviors on a five-point scale ranging from never to ten or more times.[12] These included such actions as: *discussed instructional issues with you, observed your classroom instruction*, and *provided or located resources to help staff improve their teaching.*

We examined qualitative evidence from our interviews with district office leaders and principals across the site visit districts to address the third question. Interviews in all three rounds of site visits elicited information about district improvement priorities and strategies. In an open-ended way, we explored which school factors accounting for a school's success attracted the attention of district office leaders, and what were they doing about it. This analysis allowed us to identify differences among districts in how their leaders defined and responded to needs for improvement; the analysis also revealed how individual districts provided support to different schools.

We summarize our results in subsequent sections of this chapter.

Principals' Assessments of District Instructional Foci

Six questions in the second principal survey tapped principals' assessments of the priority given by their district administrators to teaching and learning. The figures that follow show that principals generally believed that their districts were clearly focusing on this area. However, these responses also suggest some differences. For example, principals give highest ratings to their district's ability to clearly communicate standards for instructional improvement: *Clearly communicate expected standards for high-priority areas of instruction* had a mean of 4.9 on a six-point scale. Also highly rated was *Have a detailed plan for improving instruction across the district* (mean = 4.8).

Principals were slightly less generous in their general assessment of the degree to which their districts *Are active and effective in supporting excellent instruction* (mean of 4.67). When they rate specific actions, however, they are even more discriminating.

FIGURE 12.1 PRINCIPAL PERCEPTIONS OF DISTRICT ACTIONS RELATED TO IMPROVED TEACHING AND LEARNING

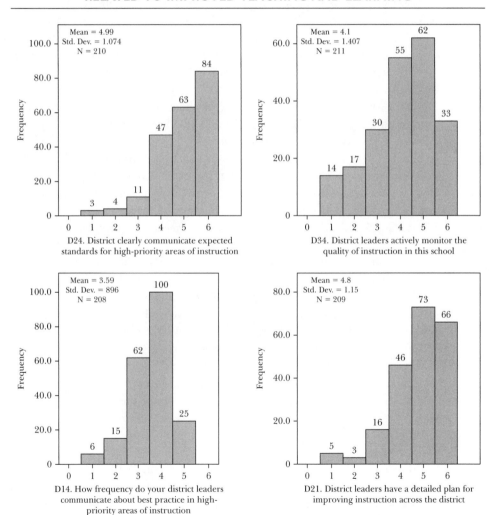

FIGURE 12.1 (*continued*)

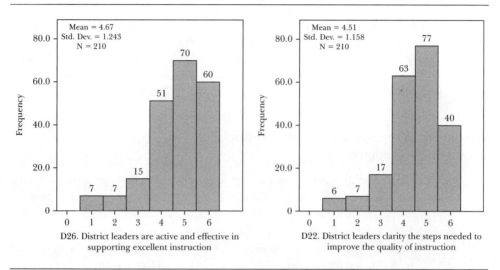

D26. District leaders are active and effective in supporting excellent instruction

D22. District leaders clarity the steps needed to improve the quality of instruction

The district's ability to *Clarify the steps needed to improve the quality of instruction* has a mean of 4.5, whereas the question of how frequently they *Communicate about best practice in high-priority areas of instruction* has a mean of 3.6, which falls between the categories of *occasionally* and *often* on the five-point survey rating scale. These findings suggest that, although there is a high degree of convergence across districts in terms of the priority accorded by district leaders to improving instruction as a focus for improving student learning, there remains considerable variability in the concrete actions taken to support this priority.

Responses to the six questions did not differ significantly by school level (elementary, middle, high school), school size, or characteristics of the student population (percent nonwhite and percent eligible for free and reduced-price lunch).[13] In addition, there was no significant difference between the responses of principals and assistant principals.

In sum, although principals believed that their districts prioritized improved instruction, they differed in response to particular questions about whether principals receive clear guidelines and support for making changes at the school level. These differences suggest that in some districts there may be a gap between the "vision" and the strategic plan for improved instruction, on the one hand, and on the other, the way in which specific support for improved instruction is delivered at the school level. As we saw in the case of professional development for principals in Chapter Nine, the gap between a set of high standards and tangible support for those standards may be critical in determining how well principals can respond within their school settings.

We are mindful, however, that it may be easier to generate data and consensus about the presence of a problem (for example, 30 percent of grade 6 students are not performing well in expository writing) and a general strategy for solving that problem (further develop teachers' repertoire of instructional methods to improve those students' writing competencies) than it is to be explicit about what changes in instructional practices are most likely to actually yield the desired improvements in those students' learning.

District Focus on Instruction and Principals' Instructional Leadership

We assume that improving building-level leadership is one of the most promising approaches districts can take to fostering change. Current research suggests that not only must districts have a coherent leadership development program grounded in data and aligned with district improvement targets (as we have suggested in our investigation of professional development in Chapter Nine and of data use in Chapter Eleven), but they must also consistently emphasize the improvement of instruction as a primary goal and means for improving student performance in the district.

This finding is quite remarkable. It suggests that district policies and practices focused on instruction are sufficiently powerful that they can be *observed* by teachers as an animating force behind strong, focused leadership by principals. Although we do not, in this section, look for a relationship between district practices and student learning, we have already established that instructional leadership by principals has an impact on teachers' classroom practices (especially combined with a strong professional community of teachers). This impact in turn affects student learning. This is perhaps our most powerful finding regarding the indirect connection between the choices and priorities set by districts and the classroom experience of students. In the research literature on district roles in school improvement, this finding stands out as one of the few empirical demonstrations of the influence of district-level practices on the quality of instructional leadership. Most research makes this claim by inference, not by measured effects.

Additional analysis demonstrated that both school characteristics (size and level) and student characteristics (percentage of minority and percentage qualifying for free and reduced price lunch) had a substantial effect on principals' instructional leadership behaviors.

How District Leaders Address Differences in School Performance and Implement Local Improvement Efforts

This chapter and some preceding chapters examine the influence of particular strands of district direction and strategies for improvement on school leadership, teaching, and learning, such as target setting, data use, professional development, and communicating and taking actions that emphasize a focus on improvement in instruction. Results described here offer a different perspective on district improvement activity. We asked what central office leaders identify as key levers for improvement among schools in their districts, and whether those key levers varied across districts that are quite different in their political, geographic, and demographic contexts.

Our results are organized around those focuses for district-led school improvement activity that are most commonly mentioned by district administrators and staff:

- Student performance on standards and indicators
- District support and pressure for improvements in curriculum and instruction
- School progress in implementing district expectations (curriculum, instruction)
- Principals' leadership expertise for school improvement
- School-based factors that explain differences in student performance and program implementation (for example, instructional expertise, curriculum implementation, learning gaps, staffing, leadership, material resources)

For this analysis we examined central office interview data from site visit districts with particular attention to differences between districts that were higher and lower performing in terms their student achievement test scores. Where possible, we suggest local factors that were contributing to those differences, though we caution against overgeneralizing findings from this relatively small sample of districts.

Student Performance on Standards and Indicators Not surprisingly, district administrators were highly sensitive to how well their schools were performing against state proficiency standards and Adequate Yearly Progress (AYP) targets. In the higher-performing districts, central office staff corroborated the survey findings about the importance of developing local instructional foci and learning standards. Interviews suggest that district leaders in the higher-performing districts uniformly described the district targets as aligned with, but exceeding, those of the state. Sometimes, as in both an urban and a large suburban district, this was articulated in terms of broad goals, such as college readiness for all. More commonly, respondents claimed that district expectations for student learning were more rigorous than (yet compatible with) those mandated by the state. This was particularly evident in settings where district leaders supported the development of district-level curriculum content and performance expectations across all areas of curriculum (not only in externally tested subjects). In the two districts in our study, for example, district personnel also told stories of multiyear, district-wide curriculum development projects resulting in production of curriculum frameworks and materials that satisfied both state and local goals for student learning.

We encountered similar findings in some small rural districts, notwithstanding the fact that they had fewer central office staff. One rural district with only two full-time professional employees volunteered to participate in the pilot phase of the state's decentralized curriculum and accountability system. Classroom teachers, led by the curriculum director, developed a district curriculum consistent with state curriculum expectations. District and school personnel in these small but active settings talked enthusiastically about implementing their curriculum, and they spoke positively about achievement results for their students as evidence of its quality. In contrast, in other districts, local educators talked mainly about implementing both their state-mandated curriculum and externally developed programs to satisfy state-level expectations. The benchmark for success was performance on state-mandated tests, and they communicated little sense of striving for more ambitious goals for student learning.

In sum, where district administrators believed that their local standards were aligned with and exceeded external standards and accountability measures, and where results on state tests were above average, administrators tended to emphasize their own benchmarks as a focus for school improvement efforts. District personnel in settings where students were performing less well on state tests were more likely to see themselves as driven by external standards and assessments and to view the district as less able to determine local priorities and needs, although this was not always the case, as we shall see in the next chapter. District administrators in higher-performing districts were also more likely to be positive about the validity of state accountability indicators than those in districts that were performing less well.

Most of the schools in our case study sample were not under sanctions for failing to meet state and federal guidelines for improvements in student achievement. There was, however, variability in the degree to which districts felt insulated against potential sanctions.[14] In higher-performing settings, district leaders were more likely to pursue continuous improvement goals for students and schools already meeting the minimum standards, in addition to specifying targets for students and schools struggling to meet standards. In several of the higher-performing districts in our sample (including urban, suburban and rural districts), district leaders and school personnel described recent and ongoing district-wide efforts to support teacher implementation of differentiated instruction. In one rural Midwestern district, for example, the superintendent championed a multiyear initiative focused on differentiated instruction. Teams of teachers were sent each summer to external professional development programs and were then were expected to lead school-based in-service training activities the following year. The explicit rationale provided by this and other districts was to help teachers ensure that the needs of "high-ability learners" were not being ignored in the face of state emphasis on closing the achievement gap between low- and high-achieving students. In these settings, local goals and related initiatives were often framed in terms of satisfying local community expectations—an argument that is most frequently heard in districts where there are few or no schools performing below state standards.

District Support and Pressure In higher-performing districts, leaders did not expect improvement in lower-performing schools to occur merely by means of inputs required under federal and state policies (for example, school choice, tutoring, prescribed needs assessments and school-improvement planning, curriculum audits, advice from external consultants). They adopted additional, district-level intervention strategies. In one higher-performing Midwestern urban district, for example, two schools became a focus for district intervention during the final year of our study because they failed to meet AYP targets (the first two schools to be designated in that status). In addition to taking advantage of additional funding from the state, and attending mandatory workshops offered by the state for all schools identified as not meeting AYP, district leaders (curriculum superintendent, curriculum directors, school improvement director) conducted their own investigations of the problems in student performance and followed up with district support tailored to each school's needs.

In contrast, a middle school in a smaller, high-poverty district in one of our Southern states also failed to meet AYP targets (the district had a history of adequate but not high performance on state proficiency tests across its schools). In compliance with state requirements, an external school improvement consultant was brought in. The school staff had little positive to say about that consultant's input, and district leaders did not report any initiatives to deal with the situation other than general support and their reliance on the school personnel to find a solution. Similar criticisms about the effectiveness of state interventions for low-performing schools were voiced in a large, high-poverty, low-performing urban school district—where (again) the district developed no plan for systematic intervention to ameliorate the problem.

In higher-performing settings, district leaders often proactively monitored trends in schools' academic performance and in their community contexts (such as demographic trends). Leaders did this in order to identify schools *potentially* at risk of not meeting AYP targets in future years, in order to target those schools and students for intervention. In one large, higher-performing suburban district (with 90 percent or more of students in most schools achieving at or above state proficiency standards), district leaders identified demographic changes occurring in several elementary schools in which there was an increasing population of low-income families from the adjacent city. District leaders became concerned that school achievement results might decline unless something was done to support teachers and principals to respond effectively to the needs of the new students, so they reallocated resources to them. In this and other higher-performing districts, personnel talked about the financial and human resource challenges they faced in providing effective support for increasing numbers of schools that required special interventions under the Adequate Yearly Progress provisions of the No Child Left Behind Act.

Administrators in all districts identified the need for (and use of) diagnostic and formative assessments of student progress throughout the school year to supplement state test data. Leaders in higher-performing districts guided the development of local assessment instruments that were deliberately aligned with state and local curriculum standards. Teachers were expected to administer them at designated intervals and to use the results for instructional planning (see examples in Chapter Nine). In other settings, school personnel relied mainly on assessment tools provided or endorsed by their state education agencies, perhaps supplemented by assessments developed by classroom teachers in their own schools.

All districts used internal and external expertise to help teachers implement district expectations for curriculum and instruction. For obvious reasons, larger districts made greater use of their own curriculum and instruction staff than small districts did. Smaller districts relied more on state-supported regional education centers and local universities for in-service training and assistance and for brokering contacts with other external consultants. Having district-level expectations for curriculum and instruction makes it easier for district leaders to monitor and respond to school-level implementation. In fact, principals in many districts pay more attention to meeting local standards than to meeting state standards, in part because of the systems described earlier.

Reliance on outside assistance for implementation can be challenging because of the costs, the potential problems of fit with local conditions, and the absence of easily available follow-up assistance to address school-specific needs. Having a central office curriculum and instruction unit did not, however, guarantee the coherence and effectiveness of district support for implementation of district-wide programs. Our evidence indicates that teachers from smaller districts reported more positive assessments of district support than did teachers from medium- or larger-sized districts. This suggests that size and district resources cannot account for the value-added effect of support for improved instruction. It is possible that larger districts pay less attention to the quality and utility of support for teachers because they assume that they have greater quality control over employees, whereas smaller districts are more attentive to the quality and utility of their "purchases."

Another explanation may lie in the relatively easier and more consistent communication that occurs naturally in smaller districts. Higher-performing districts made communication and coordination among different central office units in their interaction with teachers and principals a priority. In larger districts, the interdependent response to district-wide and school-specific needs occurred partly through interdepartmental coordinating structures and a team approach to assessing and responding to school-specific needs for help with implementation, depending on the problem. For example, in one of the large (over twenty-five thousand students) suburban districts in our sample, when school-specific concerns about student performance were raised by principals, district office supervisors, or professional staff, the district curriculum director organized a "curriculum support visit" to investigate the concern, in collaboration with the principal and teachers. The district team included assistant superintendents, appropriate curriculum division staff, and staff from the district assessment and evaluation unit.

In addition, some district leaders in both smaller and larger schools actively facilitated networked communication, sharing, and joint problem solving among schools. This occurred through district-organized opportunities for principals to speak to one another in principals' meetings, leadership programs, or peer-coaching arrangements. Larger districts sometimes created systems of teacher leaders linked through district curriculum and instruction specialists. Networking between schools helps district leaders to identify differences in school needs and to enable school personnel to find solutions among themselves, rather than relying solely on the district for help.

Monitoring School Progress in Implementing District Expectations Districts varied in the range and specificity of locally mandated expectations for professional practice—in particular, for curriculum and instruction. We are hesitant to claim that district leaders in higher-performing districts uniquely promoted more standardized, district-wide curriculum content and materials, because the trend everywhere is to increase standardization. Compared to others, however, district leaders in higher-performing districts appeared to have invested in district-wide curriculum development over a longer period of time, using well-institutionalized district curriculum systems.

As that development unfolded, there was an increase in efforts to align and coordinate other strands of district support, such as teacher development, school leadership development, school-improvement planning, and performance monitoring. Sustained development of district support systems was more likely where district leadership was stable. Progressive alignment, refinement, and synergy among dimensions of district support may be more responsible for higher performance than is curriculum standardization, per se.

In addition to focusing on curriculum and sustained professional development, leaders in higher-performing districts were more likely than others to promote and support implementation of particular instructional strategies regarded as effective. Expectations for uniformity in instructional practices included both general or subject-specific teaching methods defined by district staff as "best practices" (for example, cooperative learning, guided reading, technology use, methods of differentiating instruction) and more prescriptive programs with uniform teaching and learning activities and materials. In addition to providing or recommending teaching methods, leaders in higher-performing districts provided direction and support for the use of common methods of assessing and reporting student learning.

In one of our higher-performing districts, for example, all new elementary school teachers were required to participate in district-developed year-long courses on effective strategies for teaching beginning and more advanced readers. In another higher-performing suburban district, sample lesson plans replete with suggested teaching strategies, learning activities, and curriculum resources were built into the district's online curriculum guide for teachers. Although teachers were not formally required to implement these lessons, they had to adhere to a lesson-design format that required them to target district curriculum objectives, integrate computer-based learning activities into every lesson, and engage students in small group and independent learning activities. Teachers reported that the district guidelines exerted a strong influence on their practices. However, this level of specificity about district-supported effective instructional practices was rare across the districts.

In those districts where initiatives to create more systematic pedagogic expectations prevailed, many teachers appeared to appreciate the greater clarity of expectations and access to instructional tools (for example, course scope or sequence, lesson plans, materials, assessments) that often accompany district-wide curriculum development and support for implementation. Their receptivity to standard forms of instructional practice, however, was conditional on the quality of district support for implementation (staff development, materials, supervision), perceived fit with state or district curriculum requirements, evidence of student impact, and opportunities for teacher discretion within the boundaries established by the district.

Leaders in higher-performing settings not only worked to establish and communicate clear expectations for curriculum and instruction but also monitored the implementation of district expectations through supervision systems and school-improvement plans. In the most elaborate support systems, district leaders initially ensured common training and resources across relevant sectors of the district. Then they used monitoring systems to gather information about compliance and progress in school-level implementation. They also provided differentiated follow-up assistance. In some cases, this was to help school personnel master and comply with district expectations; in others cases, in which compliance was no longer an issue, it was to help school personnel use programs to obtain better results.

Principals' Expertise in Guiding School Improvement Although most central office administrators spoke about unevenness in the leadership strengths of their principals, leaders in higher-performing districts expressed greater confidence in their ability to improve the quality of school leadership through hiring practices, in-house leadership-development programs, school placement, and supervision.

In a minority of the districts we studied, district administrators attributed principal effectiveness to innate rather than learned capacities, and low school performance was viewed as a consequence of external factors (state policies, school community characteristics) rather than district and principal leadership. District leaders faced with struggling schools were less rather than more likely to sponsor leadership-development initiatives or to provide strategic help to principals. They focused instead on recruiting a different sort of administrator. In one of the large, low-performing urban districts in our sample, district administrators expressed the belief that principals were essentially born, not made. They talked more about the need to replace principals in low-performing schools than about prospects for developing their leadership skills. Not surprisingly, in this setting, district leaders did not describe any local professional-development programs for principals.

In higher-performing districts, central office leaders not only believed in their capacity to develop principals but also set expectations for implementation of specific sets of leadership practices. This required focusing on specific areas of leadership practice separately (for example, methods of clinical supervision, school-improvement planning, classroom walk-throughs, uses of student performance data), or within comprehensive guidelines or frameworks for leadership practice.[15] In one of the higher-performing urban districts in our sample, district officials organized a three-year principal-development program based on Marzano's balanced leadership program. They supplemented this with additional training in clinical supervision. They designed district-wide in-service programs for principals, focused specifically on new curriculum initiatives (such as revision of the elementary mathematics program) or school-improvement initiatives (such as a professional learning communities effort extending to all schools). In addition, the associate superintendent for curriculum and instruction dedicated portions of each monthly meeting with elementary and secondary school principals to collective leadership-development activities. Of course, small (often rural) districts with only a handful of principals and relatively infrequent turnover have less capacity and need for comprehensive development programs for aspiring and practicing principals.

What we observed in several of the higher-performing small districts, however, were examples of principals (both elementary and secondary) engaging in joint learning experiences with district support outside the district. In one of the rural districts, for example, the team of three principals and assistant principals took part in external professional development activities together on such topics as differentiated instruction, conducting classroom walk-throughs, and strengthening teachers' professional community over the three-year course of our site visits to the district.

District leaders in higher-performing settings invested in the development of common professional learning experiences for principals, focused on district expectations for instructional leadership and administration. They did not rely chiefly on principals' participation in state certification programs or on support for individual principals' professional interests (addressed in external workshops, conferences, and university programs; see also Chapter Six). Leaders in higher-performing districts communicate explicit expectations for principal leadership, provide learning experiences in line with these expectations, monitor principal follow-through, and intervene with further support as needed. This kind of supervision was not limited to formal procedures for appraisal by principals, but relied on ongoing monitoring and discussion about school performance and improvement plans. Where gaps in leadership skills were identified, district leaders were more likely to intervene personally—advising and coaching the principal—than to call on outside expertise. This pattern of interaction stems not only from the clear expectations for practice that are characteristic of higher-performing districts we studied but also from district leaders' confidence in their capacity to help principals master those practices.

School Factors Related to Differences in Performance In higher-performing settings, district leaders understood that the reasons for differences in student performance, or in implementation of district initiatives, were particular to the setting. Similar problems (for example, declining test scores, weak follow-through with a district professional learning communities initiative) might result from different contributing conditions in different schools. Therefore, standard solutions were considered unlikely to apply in all situations.

Leaders in these districts engaged school staff members in collaborative inquiry about the unique circumstances affecting student learning or teacher performance in their schools. They then tailored district support for improvement to the analysis of school-specific needs, rather than relying primarily on centrally determined interventions based on categorical differences among schools and their students (for example, size, SES, ELL, facilities) or set performance cutoff levels. They invested in external and locally created databases to inform inquiry and decision making related to differences in student outcomes and degrees of program implementation.[16]

Challenges and Trends

Our efforts to attain greater precision in understanding "the district difference" were both fascinating and frustrating. Our quantitative data point to a strong district effect, noted particularly in the relationship between the district's policies and practices and the teachers' reports of principals' instructional leadership. This finding is particularly significant because it provides empirical evidence, on a wide scale, that district-level policies and actions actually make a difference in principals' instructional leadership behaviors as experienced by teachers. Our "district instructional focus" scale was useful for demonstrating that effect, but the items that scale comprises should not be read as the only things that district leaders need to do to strengthen principals' instructional leadership (see prior analysis of other strands of district policy and action in Chapters Seven through Nine and in the following section of this chapter). The survey items go beyond the mere provision of professional development for instructional leadership. They combine setting and communicating high expectations, identifying clear priorities for improvement in instruction, developing explicit plans for improvement, following through with active support for principals and teachers, and monitoring.

Our overall conclusion is there is no simple list of actions that will allow district leaders to create the conditions that promote improved instruction and student learning. Instead, district leaders' actions in relation to key policy conditions are highly interdependent and require steady work on multiple fronts. Most district policies and practices that can be linked to real improvements for teaching and learning evolve over relatively long periods of time. This finding points to the critical importance of patience and of sustained, continual efforts aimed at improvement. That focus is present in the more successful districts (even where there have been leadership changes), but it was distinctly lacking in districts with frequent district leadership turnover or inconsistent policy development.

Our evidence for district-wide approaches to improving and sustaining the quality of teaching and learning pointed to some key challenges and trends faced overall—and, in particular, by higher-performing districts in our sample. Leaders in these settings were explicit about their commitment to ambitious learning goals for *all* students, not just for those not performing at acceptable proficiency levels. But they also spoke about the difficulty of establishing clear goals and plans for improvement where students were performing at or above state standards—which often led to satisfied parents. In higher-performing settings, district leaders were likely to be vigilant and strategic about sustaining good performance where it was happening. Anticipating where problems might arise goes against the grain of the prevalent accountability focus, which targets attention and resources on existing low performance and remediation. Thoughtful district administrators were equally concerned about sustaining good performance and establishing agendas for student learning beyond proficiency scores on standardized tests; the latter requires altering the public definition of low performance.

Increasing standardization of curriculum, instruction, and assessment appears to be a universal trend in the United States at the district and state levels, notwithstanding the emergence of diverse provider systems in a few large urban districts.[17] Our evidence from higher-performing districts suggests that it is not standardization of expectations for curriculum and instruction per se that improves student learning. Rather, standardization leads to improvement only insofar as it creates a platform for improving the quality of leadership, instruction, and learning. Using this platform, district leaders can develop support systems that promote quality implementation of the common expectations. The creation of such support systems takes time and skill, and it requires extensive communication and organizational learning to figure out what works well. Unfortunately, not all districts benefit from the leadership continuity, skill, and resources needed to develop equally effective support systems in a context of standardized expectations—and often those underperforming districts that may need it most lack both the stability and the internal arrangements to sustain a developmental focus.

From district leaders in our higher-performing settings, we have learned that once standard expectations for curriculum, instruction, and leadership are implemented and sustained with a reasonable degree of fidelity and quality, the next step requires additional solutions grounded in local analysis of learning needs and circumstances of struggling students. In effect, in these districts three levels of support for school improvement were observed:

- Level one encompasses common inputs to all schools to develop the basic knowledge, skills, and resources necessary to understand and work towards district expectations.
- Level two supports efforts to provide additional input and assistance to schools and school personnel that are at risk or struggling to meet expectations for professional practice and student achievement.

- Level three support occurs when there is cross-school collaborative inquiry into important problems and a search for solutions that go beyond current knowledge and expectations.

The findings presented in this chapter do not lend themselves to easy categorizations of the ways in which district leadership and support for improvement varies between higher- and lower-performing districts. There is convergence on the role of evidence from standardized achievement tests as the basis for judging school quality and as the focus for district and school targets for improvement. What is not uniform is how this approach is combined with other strategies for improvement that emphasize support for improvement, not just pressure. In particular, we saw these elements:

- Efforts to develop principal and teacher capacity to implement targeted improvements in teaching and learning (professional investment)
- Efforts to identify and support the diffusion of effective practices linked to specific needs for improvement (innovation implementation)
- Continuous monitoring of the process and effects of improvement efforts on leadership, teaching, and learning, with changes in practices where needed (evolutionary planning)

The coherence achieved by some districts, which contributed to their overall effectiveness in improving and sustaining quality teaching and learning, appears to depend on several key factors at the district level. One is the degree to which district leaders are able to develop a collective sense of ownership and responsibility among district and school personnel for the curriculum and the outcomes of curriculum delivery. When this is done well, principals and teachers define their work in ways that are consistent with ambitious local expectations for teaching and learning. A second factor influencing coherence is the extent to which district leaders are able to create and sustain a local support system and working conditions to enable principals and teachers to competently and creatively address district expectations and priorities for improvement. Third is the degree to which district leaders are able to create a culture of teamwork in identifying and addressing the challenges of improvement across district units, and in collaboration with school personnel. Effective district leaders created district-wide systems of improvement that were centered less on rules and processes than on interaction around shared goals, collaborative planning, and coordinated action. A final factor influencing coherence is the deliberate and systematic search for and use of local evidence (including but not limited to test data) to identify improvement needs and targets, to probe the circumstances underlying those needs, and to monitor progress in improvement plans.

Together, these four factors contribute to what we have reported as a strong sense of collective efficacy in the higher-performing and improving districts—a sense that local educators working together are capable of identifying and addressing the local challenges for improvement.

Implications for Policy and Practice

Five implications for policy and practice emerged from this section of our study.

1. District leaders need to establish clear expectations across multiple dimensions of improvement activity as the bases for increasing coherence, coordination, and synergy in the effectiveness of district improvement efforts over time.
2. District leaders should combine a common core of support for efforts to implement district expectations, with differentiated support aligned to the needs of individual schools.
3. District leaders should appreciate that effective school-leadership practices can be acquired through intentional leadership-development efforts, which include both formal professional development activities and collegial work.
4. Districts should strive for continuity in district leadership; such continuity is integral to the development and implementation of a coherent and effective support system for improving and sustaining the quality of student and school performance.
5. District leaders should take steps to monitor and sustain high-level student performance wherever it is found and to set ambitious goals for student learning that go beyond proficiency levels on standardized tests. Focusing improvement efforts solely on low-performing schools and students is not a productive strategy for continual improvement in a district.

Reflections

1. How do the opportunities for school leadership development provided by the higher-performing districts described in this chapter compare with the opportunities you have experienced?
2. What capacities will be required of newly appointed district leaders aspiring to the features of high performance described in this chapter?
3. According to this chapter, what is the most important thing a district can do to improve student achievement? What is the reason for such influence on students?

CHAPTER THIRTEEN

CASE STUDIES

District Responses to State Leadership

Karen Seashore Louis, Stephen E. Anderson,
and Emanda Thomas

Key Findings

- Superintendents and associate superintendents see state policies as a vehicle for achieving local goals.
- Smaller districts are more likely to regard the State Education Agency (SEA) as a source of support; medium-sized and larger districts have other sources that are more important.
- Larger districts vary based on their reputation as "historically troubled urban districts" versus being less "inner city." The urban core districts tend to resist state interventions, whereas the larger non–urban core districts tend to view the state as less important.
- The reaction of district officials to state policies and actors varies based on the political culture of the state.

This chapter examines whether centrally developed initiatives at the state level in the United States have an impact on how school districts think about their role in providing direction and support for student learning, and it also examines how districts view the strategies that state government uses to initiate change at the local level. Our focus is on smaller and medium-sized districts, a context that has been underexamined in recent investigations of the effects of the changing educational policy environment. We will, however, pay some attention to the reactions of larger districts in our sample.

Our framework draws on perceptions of *power*, *networking*, and *loose coupling* to examine district responses to state policy makers and administrative agencies. Our study suggests that there is considerable variation in how districts react to state standards and accountability, but none of the districts we analyzed in detail describe their situation in ways that suggest they feel besieged or victimized by state standards. All saw themselves as being able to harness state policy to local priorities. There were, however, differences among the districts that correspond to the larger political culture of the state in which they are located.

The relative lack of comparative empirical research on the state-district relationship, particularly in rural schools, led us to frame an exploratory set of questions to guide this investigation:

1. How do smaller districts interpret their relationship with state policy makers and agencies? In particular, do district administrators' interpretation of the state's role in policy making correspond to the frameworks we have just described?
2. Do differences between states help to account for differences in the ways in which district administrators interpret district-state relationships?

Previous Research

Many recent studies have focused on the internal organization and decision-making processes in districts, illuminating the complexity of districts' struggles to create and sustain improvements in schools[1] or to show the way in which district office personnel work with schools.[2] Relatively fewer look at the district's role in interpreting state policy initiatives, in spite of early attention given to the role of the district as a (re)interpreter of state policy.[3] However, existing research contains a variety of lenses that may help to explain the relationships between policymakers at one level and those at another. In this analysis we examine three.

○ *Hierarchical Power: States and Systemic Coherence*. A number of authors regard the state as a superordinate actor and local governments as subordinate. Without making any extreme assumptions about powerlessness at the local level, we can say that the role of the state as the constitutionally legitimate actor in education is powerfully embedded in many classical articles and analyses of the state's role.[4] Under this model (which also characterizes the operating assumptions of both state and federal programs, as well as those of some foundations), states provide funding and monitor what the district does with it.[5] Although states vary in the degree to which they provide strong structure and legislative and financial foundations for local education, their legitimate authority over local decisions in at least some educational arenas is largely uncontested, and it has increased substantially in the last few decades.[6]

○ *Networks of Power and Influence.* Some analysts of state and local activities emphasize that districts rarely respond to states based solely on the state's legitimate power position. Instead, they are actors in the policy system, vying with other state actors at all stages of the policy-making process to ensure that policy actions, when taken, are acceptable to most key groups, including local education agencies.[7] In addition, after state policies have been passed they still must be implemented, and local education agencies and state agencies use personal contacts to negotiate how both parties can best respond.[8] Thus, even though states have legitimate authority, it is exercised judiciously and often through informal and formal networks that help to shape local discussions about state policy.

○ *Loose Coupling.* The notion that educational organizations are "loosely coupled" was first introduced by Weick (1976) to explain why policies enacted in one part of the educational system often had limited impact in other parts. Further, a variety of studies in the '70s and '80s affirmed the limits of higher "levels" of the educational hierarchy and the relatively weak impact of state policy on student outcomes.[9] More recently, a new approach to loose coupling argues that schools are busy developing their own policies and initiatives, and they pay attention to demands from "outside the system" only when they are consistent with the direction in which the organization is already moving.[10] In other words, local education authorities have a sense of their own as responsible actors and pay attention to policies developed by the state only when they can be woven into the local story.

○ *New Research.* For this chapter, we limit our in-depth presentation to interviews with key district personnel (superintendents and associate superintendents) in two smaller districts with six or fewer schools (in Texas and Missouri) and two medium-sized districts (in North Carolina and New Jersey). These districts were selected, in part, because our previous work examining their states' political cultures and policy initiatives indicated the states in which they are located have taken distinctive approaches to school improvement and reform that are consistent with enduring and well-understood approaches to solving educational problems within the state. We have tested the findings of the cases presented here in cross-case analyses of eight additional districts.

Our rationale for selecting districts of varying size is based on the assumption that they provide different environments for looking at the three theoretical lenses. Smaller districts tend to have limited resources and must rely on partners in order to achieve their improvement goals. In contrast, larger districts often have staff resources in their curriculum, testing, and professional development offices that may exceed those available in state agencies. And medium-sized districts are, according to most observers, more powerful actors in the educational policy system, sometimes driving state action rather than being responsive to it. Additionally, smaller districts tend to have only a few schools that share similar characteristics, whereas the larger the district, the more likely they are to be forced to adopt nonuniform policies and practices in terms of stimulating standards and accountability (Elmore & Burney, 1998). We also draw on analyses of larger districts, although we do not present the case materials here.

Although our findings are based on the analysis of all of seven districts, we will illustrate our findings using examples from the aforementioned two smaller districts in Texas and Missouri and two medium-sized districts in North Carolina and New Jersey. In our interpretation, we also draw on analyses of additional small, medium, and large districts located in the same states. The states that we highlight in this section have different traditions in terms of their educational and political cultures:[11]

   ○ *Texas and North Carolina:* Both exhibit traditional political cultures characterized by elite influence, strong state efforts to direct schools, and evolving accountability policies that have persisted over a long period of time. North Carolina was among the states with the most positive principal assessments; Texas was average in 2005, with unreliable data in 2008.
   ○ *Missouri and New Jersey:* Both states have highly individualistic political cultures characterized by many competing interest groups, lobbying, and modest state efforts to create coherence. Missouri is a relative latecomer to state testing but has a longer history of general state standards. New Jersey, although a bit earlier to establish state tests, has focused its quality initiatives on a small group of low-performing ("Abbott") districts. Missouri's principal ratings were positive in both 2005 and 2008; New Jersey's ratings went from average to well below average.

How State Policy Affects Small District Leadership for Improvement

This section draws on evidence from two districts to examine perceptions of policy hierarchy, networks, and loose coupling.

Tortuga Shoals School District (Texas)

Situated in south Texas, Tortuga Shoals is a largely Hispanic community with a mix of long-time residents and more recent immigrants. Major sources of employment are the service industry for hotels and restaurants (tourism is a burgeoning sector) and shrimping (on the downturn). Tortuga Shoals has clearly delineated higher- and lower-income residential areas, including some subsidized housing apartments. The district superintendent, Dr. Alba Cruz, was quite familiar with the district when she arrived in July 2003 because she had previously served as a principal in the district before moving to a district level position elsewhere. Additional district personnel included a new assistant superintendent, a business officer, federal and state program officers, and an instructional facilitator in the curriculum and instruction unit. Three of four principals were new to their positions (in their first or second year).

The superintendent's top priority was improving the quality of student learning as reflected in local indicators (course failure and high school graduation rates) and state test results (which declined after the state introduced a new curriculum and tests in 2001–2002). Additional priorities included developing vocational programs aligned with local employment opportunities, and addressing social issues related to student retention, such as teen pregnancy, and low aspirations for post-secondary education.

Perceptions of Policy Hierarchy A strategic theme emphasized by Dr. Cruz was that more authentic compliance with state and local policies was essential to achieving local improvement priorities. These views were not universally shared among school personnel, who pointed to a track record of good results on the old state test and rankings, in which Tortuga Shoals was always in the top 10 percent of the districts in the region. To legitimize these directions for improvement, the superintendent commissioned a systemic curriculum audit by outside consultants, with the expectation that this would lead to a new district improvement plan.

In the past, the district had taken a decentralized approach to policy implementation. Program units at the district office level managed their policy portfolios relatively independently, and responsibility for implementation was delegated to schools. The orientation to state policy was characterized by district compliance with bureaucratic requirements and trust in school personnel to ensure positive results. As student test results began to slip under the new state requirements and more stringent NCLB criteria, the percentage of students not meeting minimum standards increased, but so did those of other schools in the region: Tortuga Shoals schools remained relatively high-performing. The new superintendent, however, began to challenge the local culture of formal compliance and decentralization. Dr. Cruz and her assistant saw a need for a more authentic and coherent approach to state policy expectations for curriculum and teaching.

The district capacity for reform was affected by state funding policies, which redistribute tax revenues from high- property-tax districts like Tortuga Shoals (with its strong tourist industry) to low-wealth districts. Although local officials decried the loss of revenue, the district received significant supplementary funding because of the high poverty levels among the student population. Recent state funding cuts, however, resulted in the loss of an instructional facilitator position as well as support for a recently introduced mathematics program. The district, by necessity, had to rely on principals' instructional leadership and on expertise from the regional education center or independent consultants to support school and district-wide improvement initiatives.

Networks District and school personnel reported little direct contact with the Texas state education department, but relied on the state-supported regional education service center (RESC) as a key source of information about state policies and as a provider of professional development. The RESC's professional development offerings focused largely on state initiatives (such as improving Gifted and Talented programs and classroom technology use) that were not always linked to local priorities for improvement. Education service center staff also provided technical support for analysis of performance data.

Dr. Cruz, along with the assistant superintendent, participated regularly in district administrator meetings organized by the education service center, and she reported that these were important to her. Neither she nor the assistant superintendent discussed other important networks they relied on, but they talked about personal communication with close colleagues from neighboring districts and about attending annual meetings of state professional associations. The district was not involved in university partnerships focused on local improvement efforts.

The year prior to Dr. Cruz's appointment, the district had entered into a multiyear contract with a commercial mathematics program developer, but after several years, at the point of renewal, the district terminated the contract for materials and professional development because of the cost, concerns among the elementary schools regarding its effectiveness, and the weak program fit with a state mathematics textbook adoption. School principals independently continued to use external consultants related to their own priorities for improvement. An elementary principal, for example, arranged for in-service training inputs on reading strategies for her teachers, whereas the junior high principal recruited external in-service expertise to support her vision for more constructivist forms of pedagogy.

The superintendent was also responsive to input from local community groups, such as the Tortuga Shoals Education Foundation. The Foundation, created by stakeholders associated with the tourist industry, was the key source motivating the superintendent's interest in expanding high school vocational programs.

Dr. Cruz and her district colleagues did not portray themselves as influential participants in the state policy-making process. Rather, they emphasized their responsibility for ensuring effective implementation of state and federal policy directions and intentions, in contrast to the laissez-faire approach to policy implementation of the prior administration.

Loose Coupling Loosely coupled certainly describes the district prior to Dr. Cruz's arrival. A district improvement plan existed on paper, but it was not an active document guiding district improvement efforts, and the district emphasized on-paper compliance with state policies. Although there were programmatic initiatives under way (the elementary mathematics program, a federally sponsored program intended to motivate high school students to pursue post-secondary studies, and a government-funded after school program to provide positive options for teen social behavior), there was no overall consensus on needs, goals, and a strategy for improvement. The district's initial response to the new state curriculum and tests and to the decline in student test results was mainly to direct and to provide small grants for principals to organize school-based curriculum writing projects, which was being carried out with little centralized district guidance or input.

During her first year as superintendent, Dr. Cruz identified some key directions for improvement in student learning. First, she was disturbed and puzzled by the fact that student course failure rates, which principals were required to report every six weeks, were unacceptably high (namely, 29 percent at the high school level), despite the history of formally satisfactory student results on state tests and school accountability ratings.

Second, while Dr. Cruz expressed uncertainty about the causes of student failure, the discrepancy between local and state assessments of student learning fueled her growing belief that the state test results were an inadequate indicator of the quality of student learning. She strongly suspected that teachers were not challenging students to the cognitive level of the new curriculum and that too much effort was being devoted to test preparation. Third, Dr. Cruz took the position that a major obstacle to further improvement in student performance was a weakness in vertical curriculum coordination and coherence from kindergarten to grade 12 between schools across the district and the central office. Dr. Cruz and her assistant realized that without additional evidence, district and school personnel would be unlikely to support these views; this led to their decision to ask the board to fund a systemic curriculum audit.

Dr. Cruz also took steps in her first year to begin to break down the institutionalized organizational culture of autonomous schools and autonomous units, noting: "When I walked into this district again, it was very fragmented. So since day one I have been working on building a culture of togetherness." Her emphasis on teamwork across schools and organizational units was a key element of her strategic agenda to develop greater consensus and coordination around directions for improvement and alignment with state and local goals for curriculum, teaching, and student development.

Summary Dr. Cruz's approach to change and improvement in student performance across the district embraced state policy expectations for curriculum, teaching, and learning. Dr. Cruz believed the path to improvement in student learning would require strengthening compliance with new state curriculum expectations, better vertical alignment of curriculum delivery across the schools, and more effective collaboration within the district. She did not, however, go beyond the state standards or collect additional data. Her focus was almost exclusively on understanding and complying with state initiatives and using the state's priorities to stimulate change at the school level. Both Cruz and others on her team were actively collecting and looking at state and local performance indicators, but they lacked the capacity to gather or use information that would help them interpret it, which limited their ability to explain performance problems (other than curriculum alignment).

Middle Region School District (Missouri)

Middle Region is a small suburban district located in the south of a major metropolitan city. Over the last fifteen years the demographic character and academic rigor of the district has changed. What was once a largely white and affluent population became predominantly nonwhite, with more than half of the students in the district receiving a free or reduced-price lunch. Along with the change in demographics of the student population, the academic performance of the school district gradually worsened. Contributing factors, as explained by district staff, were teachers working in isolation and low expectations for the newer students. The school board had growing concerns about the need for change throughout the district, especially in the high school.

A new superintendent, Dr. Ken Leslie, was hired in 2001, with the task of turning around this challenging school district. Dr. Leslie's first priority was to shift the prevailing culture among educators in the district, and his second was to improve student achievement through increased rigor, alignment of state standards to classroom practices, and implementation of higher math standards than the state's. The district's strategy for achieving these priorities involved replacing principals, creating a more rigorous curriculum aligned with state standards, and providing external support to schools to assess progress. The underlying assumption of Middle Region District is that local accountability and standards are critical to (1) achieve academic gains among students, and (2) successfully achieve or exceed state standards.

Perceptions of Policy Hierarchy The relationship between Middle Region District and the state has changed dramatically in recent years. Prior to the arrival of Ken Leslie, the legitimacy of state authority was low. State standards and curriculum were poorly implemented and largely ignored. What appeared to be more important among both teachers and administrators was the belief that students should feel validated and supported, which effectively replaced academic expectations and achievement in many classrooms. With the current superintendent, this has changed dramatically.

The district is now more attuned to state policies and guidelines, and it implements them appropriately, according to both teachers and administrators. However, the superintendent explained that this began with a sense of urgency, noting that his analysis of the data suggested a need for dramatic and sustained action to improve. Being in step with state directives for education is a clear focus of the current superintendent. The district actively seeks and expands on state direction for curriculum, standards, and assessment planning as a baseline for professional practice and student achievement. It also actively seeks support from the state.

In this small district, the superintendent's vision determines how others see the state, because there are few layers between him and the teachers. The district office frames local goals for student achievement in terms of student performance relative to the state curriculum and learning standards. Unlike Tortuga Shoals, which focused on state tests and standards, at Middle Region the teaching priorities and grade level expectations are based on national as well as state standards and accountability. District goals for elementary students emphasize grade level readiness; at the middle and high school grades, goals emphasize increasing math rigor. Overall, goals and initiatives are targeted at student learning gaps by income level and race, challenges unique to grade levels, and transitions into higher grades. The district collects additional data (including action research) and uses data-driven decision making to determine priorities for curriculum and standards alignment, and expectations for educators within a larger context of state standards.

The district goes beyond the state's requirements; it actualizes policy coherence by aligning state standards with district initiatives. State standards have recently been revised to lay out and measure grade level expectations. Effectively, the district has reformed its curriculum and assessments to reflect such policy changes. In addition to making efforts to transform itself and move in the direction of the state, the superintendent emphasizes that the district has also set its math standards higher than those of the state. Ken Leslie has placed such importance on increasing the rigor in math curricula that the district is shifting toward elementary pre-algebra to better prepare students for eighth grade algebra.

Transparency of district goals has been accompanied by efforts to increase capacity for district reform. Through the leadership of the superintendent, the district replaced most principals throughout the district, with the intention of establishing a new culture of leadership based on an attitude favoring students' capacity to learn, increasing academic rigor, and instructional background. The superintendent explains that what students need are principals who have high expectations of students and have records of turning around schools, and teachers who will emphasize learning rather than just trying to make students feel better.

Networks The superintendent of Middle Region District does not merely respond to state policy—he helped to create it and still influences it. There is evidence of a strong network of influence between the district and the state that affects district initiatives and policy alignment to state initiatives. Because Dr. Leslie formerly held an influential role with the state, his expanded set of relationships includes people in the state department of education, district superintendents, and other educators. His former role and reputation enable him to influence state forums, and he continues to engage in policy discussions with state actors. He is vocal about his concerns regarding limitations of state policy with state staff, and he pushes for the inclusion of principles that support the vision and goals of Middle Region District. The superintendent also communicates with other district superintendents for fresh ideas for growth. However, his background appears to be the greatest influence on district policy priorities, because it allows him close ties with and access to state department staff.

Although external networks are an important factor in the district and its transformation, the superintendent places a greater emphasis on internal district networks. One of the most important networks emphasized by the superintendent is the one that he maintains with school principals, whom he sees as key sources of leadership, school culture, and implementation of district goals and state policies. Due to the significance of their role, the superintendent established biweekly principal meetings and requires principals to attend school board meetings.

The emphasis of network interactions within and outside the district is not based on a goal of state policy coherence. Rather, it is based on the superintendent's thorough understanding of the strengths and weaknesses of state curriculum standards and his efforts to move Middle Region District forward in growing its local priorities, which are, in turn, moving the district ahead of its peers.

Loose Coupling The previous superintendent's administration emphasized loose coupling with state policy initiatives, which were viewed as marginally relevant to the district's demographic changes. The current superintendent helped develop a common agenda for the strategic direction of the district, including increasing expectations for student success, academic rigor, reporting, professional development, and alignment to state standards and assessment. To address his concerns about a weak performance culture in the early grades, the district revamped the curriculum at lower and middle grades based on the goals of grade level preparation, academic rigor, and preparing students to become part of a more challenging workforce, one that requires a background in algebra. In addition, new district report cards are linked to state standards, and they report reading levels to eliminate ambiguity (or teacher latitude) in reporting student progress. This change has decreased the former practice of giving passing grades to students who did not earn the grade, and it has supported an increase in proficiency by 30 percent for third graders in the district. Curriculum has been aligned to state and national standards.

The district has also set more rigorous expectations for teachers and principals in their pedagogy and expectations of students. Consequently, the district emphasizes state standards and getting teachers to base their practices on the standards, using course guides, which were previously ignored. In response, the district (with external consultation) developed a curriculum management tool to help teachers align curriculum with the new grade level expectations, state and national standards, assessments, suggested teaching strategies, and resources.

Summary In this case, the coupling of district and state initiatives largely depended on district leadership. Both Cruz and Leslie identified the need to change local teacher culture and to achieve more effective alignment with state standards for classroom practice. However, Leslie, located in an individualistic state policy context, felt free to establish standards and goals for local performance that exceeded state standards, whereas Cruz, in a more traditional "top down" state, still operated with compliance. Most notably, the commitment and actions of Superintendent Leslie, aligning district efforts with state curriculum standards, determined how state policies were "felt" within schools and encouraged both the district and schools to collect and analyze local data rather than relying only on what the state provided. Furthermore, as the district coupled its efforts more closely to state standards (and beyond), there were also improvements in achievement, as well as increased board support.

How State Policy Affects Medium-Sized District Leadership for Improvement

This section draws on evidence from two districts to illustrate the influences of state policy on district leaders' improvement efforts.

Danhill Regional School District (New Jersey)

Danhill is located in a quiet corner of New Jersey, but like much of the state is undergoing rapid development. Until recently it consisted of dairy and egg farmers, with a bit of tourist industry on the side, but it has increasingly become a desirable retirement area and is also within (long) commuting distance from larger cities. Although the district is medium-sized in terms of student population, because it is quite spread out the schools retain their small-town identity—along with some of the demographic differences.

The overall economy is increasingly dependent on "outsiders," and the superintendent estimates that about 50 percent of the young families are newcomers. Because the district covers a relatively large area, there is considerable diversity among the schools. Some elementary schools, for example, are affluent and almost exclusively white, whereas others have higher levels of poverty and minority enrollment.

Overall, the district performs well on state assessments, but several of the schools have not met AYP targets for several years running. Nevertheless, the district has a strong reputation within the state, which continues to attract support from local residents—in part because the district has worked to maintain the viability of small, decentralized schools that are responsive to local communities. Contributing to the small-town feel of the schools is the stability among professional educators and administrators. Most of them grew up in Danhill, and in the district office, almost all have been in the district for twenty-five or more years.

In some ways, the district is family-like, with a district elementary school supervisor claiming to know at least 75 percent of the teachers in the ten schools that he visits. This is a result of policy, not accident. As the superintendent noted, "We make a habit of trying to hire our graduates when they come back, for the obvious reason that they have a connection. You want your people to be connected to your district, feel a part of ownership."

Perceptions of Policy Hierarchy There is a clear acceptance of the state's role in setting curriculum standards and accountability expectations among all administrators, but a clear sense of the state as an adversary runs through the district conversations about policy and change. As one associate superintendent put it, "So much of what we see on a daily basis is so punitive. I don't think that is going to change. . . . I think that the nature of government is just what we have in New Jersey." There is a strong sense that the state is a remote entity that does not understand the realities of student learning. As the superintendent noted, the issue was not with No Child Left Behind per se, but with New Jersey's interpretation of the law, which allowed state ratings to be based on a small number of students in any grade level. Another concern revolved around the constantly changing expectations related to student testing, coupled with relatively weak communication. For example, there was uncertainty whether the state's high school proficiency test, taken in the beginning of the eleventh grade test, would assume that all students had taken Algebra II, as well as uncertainty about what would happen to students who did not pass. One associate superintendent noted, "They are moving . . . and they are not giving us enough answers." On the other hand, the district has very good relations with the regional office of the state department, which they regard as very responsive and helpful. District administrators separate their criticisms of state policy and implementation from the overall policy goals of accountability, which they see as a stimulus to innovation and improvement. The real issue that concerns the district, however, is not the communication around accountability, but the state's funding equalization policies, which they believe have left them in difficult circumstances.

Networks Danhill sees itself as a willing partner with other districts (the administrator with responsibility for technology talked about the networking that goes on with others in similar positions) and also with regional institutions of higher education (two universities were mentioned by several people) and the Educational Testing Service in Princeton, New Jersey. Students are encouraged to take courses at a local community college, which has helped to expand post-secondary offerings within the high schools.

More importantly, although Danhill is a mid-sized district, in the context of New Jersey's many very small districts it has significant capacities that others lack. Thus when Danhill administrators think about networks, they are more likely to consider how they provide assistance and resources to others, rather than their role as recipients.

In contrast, internal networking is very important. The superintendent meet with all of the district administrators at least once every two weeks, and they have many informal meetings on-site as well. Internal networking, including informal meetings with subcommittees of the school board, is what keeps Danhill's new ideas circulating and discussed before any decision is taken (with the exception, as noted, for state mandates). As one administrator noted, the strategy is to create consensus through discussion. In addition, the superintendent focuses on networking within the diverse communities that are served, making sure that he has an eye on what will create support for innovation and new policies. Because of the socioeconomic variation among the schools, the message needs to be adapted to meet different perspectives. The superintendent noted that many people do not fully understand the changes in the economic environment and their implications for education, but the schools cannot be too far ahead of public opinion.

In general, the administrators in the district appeared to be disconnected from state policy making and initiatives, and they did not discuss working through professional or other groups to change the aspects of state policy that seemed most onerous.

Loose Coupling The district's response to the increasing financial and accountability pressures, and to the weak support from the state, has been to become more entrepreneurial. In the past few years, there have been many cuts in administrative positions and constant reorganizing of the job responsibilities of those who are left. This has been done through retirements and outsourcing rather than wholesale reductions in the work force. On the whole, those who are left in the district office feel that it is working reasonably well. Perhaps more unique is the effort to change the revenue streams for the district in significant ways to compensate for the state's emphasis on finance equalization for very poor districts. A few years ago, the superintendent noted that they were paying a great deal of money to rent the building in which the district office was located. He suggested buying it and turning the unused space into services for the community as well as the district. The services provided by the district include a cafeteria that is open to the public, a copy and publications center, technology support, and space rental.

The approach to innovation in the districts is to focus on supporting continuous improvement rather than visible reforms—either those that the state promotes or those that are more popular in professional circles. In addition to the business revenue generation plan, the district increased its capacity for promoting innovations and professional development among teachers while reducing administrative costs, by implementing a supervisor position at the building level. Because supervisors are classified as administrators, they can serve the functions of instructional coaches and evaluators. The coaching strategy extends throughout the district staff. The superintendent, for example, reports that he regularly wanders around to carry out informal development with everyone from teachers to groundskeepers.

In all cases, the district prided itself on going beyond what state policy might require. One example was the teacher induction program, which in addition to the state's mandate for a mentor involved lots of initial assessment and tailored professional development. The idea for the program came not from a local contact but from a visit an administrator made to a district in New York. Local efforts to create a more rigorous high school curriculum were stimulated by internal analysis and by resources acquired from a National Science Fund (NSF) project involving two universities. Administrators were clear that their efforts predated the state's efforts to increase graduation requirements.

Summary The emphasis in Danhill was on adapting external resources (curriculum, software, and the like) to local needs, and on creating local support for district improvement actions. For the most part, this has been successful: until recently, the district had never been turned down in a bond request. Little attention was paid to the state's mandates, with the exception of meeting testing requirements. Although district officials complain that New Jersey's interpretation of the No Child Left Behind requirements makes little sense in the small schools in their district and unfairly penalizes schools with just a few students who are struggling, they have not paid a great deal of attention to a systemic response. Instead, they hew to the course that has been their consistent strategy for more than a decade: to grow support and revenues within the district and to make gradual changes that can be adapted to the variety of constituencies served by the schools. Although the state is a player, it is not important compared to the goals that are generated from within.

North White Pine County (North Carolina)

North White Pine County School System has 36 schools and approximately 29 thousand students. The district has faced high student and teacher mobility because it is located near a military base. District-level leadership, on the other hand, has remained uncharacteristically stable compared to other districts in the state. Superintendent Samuelson served for 16 years in the district and the superintendent before him served for 19 years; therefore the staff has been able to work through issues and challenges in a systematic way, especially with the board of education and county level commissioners. During the last year of our study, Superintendent Samuelson, along with three other district-level leaders, retired, and a new superintendent, Sheila Wauters, took over the district. The transition went smoothly because all of the new district-level administrators were brought up through the ranks in the North White Pine County system and were well known and well liked before they took their new positions.

One of the biggest challenges for the district has been meeting the Highly Qualified Teacher rule because of the high teacher turnover. Every year the district has had to hire between 300 and 350 new teachers because of the reality of revolving military families and state-wide teacher shortages. The teacher shortage has become an even greater problem because the student population in North White Pine County continues to grow.

Perceptions of Policy Hierarchy At the district level, policies and initiatives have always first been piloted by schools on a focused and invitational basis before they became adopted system-wide. The motto at the district has been to start new initiatives and reforms slowly before they fast-track them into the system. Superintendent Samuelson said: "Rather than racing in and then you have to back up and race out again, we have tried to fine-tune and refine what we are working on so that as someone sees the value of that and buys into it, it is already a product that fits us and fits our needs."

Because the district liked to take things slowly, the staff had problems with the state-mandated policies that had to be implemented all at once. District officials described the state as largely driven by the preferences of the governor. For example, during Superintendent Samuelson's tenure, the governor made early preschool education a top priority and mandated that all districts either create their own early preschool programs or align themselves with community agencies providing those services in the state. The governor ended up forming a political partnership with community agencies like Head Start, but offered no additional resources. The district's reaction to that initiative was mixed, as it was to a class size reduction mandate, also accompanied by no new resources. Reaction to new mandates is generally mixed, because in many cases the superintendent agrees with state goals, and uses the initiatives as an opportunity to stretch her staff, asking teachers to consider questions such as: "When the state comes out and says we are going to prepare students to be globally competitive, what does that mean? What does that mean to you in the classroom and what does that mean to our school system in terms of what we need to be doing?"

District administrators note that their legislative delegates at the state level listen to the school district, but that sometimes the vote does not go their way because the governor is able to create other alliances that support his priorities. For example, all of the school districts wanted to maintain local control and site-based decision making on several issues, especially when it came to having control over the school calendar, but the legislature ended up voting with the tourism industry to start the school year after Labor Day. The districts thus tried to pay attention to the winds that are blowing at the state capital, including the election of a state superintendent of public instruction (largely a figurehead position with limited authority) from a business rather than an educational background.

Superintendent Wauters said she and her district staff spent her first year doing that kind of sense-making around the state's focus. In addition, she partnered with community members and engaged with university and community college partners in the process. Superintendent Wauters said that even though the state has been influential, people at the state's Department of Public Instruction were "floundering" because they were unable to help districts or give them steps to help them move forward with the new focus.

Networks Networking with local community groups and partnering with other county personnel has been a necessity in North White Pine County because it has been classified as a "low-wealth" district, the central office has been understaffed, and there have been teacher shortages. However, the stability of district level leadership has helped the district make the vital connections with community groups and other county staff. Superintendent Samuelson often worked with the county manager, even though most of the contact was over the phone because of travel and budget restrictions. During his tenure, the district often networked and partnered with the local universities and with community college faculty and staff to provide teacher training. For example, the district partnered with math and science professors to create a program to help build teacher math and science skills. Getting new teachers up to speed on the state's accountability policies is an ongoing challenge. The district does most of its own professional development, so they have tried to provide mentors to all teachers, preservice training, and effective in-service teacher training, but they had to scramble to partner with their local university and community colleges to make sure that teaching assistants got certified.

The assistant superintendent also reported that the district tries to connect with the state, but because of cuts at the state level, capacity has continuously been an issue. Superintendent Wauters networked even more than the previous superintendent with local community groups and associations. For example, she became involved with the Southern Association of Colleges and Schools and served as the state specialist in the area of district accreditation. North White Pine County was the first system in the state to go through the accreditation process, for which Superintendent Wauters served as the facilitator. In addition, she has also served on other state level boards and on university and community college level boards and committees. Further, she became engaged with the economic growth development group in the community.

Loose Coupling Even though the district has high mobility rates because of the large military population, the district has been highly proficient. The district scores are higher than both the regional and state averages. Several of their schools were at 90 percent or higher proficiency rates on state tests, and all were above 80 percent. One of the greatest challenges in the district, however, has been meeting federal conditions for continued academic growth or Adequate Yearly Progress under NCLB, especially because the district has close to 2,800 students who have been classified as Exceptional Children (EC).

Like Superintendent Samuelson before her, Superintendent Wauters argued at the state level about the lack of direction or resources offered to districts to help them carry out the new state focus. For example, she went to state leaders to talk about the importance of having state assessments and accountability measures align with the new state focus. She reported that many local districts have banded together to lobby at the state level to align these systems and that she has spent a great deal of time talking with a variety of stakeholders about the need to have multiple local benchmarks for quality. She has also made it clear to principals that she will assess their performance using multiple indicators, not only a single multiple choice test.

Because of her own and other district superintendents' efforts, the state has begun to align the new focus with assessment and accountability measures. In addition, the state created a new evaluation instrument for school administrators that has been aligned specifically with the standards and expectations of the twenty-first-century skills focus and goals. The state has also been in the process of implementing a similarly aligned teacher evaluation instrument.

Summary North White Pine County district has experienced problems meeting some of the mandates in NCLB because a high percentage of their students and teachers come from military families, which are highly mobile. This is their major problem, and they report the state does little to help. Because of that, the district partners with local community colleges and universities as well as other community groups to meet state and federal requirements. North White Pine County staff report that they spend a great deal of time working with their schools and their communities to make sense of and shape these mandates to fit their local settings. The district has tried as much as possible to stick to their own local philosophy by piloting new initiatives in schools that volunteer, and then refining those policies before they implement them system-wide. Like the other medium-sized district, Danhill, North White Pine County has actively tried to influence local public opinion and understanding of state policy, although the superintendents (past and current) played a more active role as actors in the state policy context.

Summary of Findings from the District Leadership Cases

A comparison of the four districts using the framework that we set out in the earlier sections of the book is presented in Table 13.1. In framing our summary, we draw on these four districts and on our analysis of additional districts that we do not present in detail.

Debates in the press surrounding the standards and accountability movement often emphasize the prescriptive nature of emerging state and federal legislation. By implication, there is a sense that local districts, as well as principals and teachers, are put in straitjackets as they struggle to comply with policies that do not always make sense in their local context. This analysis casts empirical light on the issue by examining the responses of district office staff members in four small and medium-sized districts. Size is an important feature of our inquiry, because we assumed that smaller districts, because of their limited resources, may be less able to move resources around to meet new expectations that come

TABLE 13.1 CHARACTERISTICS OF A SAMPLE OF SMALLER AND MEDIUM-SIZE DISTRICTS

	School Population	Number of Schools	Setting	Demographic Distributions (% minority, % FRP)	District Scores in Language Exam*	District Scores on Math Exam*
Tortuga Shoals, TX	1,653	4	Small town	87.13 %, 88.39 %	ES—Similar MS—Below HS—Above	ES—Below MS—Below HS—Below
Middle Region District, MO	2,349	8	Small suburb of medium-sized city	72.9 %, 62.4 %	ES—Below MS—Below HS—Below	ES—Below MS—Below HS—Below
Danhill Regional District, NJ	16,000	18	4 small towns, surrounding area	12.7 %, 13 %	ES—Above MS—Above HS—Similar	ES—Similar MS—Similar HS—Similar
North White Pine County NC	23,000	36	Large military base is located in county	36.2 %, 41 %	ES—Below MS—Above HS—Below	ES—Similar MS—Similar HS—Similar

*Comparison of districts scores to state overall scores in 2005.

from outside the district. The significance of state policy environments is also important, because states have varied quite widely in how quickly and in what ways they have reacted to public demands for increased standards.

Hierarchical Power: Do States Have a Systemic Effect?

Overall, the evidence suggests that state accountability and standards policies, including their interpretation of NCLB requirements, have modest impacts on local behavior and planning for improvement. This does not mean that schools or districts ignore state policies; rather, it means that policies and requirements are incorporated into what the district administrators want to do, rather than serving as a fixed template. Some districts complain about resources and support, but in general they agree with the intent of state policy (if not with the lack of financial support for implementation).

Although there is variation in how smaller and medium-sized districts react to state standards and accountability, districts rarely describe their situation in ways that suggest they feel besieged or victimized by the standards movement, even when they disagree with specific state policies. Three of the four districts we analyzed in detail have high-poverty or high-minority populations, yet they all welcomed the standards movement as helping them to define and achieve important (local) educational goals. They described their relationship with their states in terms that must be categorized as accepting. They acknowledge the legitimacy of state policy (even if they dislike the notion of federal mandates and bemoan inadequate state funding), and they generally find they are able to use policy to enlarge their own influence over the improvement of education in their local settings.

None of the districts describes its state agencies as a significant source of support, although three of the states (Texas, Missouri, and New Jersey) have well-funded regional service agencies whose role is to support professional development and to enlarge district office capacities. Loose coupling was evident in the actions of all four districts to develop their own improvement agenda to which the state standards and accountability agenda could be linked. Two districts (Tortuga Shoals and North White Pine County) described the state's role as defining what they were trying to do, but even in those cases district leaders saw themselves as going beyond superficial compliance. None, however, reported significant professional guidance and support from state education departments or regional service units for the implementation of locally defined needs and goals, even within the parameters of state priorities and initiatives.

There is little evidence to support the assumption that state policies bypass the district and have a direct impact on the behavior of principals. Although principal assessment of positive state influences predicts their instructional leadership behavior, state effects are overwhelmed by principals' perceptions about the role of local standards and policies.

Networks of Local Leadership Influence Senior district staff in small- and medium-sized districts have limited political professional networks, with the exception of the individual who formerly held a key state position. However, both he and the superintendent in North White Pine County saw themselves as influencing state policy making, either on their own or through professional associations. The professional networks established by most of the superintendents in our sample are largely localized within the district and with other nearby districts, and they are typically more focused on coping with state policy mandates than on shaping those policies to begin with. There is some evidence that they participate actively in lobbying or making efforts to influence state policy, but only as part of a coalition. Overall, however, the evidence suggesting that districts see themselves as potent actors in the state's policy process is modest. State superintendents' associations were rarely mentioned as important sources of influence by superintendents, just as they were rarely included in the circles of influence described by state policy makers.

Loose Coupling Senior district staff view their work as loosely coupled with the state. District's sense of engagement with their policy-making process and their SEA varies by state policy culture.

- ○ Districts located in more traditional states see themselves as working toward authentic compliance with state policies, which requires them to go beyond the mandates and expectations to tailor law to local circumstances. Data from Tortuga Shoals and North White Pines have been presented as empirical evidence for this conclusion. In both the traditional states, mandates and limited state support for implementation were assumed, but states provided the framework within which local policy was worked out. District leaders leveraged state policy to frame, focus, and mobilize local improvement efforts.
- ○ Districts located in individualistic states (Danhill and Middle Region) saw state policies as less central to their improvement agendas, and they viewed their local work as loosely coupled with state policy making. They also did not seem to be concerned about sanctions. Like the traditional states, they did not see themselves as reliant on state help, but they believed that it was up to the district to design and implement effective school improvement policies. They all expressed a sense of being responsible for designing and implementing their own policy initiatives (while complying with the details of state policy).

◦ Although we have not presented the relevant case data here, two smaller districts located in states with a clear or moderate moralistic policy culture (Oregon and Nebraska) saw themselves as collaborative partners with the state. In both cases, the district administrators believed there were people in the state agency who could assist them in finding resources—perhaps even providing them, either directly or through the state's regional service agencies. They also described ways in which they took opportunities created by the state to participate in shaping state improvement policies.

Based on our previous analysis of interviews with state-level policy actors and stakeholders, we are led to the conclusion that district actors share many of the same assumptions about "how educational policy and improvement gets done here," and they adapt their own responses to the state's traditional ways of developing and implementing policy. Although we would not go so far as to say that state policy culture determines how smaller districts respond, we suggest that our data support the idea that how districts respond to increasingly uniform standards and testing policies will be significantly affected by the state's political culture. We hypothesize that in traditional states, small and medium-sized districts are more likely to see themselves as compliant actors; in individualistic states they view themselves as freer to interpret standards in their own ways; and in moralistic states they are likely to see states as partners in improvement.

But What About Larger Districts? As was pointed out in the beginning of this chapter, our focus was on the less-studied smaller districts in our sample. We did, however, carry out analyses of the larger districts, although less deeply. As expected, we find that the largest districts in our sample, irrespective of the state in which they are located, see themselves as responsible for their own future and view the development of their internal resources as the most important key for improvement and quality. However, there are clear differences among the larger districts we analyzed:

◦ Three semi-urban districts in our sample were large, but located outside of a major urban area. Rather than being in a declining urban core, they served expanding populations that were often increasingly diverse. They typically saw themselves as disengaged from state policy because they believed that they were far ahead in their locally developed strategic improvement plans. Compliance was a given, but it did not drive or shape their priorities. In this regard they were more like Danhill and Middle Region, but with far greater resources, both financially and in the district office.

○ Four inner-city districts, on the other hand, were "resisters" who blamed the state for unfair policies that disadvantaged schools and students like the ones they served. In one case, the district had even sued the state to stop enforcement of some components of the standards and accountability procedures.

Further analyses will be carried out to articulate further some of these differences. Overall, however, our study suggests it is important to look closely at district responses to the standards and accountability movement, using a finer lens, and to avoid equating the public responses of national and state spokesmen with the more pragmatic responses of district administrators, whose primary objective is to develop local policies to improve the lives and achievement of their students.

Implications for Policy and Practice

1. State policy makers need to engage more strategically in determining how they can provide support for the development and implementation of locally defined priorities for improvement within the framework of state standards and accountability policies and the practical realities of local community contexts.
2. State policy makers and education agencies should find ways to disseminate the creative initiatives that local districts develop or evolve in order to authentically comply with and exceed state policy expectations, and to expand on those expectations in light of local needs and priorities.
3. State policy makers and education agencies need to be more responsive to the legitimacy of district concerns about unforeseen inequities arising from the implementation of well-intended government policies.
4. District authorities, particularly superintendents, should consider how best to develop quality performance benchmarks in addition to the minimum standards mandated by the state. These standards should be based on nationally normed tests as well as those established by the state.
5. District authorities should develop more consistent networks that engage with state policy development and adaptation. These networks should be consistent with the variable needs and priorities of districts with different capacities and demographic profiles.
6. District leaders are able to define and pursue local goals and priorities because they are able to shape local understanding of state policies, as well as the effects of those policies on local education services, and they should devote attention to this work.

Reflections

1. How do district administrators in your setting react to and interpret state policy?
2. To what degree are state policy initiatives viewed through a bureaucratic lens? Do administrators view state policies as having some positive potential for district improvement, or is the state viewed as a hostile agent?
3. How do local administrators in your setting use networks to increase their opportunity to influence state policy or to create greater latitude for local action? Are these networks effective in creating more opportunities for local action?
4. Are school administrators in your setting able, at least in some cases, to avoid the impact of state policies? If so, what are the consequences?

CONCLUSION

At the time it was undertaken, we believed our study of leadership for learning to be the most ambitious inquiry about educational leadership ever attempted.[1] We were unaware of any other similarly focused study as comprehensive in scope, encompassing as large a sample of classrooms, schools, and districts, extending over such a prolonged period of time, and as well funded. Looking back over the work that we have completed—much of which is summarized in this book—we believe our results contribute to the field in three ambitious ways: by using the scope and scale of the study to provide robust support for theories and claims emerging from the work of others; by pushing back against ill-founded, but often popular claims about leadership; and by offering concepts and evidence that are, if not unique, at least relatively novel to the field.

Our goal for this book was to provide a selective and largely nontechnical account of what we learned as a result of our five-year study of educational leadership across the United States. As the two main parts of the book make clear, the emphasis has been on school- and district-level leadership.[2] This conclusion revisits what we have accomplished in terms of the original goals summarized in Chapter One. In the following sections we discuss how they have been addressed and what our results contribute to educational leadership as a field of study and practice.

Our Findings: Leadership Effects

The study was designed to shed new light on the role that leadership plays in fostering student learning. As we acknowledge throughout, we are not the only scholars to have investigated this question. Our study verifies earlier (but typically smaller) studies that have established that leadership is associated with student learning. More importantly, however, the chapters of this book push the knowledge envelope by examining specific leadership practices in both schools and districts that make significant contributions to student learning. Our evidence goes some distance toward clarifying the paths by which successful leaders influence the quality of teaching and learning.

What we have learned suggests there are specific practices that are relevant for district and school administrators who aim to increase student learning. Many of these are not unique to our study. As we noted in Chapter Five, leaders who have a positive impact emphasize their contributions in four areas: *setting directions*, *developing people*, *redesigning the organization*, and *improving the instructional program*. Almost all leadership practices considered instructionally helpful by principals and teachers are specific enactments of these core practices. As the study thus replicates what is known, we have affirmed these core leadership arenas in a large study with a national random sample that includes schools with a wide range of schools.

What is new, however, is our ability to trace the interaction between leadership at multiple levels—within districts, between districts and schools, among schools, and within schools and classrooms. We have demonstrated that the effects of leadership on quality cannot be isolated in a particular unit of the particularly complex setting that is the U.S. educational system. Of course, good teaching is at the heart of student achievement—but fostering good teaching requires examining how leadership is integrated in a way that is responsive to the particular conditions facing the school.

Our Findings: Beyond Heroes and Toward Contextual Leadership

While affirming previous research, our study has taken a different perspective from the prevailing approach to examining leadership effects. Previous research, both in education and in other sectors, has focused disproportionately on the role and agency of the leader. Much of the public's image of leadership in education is derived from media accounts of heroic or exceptional leaders who have overcome the particularly challenging circumstances in which they find themselves and have accomplished extraordinary things. We only need to revisit a few Hollywood blockbusters—*Stand and Deliver* or *Mr. Holland's Opus*—to understand our national preoccupation with individuals who succeed "against the odds." We, however, were committed to examining how people's work settings affected their leadership, as heroes are in short supply but schools are plentiful.

We have, particularly in the United States, what Meindl, Ehrlich, and Dukerich (1985) term a romantic view of leadership. This perspective, which attributes almost every organizational success or failure to the actions of people who have positional authority, is as deeply embedded in the *Wall Street Journal* as it is in the rush of states to develop "turnaround leadership academies" to solve the perceived problem of school quality. A preoccupation with agency in the field of educational leadership fails to acknowledge the massive scale of the public schooling enterprise, and the demands it makes on recruitment of those who will lead the enterprise. "Raising the bar" and (especially) "closing the gap" will not be accomplished on the large scale that has now become urgent if we have to rely on only exceptional or heroic leaders. There are too few of them, and even talented and committed individuals struggle to make a difference in difficult circumstances—at least in the short run.[3]

Our focus, in contrast, looks at leadership in context, examining the specific circumstances in which leadership is exercised, as well as the broad strategies and specific practices that more and less successful leaders engage in. Our analysis of a wide range of schools and districts with highly variable student achievement also sets our study apart from many of the recent investigations that focus on schools and districts that stand out due to their apparent success. We argue that looking at modest as well as outstanding success, and even at those schools and districts that Susan Rosenholz (1989) called "stuck," allows us to provide a more realistic description of leadership in context.

Much of our evidence speaks to the interaction between individuals and their context by shining a much stronger light on the structures or settings in which people work as explanations for their behavior. Although this focus is woven throughout the book, it is the main point of Chapter Six (in which we looked at the differences in leadership practices and their effects in elementary and secondary schools) and Chapter Thirteen (in which we looked at how district size and demographic characteristics affect superintendents). These and other findings suggest that we should give less focus to developing lists of skills or practices that will lead to improved student learning, and we should pay more attention to how leaders become expert at working within the settings in which they find themselves.

A relatively novel result of our research is our effort to link the contributions of districts to leadership and even to teacher practice in schools, and our more detailed investigation of how districts respond to their contexts by adapting the resources at hand. Quite clearly, based on our data, one size does not fit all schools, whereas the vast majority of districts—not to mention states—attempt to drive change into schools using very similar sets of tools or interventions, occasionally acknowledging the need for those schools to do some "adaptation" in light of their local contexts. Several of the chapters in Part Two of this book outline in detail just how the most successful districts in our study developed nuanced and highly individualized approaches to school improvement.

Our Findings: Promoting Will and Skill for Change

Schools will not improve if the people who work in them lack the will to make difficult changes, as well as the skill to do so.[4] One of the relatively novel outcomes of our work is evidence about the very important contribution of one factor that makes significant contributions to leaders' impacts on school improvement and student learning: *collective school leader efficacy*. Leader efficacy has been the focus of attention in research on leadership in nonschool sectors but has received modest attention in educational leadership research. While individual efficacy has positive effects in schools, it is collective efficacy that appears to be among the most powerful sources of influence that districts can exercise on schools and students—in large measure because it promotes a strong identification with the goal of improving student learning but is also inherently a measure of principals' belief that they have the capacity to do so.

Our evidence about how district leadership enables school-level leadership addresses our goal of describing the ways in which, and the success with which, individuals and groups at the state, district, school, and classroom levels help others to acquire the will and skill required to improve student learning. We demonstrate that districts have an impact on student learning because they are able to create work settings that seem to increase school-based leaders' belief that they can, together, get the job done.

But developing collective efficacy is not an end in itself. Rather, it becomes a precondition for the ability of districts to develop will and skill in more targeted areas. One of our most telling sets of evidence addressing this goal concerns what successful districts did to facilitate data-informed decision making and problem solving in schools. We consider this evidence particularly telling because it made clear that, even though the popular rhetorical admonition by districts for their schools to be data driven has very little effect, it is still the default strategy for encouraging data use in schools. Indeed, much of what we learned about how districts successfully nurture data-informed practices in their schools could apply to introducing other types of valued reforms to schools. These successful districts, for example, "walked the talk" themselves, monitored their schools' progress and responded to what they learned, provided opportunities for those in the school to build new data interpretation capacities, and introduced external expertise into schools that needed it. Most reform initiatives would fare better in schools if districts moved beyond an approach to professional development for principals that involved one-off workshops, and instead worked on developing the socially networked leadership capacities that permit collective identification of problems and solutions. We might even go so far as to advocate for the development of district-wide professional learning communities for administrators.[5]

More specifically, our evidence about successful district leadership included the development of instructional leadership capacity at the school level. But it also made clear that such leadership development opportunities and the capacities that they engendered had very little payoff for schools and students, unless the district also established through its policies a well-balanced system of pressures and supports to both encourage and reward school leaders for implementing their newfound capacities. This is not a recommendation for increasingly "tight linkage" between district offices and schools. Rather, it suggests how urgent it is for districts to reenergize their focus on the development of a district-wide culture of collaboration and change, in which data use, increased emphasis on instruction, and accountability are more likely to flourish without heavy-handed sanctions.

At the school level, we also find that leadership has an effect on students primarily when it engenders a strong community of learners, typically known as a professional community. The will and skill needed to change teaching practices can, of course, be motivated through one-on-one development, but it is far more efficient for principals and other school leaders to create settings in which practice is shared and motivation to experiment is developed. We should point out that our study does not lead to a ringing endorsement of the all-too-typical implementation of PLCs in schools, where teachers are assigned to committees, given data to examine, and asked to come up with improvements within a particular time frame. Professional learning communities, in our study, represent a more organic configuration of trusting relationships among teachers in which knowledge is shared, "big questions" about classroom practices are discussed, and the identification of problems and solutions requires a combination of information from student assessments and the shared professional knowledge that teachers and administrators bring to the table.[6] They are also very important as vehicles for developing teacher leadership in instruction, which is far more important than the exercise of instructional leadership by the principal.

Our Findings: Increasing Leadership Capacities

A well-accepted but less well understood idea in the educational leadership literature revolves around the problem of heroic leadership—namely, getting more people involved in "doing" leadership work. At least a third of the chapters in the book address, from quite different perspectives, ideas and theories about collective, shared, and distributed leadership. Although research about these ideas has grown by leaps and bounds over the past decade, very little of it has addressed the primary criterion of interest to the majority of practitioners: Does it pay off for student learning? Surprisingly, the agenda for research in this area has survived the lack of evidence to answer this question. But our evidence points quite clearly to an affirmative, if complex, answer. So this is an example of providing robust support for theories and claims found in the work of others.

Because we look at different approaches to getting more people involved in leadership, we have much more to add. In particular, our analyses of collective leadership point clearly to two critical findings. First, we found that increasing the influence and leadership exercised by people who have no formal administrative authority does not decrease the influence of those who do occupy such roles. In other words, formal lines of authority and responsibility are not impeded by sharing power. Second, we found that sharing power with people who are typically excluded from studies of shared and distributed leadership—parents, community members, and students—is a key factor in distinguishing between schools and districts with more and less effective leadership in other areas. Simply put, sharing power increases engagement and effort without challenging the professional knowledge of educators.

We also show, in our qualitative analyses, that sharing leadership is hard work that pushes against the grain in many districts and schools. A relatively novel approach to sharing leadership is presented in our evidence about how districts can help "harness family and community energies for school improvement." To date, the extremely influential role of parents in the education of their children and the question of how schools might add value to parents' influence has been conceptualized and studied as a family-school problem. Our evidence paints an important role for districts—assuming that this avenue for improving student achievement is to be traveled by more than just those schools who already "get it."

It is still common to hear "All that matters is what happens in the classroom," which is often followed by policy proposals that emphasize putting more money in teacher salaries and professional development. "Principals are *the* key to school improvement" is another frequent claim, often followed by recommendations in the heroic leadership mold discussed earlier. Evidence from our study pushes back against these and several other popular claims. One recent report, for example, studied "productivity" of all U.S. districts in terms of costs versus benefits (where the benefit was scores on state tests) and found that "unproductive districts" spent a higher proportion of their funding outside of the classroom with the implication that districts don't matter much in the battle for gains in student learning.[7] This is one of the claims that our data dispel most convincingly. We believe that we have shown beyond a shadow of doubt that districts can be a significant force toward school improvement when they enact practices and policies that we have been at some pains to describe. Less obvious in our data, but no less critical, is our evidence that districts can also be an anchor around a school's neck. Districts are, in other words, forces for creating either "moving" or "stuck" schools. They are rarely neutral.

These and other findings presented in this book just begin to capture the broad and unique role of districts we found in the school improvement and student learning business. Our purpose is to help ensure that more than just the schools already leaning in the right direction are part of the solution—but not through the coercive practices so popular with some policy makers. So-called "resistant" educators often have perfectly rational reasons for what is interpreted as resistance. Successful districts listen to those reasons and learn from them.

Although we have just one chapter that focuses on the role of government leadership in promoting change and improvement, our findings here also counter a number of common myths. The first is that the "accountability movement" has hampered local change efforts by imposing standards that are unresponsive to local needs and issues. Obviously that is sometimes the case, but leaders in this study had a far more nuanced view of state leadership, and one that was largely positive. Most saw the state as an ally, and accountability and standards as adaptable conditions that allowed them to muster local levers for change. For most districts, state involvement implied resources and support rather than a straitjacket. Given that there are nine states in the study, and these represent a great range of approaches and initiatives for school improvement, we believe our data warrants that states be increasingly included as part of school leadership studies; clearly they are actors in the collective leadership model that operated positively in this study.

Final Thoughts

It is worth returning to the descriptive framework that guided our initial framework for this investigation, shown in Figure C.1. Our hope was to be able to assess the relative impact of each of the contributing elements of this model to

FIGURE C.1 SOURCE OF IDEAS ABOUT INTEGRATIVE LEADERSHIP IN EDUCATION

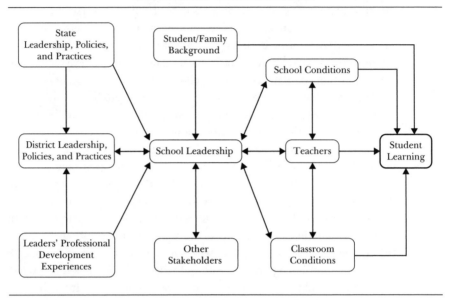

student learning. At one level, we have succeeded: each box has been explored in at least one chapter in this book, and each has been shown to be a factor that must be taken into account. Every study has its limitations, and in our case we have great breadth in our ability to touch on the role that all of the critical actors play, taking into account how they affect teachers, instruction, and students in different contexts. This strength is also a weakness. We can draw up no simple list of the leadership practices or the characteristics of schools and their context that determine student learning. We are able, however, to point to some clear priorities and conclusions.

Leadership Affects Student Learning When . . .

1. . . . it is targeted at working relationships, improving instruction and, indirectly, student achievement.
2. . . . it requires formal leaders, teachers, and other stakeholders to share power and influence.

3. . . . it develops capacity through supporting strong relationships among formal leaders, teachers, and other stakeholders that cement a common commitment to student learning.
4. . . . it strengthens professional community for all members of the school community—a special learning environment within which educators work together to improve their practice and focus their work on student learning.
5. . . . it is adaptive to the specific needs of the local setting, which includes significant variations in capacity, structure, and needs among buildings in the same district.
6. . . . it takes advantage of external pressures for change and improvement rather than fighting against them.

SCALE RELIABILITY FOR VARIABLES

Variable	Alpha	Sample Items
Focused Instruction	.77	My instructional strategies enable students to construct their own knowledge. Disruptions of instructional time are minimized. Most students in my class are capable of taking charge of their own learning in age-appropriate ways. I focus on developing a deep knowledge of the core subjects that I teach. I maintain a rapid pace of instruction in my classes.
Professional Community	.85	Most teachers in our school share a similar set of values, beliefs, and attitudes related to teaching and learning. In our school we have well-defined learning expectations for all students. How many teachers in this school take responsibility for improving the school outside their own class? How often in this school year have you invited someone in to help teach your class(es)? How often in this school year have you received meaningful feedback on your performance from colleagues?

(continued)

Variable	Alpha	Sample Items
		How often in this school year have you visited other teachers' classrooms to observe instruction?
		How often in this school year have you had conversations with colleagues about what helps students learn best?
Shared Leadership	.78	The department chairs/grade-level team leaders influence how money is spent in this school.
		Teachers have an effective role in school-wide decision making.
		Teachers have significant input into plans for professional development and growth.
		School's principal(s) ensures wide participation in decisions about school improvement.
Instructional Leadership	.82	My school administrator clearly defines standards for instructional practices.
		How often in this school year has your school administrator discussed instructional issues with you?
		How often in this school year has your school administrator observed your classroom instruction?
		How often in this school year has your school administrator attended teacher planning meetings?
		How often in this school year has your school administrator made suggestions to improve classroom behavior or classroom management?
		How often in this school year has your school administrator given you specific ideas for how to improve your instruction?
Trust	.90	When teachers are struggling, our principal provides support for them.
		Our principal ensures that all students get high-quality teachers.
		If my principal promised to do something, s/he would follow through.
		In general, I believe my principal's motives and intentions are good.
		I feel free to discuss work problems with my principal without fear of having it used against me later.
Professional Community	.85	Most teachers in our school share a similar set of values, beliefs, and attitudes related to teaching and learning.
		In our school we have well-defined learning expectations for all students.

Variable	Alpha	Sample Items
		Our student assessment practices reflect our curriculum standards.
		Teachers support the principal in enforcing school rules.
		How many teachers in this school feel responsible to help each other improve their instruction?
		How many teachers in this school take responsibility for improving the school outside their own class?
		How many teachers in this school help maintain discipline in the entire school, not just their classroom?
		How often in this school year have you invited someone in to help teach your class(es)?
		How often in this school year have you had colleagues observe your classroom?
		How often in this school year have you received meaningful feedback on your performance from colleagues?
		How often in this school year have you visited other teachers' classrooms to observe instruction?
		How often in this school year have you exchanged suggestions for curriculum materials with colleagues?
		How often in this school year have you had conversations with colleagues about the goals of this school?
		How often in this school year have you had conversations with colleagues about development of new curriculum?
		How often in this school year have you had conversations with colleagues about managing classroom behavior?
		How often in this school year have you had conversations with colleagues about what helps students learn best?

(N = 138 Schools)

ADDITIONAL EVIDENCE RELATED TO CHAPTER SEVEN

Methods

We obtained data for this appendix from responses to the first round of principal and teacher surveys and from state-mandated measures of students' achievement in mathematics. Also, for the vignettes in Chapter Seven, we analyzed data from interviews we conducted over three years with district and school staff members and community stakeholders. The surveys posed questions about principals' and teachers' perceptions of parental and community involvement in schools; they also asked about stakeholders' influence in schools, the composition of leadership teams, and principals' and teachers' perceptions of parent and community openness to and involvement in promoting student learning. For all survey items we used a six-point response scale (from *strongly agree* to *strongly disagree*). We calculated separate scales for each survey (all met conventional standards of reliability), then we used step-wise regression to analyze the principals' and teachers' surveys separately. Factors measured by the principals' survey included the following:

- *Principals' openness to community involvement.* All the items in this scale reflected our concept of *participatory democratic structures* (that is, community members are actively engaged in planning and setting school-improvement goals).

- *District support for community and parent involvement.* This scale measured the role of the district in helping or hindering principals in their efforts to obtain greater community and parental involvement.
- *Principals' perceptions of parental influence.* This scale measured the extent to which parents were involved in decision making and the perceived level of influence parents exercised in setting directions for school-improvement efforts.

We first examined elected versus nonelected site councils to distinguish between those that reflected democratic participatory structures and those that did not. (Although some schools refer to their site councils as "building leadership teams," for purposes of clarity we will use the term "site council" to refer to all such groups of people who participate together to provide guidance and occasional decisions as a means of local leadership at the building level.) We focused on formally elected school site councils that were diverse (that is, with more than three groups of people represented on the teams, meaning those that included parents and community members). Forty-three percent of the teams were elected, and elected teams were more diverse than nonelected teams.

For the first analysis of data from the principal survey, our outcome variables included (1) the diversity of membership on school-site councils, and (2) the level of principals' and teachers' openness to community and parental involvement in schools. For the analysis from the teacher survey, four variables were measured:

- *Parent-Teacher Collective Leadership.* In schools demonstrating collective leadership, principals and teachers are more likely to collaborate with parents and the community.[1]
- *District and School Leadership Influence.* Using this variable we measured the degree to which administrators at the school and district level retained control over decision making.
- *Teachers' Perceptions of Parental Influence.* Using this variable we explored the relationship between teachers' perceptions of parental influence and student learning outcomes.
- *Teacher Influence.* Using this variable we distinguished among the influence of parents, administrators, and teachers in school decisions.

We measured student achievement by reference to the school's performance on the 2005–2006 state tests in mathematics. We used poverty (the number of students receiving free or reduced-price lunches) and type of school (elementary and secondary) as control variables for all of our analyses because several studies examining community involvement specifically found them to be significant influences on parental involvement in schools. SES is also a significant factor in predicting student achievement.[2]

Regression Tables

TABLE B.1 FACTORS ASSOCIATED WITH DIVERSITY OF MEMBERSHIP ON SCHOOL-SITE COUNCILS

Predictors	Standardized Coefficients	t	Sig	R^2	Adjusted R^2
(Constant)		3.648	.000		
Percent of Free or Reduced-Price Lunch Students	.260	2.656	.009	.092	.074
District Support	.227	2.324	.022		
F = 5.092					

(N=157)
*Significant at the .05 level

TABLE B.2 FACTORS ASSOCIATED WITH PRINCIPALS' OPENNESS TO COMMUNITY INVOLVEMENT

	Predictors	Standardized Coefficients	t	Sig	R^2	Adjusted R^2
1	(Constant)		16.073	.000		
	Percent of Free or Reduced-Price Lunch Students	.027	.274	.785	.001	−.009
	F = .075					
2	(Constant)		2.130	.036		
	Percent of Free or Reduced-Price Lunch Students	.017	.172	.864	.095	.068
	District Support	.169	1.673	.097		
	Site Council Diversity	.230	2.292	.024		
	F change = 5.159*					
3	(Constant)		1.661	.1000		
	Percent of Free or Reduced-Price Lunch Students	.025	.224	.808	.096	.059
	District Support	.171	1.684	.095		
	Site Council Diversity	.231	2.289	.024		
	Elementary or Secondary School	.035	.352	.726		
	F change = .124					

(N=157)
*Significant at the .05 level

TABLE B.3 PRINCIPAL SURVEY: FACTORS ASSOCIATED WITH 2005–2006 STUDENT ACHIEVEMENT SCORES IN MATH AT THE BUILDING LEVEL

	Predictors	Standardized Coefficients	t	Sig	R^2	Adjusted R^2
1	(Constant)		17.617	.000		
	Percent of Free or Reduced-Price Lunch Students	−.416	−4.413	.000	.173	.164
	F = 19.471**					
2	(Constant)		5.196	.000		
	Percent of Free or Reduced-Price Lunch Students	−.405	−4.009	.000	.210	.175
	Site Council Diversity	.087	.856	.394		
	District Support	.096	.970	.335		
	Principals' Openness to Community Involvement	−.180	−1.836	.070		
	F change = 1.419					
3	(Constant)		5.973	.000		
	Percent of Free or Reduced-Price Lunch Students	−.496	−4.784	.000	.268	.227
	Site Council Diversity	.099	1.004	.318		
	District Support	.078	.811	.419		
	Principals' Openness to Community Involvement	−.159	−1.662	.100		
	Elementary or Secondary School	−.255	−2.649	.010		
	F change = 7.018*					

(N=157)

*Significant at the .05 level

**Significant at the .001 level

TABLE B.4 TEACHER SURVEY: FACTORS ASSOCIATED WITH 2005–2006 STUDENT ACHIEVEMENT SCORES AT THE BUILDING LEVEL

	Predictors	Standardized Coefficients	t	Sig	R^2	Adjusted R^2
1	(Constant)		117.657	.000		
	Percent of Free or Reduced-Price Lunch Students	−.458	−29.331	.000	.209	.209
	F = 860.303**					
2	(Constant)		21.916	.000		
	Percent of Free or Reduced-Price Lunch Students	−.450	−28.950	.000	.229	.228
	Parent-Teacher Shared Leadership	.097	5.468	.000		
	District-School Leadership	.004	.269	.788		
	Teacher Influence	.020	1.059	.290		
	Teachers' Perceptions of Parental Involvement	.058	3.276	.001		
	F change = 20.771**					
3	(Constant)		28.190	.000		
	Percent of Free or Reduced-Price Lunch Students	−.544	−34.111	.000	.290	.289
	Parent-Teacher Shared Leadership	.054	3.159	.002		
	District-School Leadership	.011	.683	.494		
	Teacher Influence	.021	1.153	.249		
	Teachers' Perceptions of Parental Involvement	.043	2.530	.011		
	Elementary or Secondary School	−.268	−16.672	.000		
	F change = 277.955**					

(N=4,491)
**Significant at the .001 level

NOTES

Foreword

1. Schlechty (2009); Danzig, Borman, Jones, and Wright (2007); Glickman (2002); Copland and Knapp (2006).
2. Townsend and MacBeath (Eds.) (2011).

Preface

1. See, for example, Robinson et al. (2008).
2. Marzano, Waters, and McNulty (2005).
3. York-Barr and Duke (2004).
4. Gronn (2009).
5. Leithwood, Louis, Anderson, and Wahlstrom (2004).

Chapter 1

1. See, for example, Gezi (1990); Reitzug and Patterson (1998).
2. Spillane, Diamond, Burch, Hallett, Jita, and Zolmmers (2002).
3. See, for example, Mortimore (1993); Scheurich (1998).
4. See, for example, Hallinger and Heck (1996b); Leithwood and Jantzi (2005); Marzano, Waters, and McNulty (2005); Robinson, Lloyd, and Rowe (2008).

5. Creemers and Reetzig (1996); Townsend (1994).

6. See Fredricks, Blumenfeld, and Paris (2004) for a review, especially p. 70.

7. Leithwood and Jantzi (1999a, 1999b); Leithwood, Louis, Anderson, and Wahlstrom (2004); Silins and Mulford (2002b); Silins, Mulford, and Zarins (2002).

8. Leithwood, Louis, Anderson, and Wahlstrom (2004).

9. Creemers and Reetzig (1996).

10. Elmore (1995).

11. Yammarino, Dionne, Chun, and Dansereau (2005).

12. Leithwood and Duke (1999).

13. For example, Pearce and Conger (2003).

14. For example, York-Barr and Duke (2004).

15. For example, Leithwood and Jantzi (2006).

16. Dorfman and House (2004).

17. For example, Nelson and Sassi (2005).

18. Andrews and Soder (1987); Duke (1987); Hallinger (2003).

19. Reeves (2006).

20. Lambert et al. (1995).

21. For example, Wagner et al. (2006).

Chapter 2

1. Rowan (1990).

2. Talbert and McLaughlin (1993).

3. Leithwood and Jantzi (2005).

4. Hutchins (1996).

5. Perkins (1993); Tsoukas (2005).

6. Wenger, McDermott, and Snyder (2002).

7. York-Barr and Duke (2004).

8. But see Firestone (1989); Firestone and Martinez (2007).

9. Hallinger and Heck (1996a); Pitner (1988).

10. We were able to generate data on the socio-economic composition of the student body in only seventy-six of these schools, so the calculations for tables drawing on SES have been adjusted to use this smaller sample.

11. Note that this figure is based on a structural equation model conducted with the SLISREL program. The specific statistics are available from the first author.

12. Creemers and Reetzig (1996).

13. Leithwood and Riehl (2005).

14. Hallinger and Heck (2002).

15. Pearson Product-Moment Correlation Coefficients.

16. Beck and Murphy (1998).

17. Desimone (2006).

18. Tannenbaum (1961).

19. These correlations are all significant at the 0.01 level (2 tailed).

20. Bidwell, Frank, and Quiroz (1997)

21. Avolio (1994).

22. Leithwood and Jantzi (2006); Leithwood, Louis, Anderson, and Wahlstrom (2004).

Chapter 3

1. Louis, Dretzke, and Wahlstrom (2010); Wahlstrom and Louis (2008).
2. Cohen, Raudenbush, and Ball (2003).
3. Wayne and Youngs (2003).
4. Smith, Desimone, and Ueno (2005).
5. Wahlstrom and Louis (2008).
6. Brophy (1986).
7. Slavin (1987); Slavin and Lake (2008).
8. Wiske (1998).
9. Fenstermacher and Richardson (2005).
10. Allington (2001); Knapp (1995); Taylor, Pearson, Clark, and Walpole (2000).
11. Kirschner, Sweller, and Clark (2006); Newmann and Associates (1996).
12. Wahlstrom and Louis (2008).
13. Wilson and Peterson (2006).
14. Newmann and Associates (1996).
15. These items emerged from a factor analysis of the larger battery of items in both the 2005 and 2008 surveys; they have a reliability coefficient of .74.
16. Note that this figure is based on a structural equation model conducted with the SPSS AMOS program. The specific statistics are available from the first author. All models reported in this chapter achieved strong statistical fits with the data, including RMSEA, NFI, and CFI indexes.
17. Marzano, Waters, and McNulty (2005).
18. Hallinger (2005); Mosenthal, Lipson, Torncello, Russ, and Mekkelsen (2004).
19. Camburn, Rowan, and Taylor (2003).
20. Stein and Nelson (2003).
21. Halverson, Grigg, Prichett, and Thomas (2007); Leithwood (2001); O'Donnell and White (2005); Silins and Mulford (2004).
22. Anderson (1998); Malen (1994).
23. Leithwood et al. (2007); Mayrowetz and Smylie (2004); Spillane, Halvorson, and Diamond (2004).
24. Marks and Louis (1997); Smylie, Conley, and Marks (2002).
25. Pounder (1999).
26. Chrispeels, Castillo, and Brown (2000); Marks and Printy (2003).
27. Harris (2009).
28. Marks and Printy (2003).
29. Serva, Fuller, and Mayer (2005).
30. See, for example, Bryk and Schneider (2003); Hoy and Sweetland (2001); Louis (2007); Tarter, Bliss, and Hoy (1989); Tschannen-Moran (2004).
31. Tarter, et al. (1989); Bryk and Schneider (2003).
32. Daly and Chrispeels (2008).
33. Driscoll (1978).
34. Louis (2006).
35. Wiley (2001).
36. King and Newmann (2001); Louis and Marks (1998); Smylie and Wenzel (2003).
37. Scribner, Sawyer, Watson, and Myers (2007); York-Barr and Duke (2004).

38. Hord and Sommers (2008); McLaughlin and Talbert (2002).

39. See, for example, Bryk, Camburn, and Louis (1999); Louis and Marks (1998).

40. Marks, Louis, and Printy (2002).

41. We used the maximum likelihood method for the path analysis. We assessed good-ness of fit between the model and the data via three fit indices: the RMSEA (.000), the normed fit index (NFI = .99), and the comparative fit index (CFI = 1.0). Taken together, these results indicate that the fit between the model and the data is adequate.

42. Hargreaves (2001); Leithwood and Beatty (2007); Little (1996); Zembylas (2003).

43. Spillane (2005); Stein and Nelson (2003).

Chapter 4

1. MacBeath (2005); Spillane (2006).

2. Leithwood, Mascall, et al. (2007).

3. Justification for these categories is provided in Leithwood and Riehl (2005); Leithwood, Louis, et al. (2004); Leithwood, Day, et al. (2006).

4. The interview transcripts were entered into a qualitative data analysis software database that included *leadership* as one of the core codes. We employed a three-stage process of analysis. In stage one, we created descriptions of leadership activities in each case study school. We developed a template that enabled us to construct descriptions of (1) sources of leadership linked to (2) specific actions and (3) goals in (4) specific contexts, along with (5) the coparticipants in those situations, (6) the reported effects of those actions, and (7) the reported factors influencing those leadership variables. This analysis generated fifteen to twenty-five leadership scenarios per school. In stage two we recoded each scenario according to Leithwood et al.'s (2006) core leadership func-tions (also see Chapter Five). Then we wrote an analysis of the leadership distribution patterns we discerned in the scenarios, applying concepts from prior research as noted earlier. In stage three we wrote case reports for each school structured by the research questions.

5. Evidence of this is provided by Camburn, Rowan, and Taylor (2003); Hall (1992); Heller and Firestone (1995); Leithwood, Day, et al. (2006); Spillane (2006).

6. See Leithwood, Mascall, et al. (2007).

7. Ibid.

Chapter 5

1. See, for example, Blase (1987, 1989).

2. Brewer and Hunter (1989).

3. For example, Hallinger and Heck (1998); Leithwood and Jantzi (2005); Leithwood and Riehl (2005); Robinson et al. (2008); Waters et al. (2003).

4. See Bandura's (1986) model of motivation, for example.

5. Observations covering one instructional period were conducted in Grades 3, 5, 8, and 10, in language arts and mathematics classrooms.

6. One might expect that significant variations in teaching quality across schools would be reflected in significant differences in student achievement among the HSS and LSS. But this was not the case in these 12 schools.

7. School size in the high scoring schools ranged in size from 455 to 1,980 students, with an average of 924 students. There was greater variation in the sizes of the low scoring schools (210 to 2,788 students), with an average of 1,081. In elementary and middle/junior high schools, the average population of students was larger in the HSS than in the LSS (538 vs. 378 in elementary schools; 763 vs. 549 in middle schools). In the high schools, the average population of the LSS was much larger (2317) than that of the HSS (1,561).

8. Our separate analysis of principals' responses needs to acknowledge the small size of the sample, therefore percentage differences in the principals' responses are deceptive.

Chapter 6

1. See, for example, Brookover et al. (1978).
2. For a review of changes in principal praxis and practice, see Wenglinsky (2004).
3. See, for example, Goddard (2002); Joyce, Calhoun, and Hopkins (2002); Sergiovanni (2005).
4. Hargreaves (1992); Newmann et al. (2001); Smith (1998).
5. See, for example, Creemers and Reetzig (1996); Hallinger and Heck (1998); Spillane, Halverson, and Diamond (2004); Wenglinsky (2002).
6. Spillane (2004).
7. Stein and Nelson (2003).
8. MDRC (2007).
9. To address the possibility that the results of the principal component factor analysis were due to the two different types of question stems, we also ran a principal axis analysis, which confirmed the initial results.
10. See the methodological appendix of the final report for details on how we computed achievement scores, in Louis, Dretzke, and Wahlstrom, (2010).

Chapter 7

1. Anderson (1998, 1999); Schuller, Baron, and Field (2000).
2. Anderson (1998, 1999); Crowson and Boyd (2001); Driscoll (1998); Keith (1999); Lee et al. (1993); Riley and Louis (2004).
3. See Riley and Louis (2004, p. 9).
4. Anderson (1998, 1999); Beck and Murphy (1998); Mawhinney (2004); Riley and Louis (2004).
5. Hess (1999); Malen (1994, 1999); Malen and Ogawa (1988).
6. Hess (1999); Malen (1994, 1999); Malen and Ogawa (1988).
7. Anderson (1998). This finding is challenged by some European studies; for example, Møller (2006).
8. Malen and Ogawa (1988, p. 265).

9. Hess (1999); Malen (1994, 1999); Malen and Ogawa (1988); Tschannen-Moran (2001).
10. Leithwood, Jantzi, and Steinbach (1999).
11. Miretzky (2004).
12. Abrams and Gibbs (2002, p. 384).
13. Mediratta, Fruchter, and Lewis (2002); Mediratta, Shah, and McAlister (2008).
14. Opfer and Denmark (2001).
15. Goldring and Sims (2005); Honig (2006).
16. Giles (2006).
17. Bauch and Goldring (2000).
18. Tschannen-Moran (2001).
19. Smrekar and Cohen-Vogel (2001).
20. Patrikakou and Weissberg (1998).
21. Epstein and Dauber (1991).
22. Kruse and Louis (in press).
23. Henderson and Mapp (2002).
24. Fan (2001); Lee and Bowen (2006).
25. Lee, Bryk, and Smith (1993).
26. Jeynes (2003, 2007).
27. Fan (2001); Feuerstein (2000); Jeynes (2007); Lee and Bowen (2006); Sanders (1998); Sheldon (2003).
28. Other factors affecting family involvement in schools include race, SES, family size, parent self-efficacy, geographic location of school, educational attainment of parents, and grade level of child. See Bandura (1996); Chrispeels and Rivero (2001); Epstein and Dauber (1991); Fan (2001); Feuerstein (2000); Grolnick et al. (1997); Hoover-Dempsey and Sandler (1995); Lee and Bowen (2006).
29. Sheldon (2005).
30. Gordon and Louis (2009).
31. Henderson and Mapp (2002); Ho Sui-Chu and Willms (1996); Shaver and Walls (1998).

Chapter 8

1. See Bandura (1982, 1986, 1993, 1997a, 1997b).
2. Bandura (1997a, p. 77).
3. Bandura (1993).
4. For example, Locke and Latham (1984).
5. Bandura (1993).
6. Chemers, Watson, and May (2000); Gareis and Tschannen-Moran (2005).
7. Chen and Bliese (2002).
8. Pescosolido (2003).
9. Zaccaro, Blair, Peterson, and Zazanis (1995).
10. Leithwood, Jantzi, Earl, Watson, Levin, and Fullan (2004); Togneri and Anderson (2003).
11. Leithwood and Mascall (2008).
12. Standard regression analysis.

13. Standard regression analysis.
14. See Chen and Bliese (2002).
15. For example, Lucas (2003); Smith, Guarino, Strom, and Reed (2003); Walberg and Fowler (1987).
16. DeMoulin (1992); Dimmock and Hattie (1996).
17. Hargreaves and Fink (2006); Macmillan (1996).

Chapter 9

1. More information about our analytic methods can be found in Leithwood, Strauss, and Anderson (2009).
2. For example, Bandura (1997a, b).
3. These techniques and the detailed results can be found in our final research report (Louis et al., 2010, section 2.2).
4. Based on analyses not shown here, we chose not to include individual principal efficacy as a mediating variable. Individual efficacy has no significant relationship with achievement, and the more complex model explains no additional variance.

Chapter 10

1. See Fink (2010) for example.
2. Blackmore (1996).
3. Hargreaves et al. (2003).
4. Macmillan (2000).
5. Fink and Brayman (2006).
6. Heck (2007).
7. Deal (1993); Macneil, Prater, and Busch (2007); Nanavati and McCulloch (2003); Senge (1990); Stoll (1999); Stolp (1994).
8. Patterson and Rolheiser (2004); Sarason (1982); Schein (1993); Tschannen-Moran, Woolfolk Hoy, and Hoy (1998).
9. Ross and Gray (2006); Waters, Marzano, and McNulty (2003).
10. Bruggink (2001); Grusky (1963).
11. Corbett, Dawson, and Firestone (1984).
12. Davidson and Taylor (1998, 1999); Fullan (1992); Ogawa (1995).
13. Partlow (2004).
14. Macmillan (2000).
15. Reynolds et al. (2008).
16. Hargreaves et al. (2003).
17. Macmillan (2000); Macmillan, Meyer, and Northfield (2005).
18. Hargreaves et al. (2003).
19. Miskel and Cosgrove (1984); Miskel and Owens (1983); Ogawa (1991).
20. Boesse (1991); Rebhun (1995).
21. Harris (2009).

22. Gronn (2002); MacBeath (2009); Spillane (2006).
23. To measure student achievement across schools, we collected data from state websites. These data were school-wide results on state-mandated tests of language and mathematics at several grade levels over four years (2003 to 2006). For purposes of this study, a school's student achievement level is represented by the percentages of students meeting or exceeding the proficiency level (usually established by the state) on language and mathematics tests. We averaged these percentages across grades and subjects in order to increase the stability of scores, producing in a single achievement score for each school for each of four years. Our data on student achievement for these schools covers only the most recent four years, yet the turnover of principals is measured over the past 10 years. The premise is that there would be a cumulative effect of principal turnover during this time, which would appear as an overall low level of achievement in the schools in the most recent four years.
24. This model is a good fit with the data according to the conventions indices (RMSEA = .00; RMR = .01; AGFI = 1.00; NFI = 1.00).

Chapter 11

1. Linn (2003).
2. Honig and Coburn (2008); Wayman, Jimerson, and Cho's (2010); Wolhstetter, Datnow, and Park (2008).
3. Wolhstetter, Datnow, and Park (2008).
4. Copland, M. (2003); Boudette and Steele (2007); Love (2009).
5. Anderson, Leithwood, and Strauss (2010); Ikemoto and Marsh (2007); Massell and Goertz (2002); Wayman, Cho, Jimerson, and Snodgrass Rangel (2010).
6. Anderson (2006); Cawelti and Protheroe (2001); Leithwood (2010); Murphy and Hallinger (1988); Snipes, Doolittle, and Herlihy (2002); Togneri and Anderson, (2003); Zavadsky (2009).
7. Coburn, Touré, and Yamashita (2009).
8. Linn (2003); Wayman, Cho, Jimerson, and Snodgrass Rangel (2010); Wohlstetter, Datnow, and Park (2008).
9. Anderson (2006); Sammon (1999).
10. Anderson (2006).
11. This analysis used the AMOS structural equation modeling program that is part of the SPSS statistical package. The various statistical measures to determine the fit between the data and the model (RMSEA, CFI, NFI) all suggest that the model is a relatively robust one.
12. Datnow, Park, and Wohlstetter (2007); Togneri and Anderson (2003); Wayman, Jimerson, and Cho (2010).
13. See also Datnow, Park, and Wohlstetter (2007).
14. See Chapter Nine.
15. Herman and Haertel (2005)
16. McDonnell (2005).
17. Carnoy and Loeb (2002); McDonnell (2005).
18. Coburn et al. (2009); Ikemoto and Marsh (2007); Spillane et al. (2002).
19. Ikemoto and Marsh (2007).

20. Frederiksen (1984).
21. Argyris and Schön (1974).
22. Starbuck (1996).

Chapter 12

1. Floden et al. (1988); Tymms et al. (2008).
2. Tymms et al. (2008).
3. For example, Corcoran et al. (2001).
4. Murphy and Hallinger (1988).
5. Rosenholtz (1989).
6. See, for example, Cawelti and Protheroe (2001); Elmore and Burney (1997); Sharratt and Fullan (2009); Snipes, Doolittle, and Herlihy (2002); Snyder (2002); Supovitz (2006); Togneri and Anderson (2003).
7. Murphy and Hallinger (1988); Waters and Marzano (2006).
8. For example, Leithwood (2010).
9. Elmore and Burney (1998).
10. Childress et al. (2007).
11. See Chapters Six and Seven for a multidimensional view of district leadership for improvement.
12. We also investigated the relationship between district focus on instruction and principals' self-assessments of their expertise in providing instructional support to teachers. We argue, however, that a stronger test of the importance of the district's role is to look for the reflection of improved principal leadership on the part of those who experience it.
13. Based on an analysis of variance.
14. By the 2006–7 school year, one district in the sample was labeled as a district in need of improvement, while a few others had several schools that were either in need of improvement or had the potential of becoming so identified.
15. For example, Marzano, Waters, and McNulty (2005) on balanced leadership; Dufour, Eaker, and Dufour (2005) on professional learning communities; and Fullan (2001) on leading in a culture of change.
16. See Chapter Eleven for specific examples related to district support for data use in schools.
17. None of the randomly sampled districts in our sample had more than a few charter schools or other providers; this was not raised as an important issue (Boyd, Kerchner, and Blyth, 2008).

Chapter 13

1. Anderson and Rodway-Macri (2009); Coburn and Talbert (2006); Firestone and Martinez (2007).
2. Stein and Coburn (2007).
3. Spillane, Reiser, and Reimer (2002).

4. Haskew (1970); Lutz (1986).
5. Timar (1994); Wong (1991).
6. Fuhrman (1987).
7. Marshall, Mitchell, and Wirt (1986); Mazzoni (1993).
8. Firestone and Nagle (1995); Spillane (1998).
9. Marshall (1988).
10. Honig and Hatch (2004).
11. Evidence to support these categorizations has been presented elsewhere. See Louis et al., 2008).

Conclusion

1. Other large studies, such as the Lolso project in Australia, are either geographically limited or confined to one type of school (Silins and Mulford, 2002a, 2002b).
2. A significant emphasis within our study also concerned the role of states and state leadership, but we have limited our attention to that analysis in this volume. See our final report (Louis et al., 2010) and several publications (Louis et al., 2010).
3. We commend two of the public television series developed by Education Matters, one of which deals with a principal selected to turn around a failing school, and the other with the efforts of Michelle Rhee to make a difference in Washington, DC, in a short time period. These are archived at http://learningmatters.tv/
4. Miles and Louis (1990).
5. Katz, Earl, and Ben Jafaar (2009).
6. For a critique of the "PLC movement," see Louis (2009) and Hord and Sommers (2009).
7. Boser (2011).

Appendix B

1. See, for example, Goldring and Sims (2005); Tschannen-Moran and Hoy (2000).
2. Henderson and Mapp (2002); Ho Sui-Chu and Willms (1996).

REFERENCES

Abrams, L. S., & Gibbs, J. T. (2002). Disrupting the logic of home-school relations: Parent involvement strategies and practices of inclusion and exclusion. *Urban Education, 37*(3), 384–407.

Allington, R. L. (2001). *What really matters for struggling readers: Designing research-based interventions.* New York: Longmans.

Anderson, G. L. (1998). Toward authentic participation: Deconstructing the discourses of participatory reforms in education. *American Educational Research Journal, 35*(4), 571–603.

Anderson, G. L. (1999). The politics of participatory reforms. *Theory into Practice, 38*(4), 191–195.

Anderson, S., Leithwood, K., & Strauss, T. (2010). Leading data use in schools: Organizational conditions and practices at the school and district levels. *Leadership and Policy in Schools, 9,* 292–329.

Anderson, S., & Rodway-Macri, J. (2009). District administrator perspectives on student learning in an era of standards and accountability: A collective frame analysis. *Canadian Journal of Education, 32*(2), 192–221.

Anderson, S. E. (2006). The school district's role in educational change. *International Journal of Educational Change, 15*(1), 13–37.

Andrews, R., & Soder, R. (1987). Principal leadership and student achievement. *Educational Leadership, 44*(6), 9–11.

Argyris, C., and Schön, D. (1974). *Theory in practice: Increasing professional effectiveness.* San Francisco: Jossey-Bass.

Avolio, B. J. (1994). The alliance of total quality and the full range of leadership. In B. M. Bass & B. J. Avolio (Eds.), *Improving organizational effectiveness through transformational leadership* (pp. 121–145). Thousand Oaks, CA: Sage.

Bandura, A. (1982). Self-efficacy and mechanism in human agency. *American Psychologist, 37*(2), 122–147.

Bandura, A. (1986). *Social foundations of thought and action.* Englewood Cliffs, NJ: Prentice Hall.

Bandura, A. (1993). Perceived self efficacy in cognitive development and functioning. *Educational Psychologist, 28*(2), 117–148.

Bandura, A. (1996). *Self-efficacy in changing societies.* New York: Cambridge University Press.

Bandura, A. (1997a). *Self-efficacy: The exercise of control.* New York: Freeman.

Bandura, A. (1997b). Self efficacy: Toward a unifying theory of behavioural change. *Psychological Review, 84*(2), 191–215.

Bauch, P., & Goldring, E. (2000). Teacher work context and parent involvement in urban high schools of choice. *Educational Research and Evaluation, 6*(1), 1–23.

Beck, L., & Murphy, J. (1998). Site-based management and school success: Untangling the variables. *School Effectiveness and School Improvement, 9*(4), 349–357.

Berman, P., & McLaughlin, M. W. (1977). *Federal programs supporting educational change: Volume VII. Factors affecting implementation and continuation.* Santa Monica, CA: RAND.

Bidwell, C., Frank, K., & Quiroz, P. (1997). Teacher types, workplace controls, and the organization of schools. *Sociology of Education, 70*(4), 285–308.

Black, P., & Wiliam, D. (2004). The formative purpose: Assessment must first promote learning. In M. Wilson (Ed.), *Towards coherence between classroom assessment and accountability (103rd Yearbook of the National Society for the Study of Education)* (pp. 20–50). Chicago, IL: University of Chicago Press.

Blackmore, J. (1996). Doing 'emotional labour' in the education market place: Stories from the field of women in management. *Discourse: Studies in the Cultural Politics of Education, 17*(3), 337–349.

Blase, J. (1987). Dimensions of effective school leadership: The teacher's perspective. *American Educational Research Journal, 24,* 589–610.

Blase, J. (1989). The micropolitics of the school: The everyday political perspectives of teachers. *American Educational Research Journal, 25,* 377–407.

Boesse, B. D. (1991). Planning how to transfer principals: A Manitoba experience. *Education Canada, 31*(1), unpaginated.

Boser, U. (2011). Return on Educational Investment: A District-by-District Evaluation of U.S. Educational Productivity. http://www.americanprogress.org/issues/2011/01/educational_productivity/report.html

Boudette, K., & Steele, J. (2007). *Data wise in action: Stories of schools using data to improve teaching and learning.* Cambridge, MA: Harvard Educational Pub Group.

Boyd, W. L., Kerchner, C., & Blyth, M. (2008). *The transformation of great American school districts: How big cities are reshaping public education.* Cambridge, MA: Harvard Education Press.

Brewer, J., & Hunter, A. (1989). *Multimethod research.* Newbury Park, CA: Sage.

Brookover, W. B., Schweitzer, J. H., Schneider, J. M., Beady, C. H., Flood, P. K., & Wisenbaker, J. M. (1978). Elementary school social climate and school achievement. *American Educational Research Journal, 15,* 301–318.

Brophy, J. (1986). Teacher influences on student achievement. *American Psychologist, 41*(10), 1069–1077.

Bruggink, P. (2001). *Principal succession and school improvement: The relationship between the frequency of principal turnover in Florida public schools from 1990–91 and school performance indicators in 1998–99.* Unpublished doctoral dissertation, Florida State University.

Bryk, A. S., Camburn, E., & Louis, K. S. (1999). Professional community in Chicago elementary schools: Facilitating factors and organizational consequences. *Educational Administration Quarterly, 35*(5), 751–781.

Bryk, A. S., & Schneider, B. (2003). Trust in schools: A core resource for school reform. *Educational Leadership, 60*(6), 40–44.

Camburn, E., Rowan, B., & Taylor, J. E. (2003). Distributed leadership in schools: The case of elementary schools adopting comprehensive school reform models. *Educational Evaluation and Policy Analysis, 25*(4), 347–373.

Carnoy, M., & Loeb, S. (2002). Does external accountability affect student outcomes? A cross-state analysis. *Educational Evaluation and Policy Analysis, 24*(4), 305–331.

Cawelti, G., & Protheroe, N. (2001). *High student achievement: How six school districts changed into high-performance systems.* Arlington, VA: Educational Research Service.

Chemers, M. M., Watson, C. B., & May, S. (2000). Dispositional affect and leadership effectiveness: A comparison of self-esteem, optimism, and efficacy. *Personality and Social Psychology Bulletin, 26,* 267–277.

Chen, G., & Bliese, P. D. (2002). The role of different levels of leadership in predicting self- and collective efficacy: Evidence for discontinuity. *Journal of Applied Psychology, 87*(3), 549–556.

Childress, S., Elmore, R., Grossman, A., & Johnson, S. (2007). *Managing school districts for high performance: Cases in public education leadership.* Cambridge, MA: Harvard Education Press.

Chrispeels, J. H., Castillo, S., & Brown, J. S. (2000). School leadership teams: A process model of team development. *School Effectiveness and School Improvement, 11*(1), 20–56.

Chrispeels, J., & Rivero, E. (2001). Engaging Latino families for student success: How parent education can reshape parents' sense of place in the education of their children. *Peabody Journal of Education, 76*(2), 119–169.

Coburn, C. E., & Talbert, J. E. (2006). Conceptions of evidence-based practice in school districts: Mapping the terrain. *American Journal of Education, 112*(4), 469–495.

Coburn, C. E., Touré, J., & Yamashita, M. (2009). *Evidence, interpretation, and persuasion: Instructional decision making at the district central office.* New York: Teachers College Press.

Cohen, D. K., Raudenbush, S. W., & Ball, D. L. (2003). Resources, instruction, and research. *Educational Evaluation and Policy Analysis, 25*(2), 119–142.

Conger, C., & Kanungo, R. (1998). *Charismatic leadership in organizations.* Thousand Oaks, CA: Sage.

Copland, M. A. (2003). Leadership of inquiry: Building and sustaining capacity for school improvement. *Educational Evaluation and Policy Analysis, 25*(4), 347–373.

Copland, M., & Knapp, M. (2006). Connecting Leadership with learning: A framework for reflection, planning, and action. Alexandria, VA: Association for Supervision and Curriculum Development.

Corbett, H. D., Dawson, J., & Firestone, W. (1984). *School context and school change: Implications for effective planning.* Philadelphia, PA: Research for Better Schools.

Corcoran, T., Fuhrman, S. H., & Belcher, C. L. (2001). The district role in instructional improvement. *Phi Delta Kappan, 83,* 78–84.

Creemers, B. P. M., & Reetzig, G. J. (1996). School level conditions affecting the effectiveness of instruction. *School Effectiveness and School Improvement,* (7), 197–228.

Crowson, R. L., & Boyd, W. L. (2001). The new role of community development in educational reform. *Peabody Journal of Education, 76*(2), 9–29.

Daly, A. J., & Chrispeels, J. (2008). A question of trust: Predictive conditions for adaptive and technical leadership in educational contexts. *Leadership and Policy in Schools, 7*(1), 30–63.

Danzig, A., Borman, K., Jones, B., & Wright, W. (Eds.). (2007). Professional development for learner centered leadership: Policy, research, and practice. Mahwah, NJ: Lawrence Erlbaum.

Datnow, A., Park, V., & Wohlstetter, P. (2007). Achieving with data: How high performing school systems use data to improve instruction for elementary schools. Report for New Schools Venture Fund. Los Angeles, CA: Center on Educational Governance, University of Southern California.

Davidson, B. M., & Taylor, D. L. (1998, April). *The effects of principal succession in an Accelerated School.* Paper presented at the Annual Meeting of the American Educational Research Association, San Diego, CA.

Davidson, B., & Taylor, D. L. (1999, April). *Examining principal succession and teacher leadership in school restructuring.* Paper presented at the Annual Meeting of the American Educational Research Association, Montreal, QC.

Deal, T. E. (1993). The culture of schools. In M. Sashkin & H. J. Walberg (Eds.), *Educational leadership and school culture.* Berkeley, CA: McCutchan Publishing.

DeMoulin, D. F. (1992). *Demographic characteristics associated with perceived self-efficacy levels of elementary, middle and secondary principals.* Paper presented at the annual meeting of the Mid-South Educational Research Association, Knoxville, TN.

Desimone, L. M. (2006). Consider the sources: Response differences among teachers, principals and districts on survey questions about their education policy environment. *Educational Policy, 20*(4), 640–676.

Dimmock, C., & Hattie, J. (1996). School principals' self-efficacy and its measurement in a context of restructuring. *School Effectiveness and School Improvement, 7*(1), 62–75.

Dorfman, P., House, R. (2004). Cultural influences on organizational leadership, In R. House, P. Hanges, M. Javidan, P. Dorfman & V. Gupta (Eds.), *Cultural leadership and organizations: The globe study of 62 societies* (pp. 51–73). Thousand Oaks, CA: Sage.

Driscoll, J. W. (1978). Trust and participation in organizational decision making as predictors of satisfaction. *Academy of Management Journal, 21*(1), 44–56.

Driscoll, M. E. (1998). Professionalism versus community: Themes from recent school reform literature. *Peabody Journal of Education, 73*(1), 89–127.

Dufour, R., Eaker, R., & Dufour R. (Eds.) (2005). *On common ground: The power of professional learning communities.* Bloomington, IN: National Education Service.

Duke, D. L. (1987). *School leadership and instructional improvement.* New York: Random House.

Elmore, R. (1995). Getting to scale with good educational practice. *Harvard Educational Review, 66*(1), 1–26.

Elmore, R., & Burney, D. (1997). *Investing in teacher learning: Staff development and instructional improvement in Community School District #2.* New York: National Commission on Teaching & America's Future & the Consortium for Policy Research in Education.

Elmore, R., & Burney, D. (1998). School variation and systemic instructional improvement in Community School District #2, New York. http://www.lrdc.pitt.edu/hplc/publications/school%20variation.pdf

Epstein, J., & Dauber, S. (1991). School programs and teacher practices of parent involvement in inner-city elementary and middle schools. *Elementary School Journal, 91,* 279–289.

Fan, X. (2001). Parental involvement and students' academic achievement: A growth modeling analysis. *Journal of Experimental Education, 70*(1), 27–61.

Fenstermacher, G., & Richardson, V. (2005). On making determinations of quality in teaching. *Teachers College Record, 107*(1), 186–213.

Feuerstein, A. (2000). School characteristics and parent involvement: Influences on participation in children's schools. *Journal of Educational Research, 94*(1), 29–39.

Fink, D. (2010). *The succession challenge: Building and sustaining leadership capacity through succession management.* London, UK: Sage.

Fink, D., & Brayman, C. (2006). School leadership succession and the challenges of change. *Educational Administration Quarterly, 42*(1), 62–89.

Firestone, W. (1989). Using reform: Conceptualizing district initiative. *Educational Evaluation and Policy Analysis, 11*(2), 151–164.

Firestone, W. A., & Martinez, M. C. (2007). Districts, teacher leaders, and distributed leadership: Changing instructional practice. *Leadership and Policy in Schools, 6*(1), 3–35.

Firestone, W. A., & Nagle, B. (1995). Differential regulation: Clever customization or unequal interference? *Educational Evaluation and Policy Analysis, 17*(1), 97–112.

Floden, R. E., Porter, A. C., Alford, L. E., Freeman, D. J., Irwin, S., Schmidt, W. H., & Schwille, J. R. (1988). Instructional leadership at the district level: A closer look at autonomy and control. *Educational Administration Quarterly, 24*, 96–124.

Frederiksen, N. (1984). Implications of cognitive theory for instruction in problem solving. *Review of Educational Research, 54*(3), 363–407.

Fredricks, J. A., Blumenfeld, P. C., & Paris, A. H. (2004). School engagement: Potential of the concept, state of the evidence. *Review of Educational Research, 74*(1), 59–109.

Fuhrman, S. H. (1987). Education policy: A new context for governance. *Publius, 17*(3) (The State of American Federalism, 1986), 131–143.

Fullan, M. (1991). *Leading in a culture of change.* San Francisco: Jossey-Bass.

Fullan, M. (1992). Visions that blind. *Educational Leadership, 49*(5), 19–20.

Fullan, M. (2001). *Leading in a culture of change* (2nd ed.). San Francisco: Jossey-Bass.

Fullan, M. (2003). *The moral imperative of school leadership.* Thousand Oaks, CA: Corwin.

Fullan, M. (2010). *The moral imperative realized.* Thousand Oaks, CA: Corwin.

Gabarro, J. J. (1987). *The dynamics of taking charge.* Boston: Harvard Business School Press.

Gareis, C. R., & Tschannen-Moran, M. (2005). *Cultivating principals' sense of efficacy: Supports that matter.* Paper presented at the annual meeting of the University Council for Educational Administration, Nashville, TN.

Gezi, K. (1990). The role of leadership in inner-city schools. *Educational Research Quarterly, 12*(4), 4–11.

Giles, C. (2006). Transformational leadership in challenging urban schools: A role for parent involvement? *Leadership and Policy in Schools, 5*(3), 257–288.

Glickman, C. (2002). Leadership for learning: How to help teachers succeed. Alexandria, VA: Association for Supervision and Curriculum Development.

Goddard, R. D. (2002). A theoretical and empirical analysis of the measurement of efficacy: The development of a short form. *Educational and Psychological Measurement, 62*(1), 97–110.

Goldring, E., & Sims, P. (2005). Propelling teaching and learning: The politics of leadership academies and district-community-university partnerships. *Education Policy, 19*(1), 223–249.

Goldstein, J. (2003). Making sense of distributed leadership: The case of peer assistance and review. *Educational Evaluation and Policy Analysis, 25*(4), 397–422.

Gordon, M. F. (2010). *Bringing parent and community engagement back into the education reform spotlight: A comparative case study.* (Doctoral dissertation, University of Minnesota, 2010). Dissertation Abstracts International-A 71/04.

Gordon, M. F., & Louis, K. S. (2009). Linking parent and community involvement with student achievement: Comparing principal and teacher perceptions of stakeholder influence. *American Journal of Education, 116*(1), 1–32.

Grolnick, W. S., Benjet, C., Kurowski, C. O., & Apostoleris, N. H. (1997). Predictors of parental involvement in children's schooling. *Journal of Educational Psychology, 89*(3), 538–548.

Gronn, P. (2002). Distributed leadership. In K. Leithwood & P. Hallinger (Eds.), *Second international handbook of educational leadership and administration* (pp. 653–696). Dordrecht, NL: Kluwer.

Gronn, P. (2009). Hybrid leadership. In K. Leithwood, B. Mascall, & T. Strauss (Eds.), *Distributed leadership according to the evidence* (pp. 17–40). New York: Routledge.

Grusky, O. (1963). Managerial succession and organizational effectiveness. *The American Journal of Sociology, 69*, 47–54.

Hall, G. (1992). Characteristics of change facilitator teams: Keys to implementation success. *Educational Research and Perspectives, 19*(1), 95–110.

Hallinger, P. (2003). Leading educational change: Reflections on the practice of instructional and transformational leadership. *Cambridge Journal of Education, 33*(3), 329–351.

Hallinger, P. (2005). *Instructional leadership and the school principal: A passing fancy that refuses to fade away.* College of Management, Mahidol University, Thailand.

Hallinger, P., & Heck, R. (1996a). The principal's role in school effectiveness: An assessment of methodological progress, 1980–1995. In K. Leithwood & P. Hallinger (Eds.), *International handbook of educational leadership and administration* (pp. 723–783). Dordrecht, NL: Kluwer.

Hallinger, P., & Heck, R. (1996b). Reassessing the principal's role in school effectiveness: A review of empirical research, 1980–1995. *Educational Administration Quarterly, 32*(1), 5–44.

Hallinger, P., & Heck, R. (1998). Exploring the principal's contribution to school effectiveness: 1980–1995. *School Effectiveness and School Improvement, 9*(2), 157–191.

Hallinger, P., & Heck, R. (1999). Next generation methods for the study of leadership and school improvement. In J. Murphy & K. Louis (Eds.), *Handbook of research on educational administration* (2nd ed., pp. 141–162). San Francisco: Jossey-Bass.

Hallinger, P., & Heck, R. (2002). What do you call people with visions? The role of vision, mission, and goals in school leadership and improvement. In K. Leithwood & P. Hallinger (Eds.), *Second international handbook of educational leadership and administration* (pp. 9–40). Dordrecht, NL: Kluwer.

Halverson, R., Grigg, J., Prichett, R., & Thomas, C. (2007). The new instructional leadership: Creating data-driven instructional systems in school. *Journal of School Leadership, 17*(2), 59–194.

Hargreaves, A. (1992). Time and teachers' work: An analysis of the intensification thesis. *Teachers College Record, 94*, 87–108.

Hargreaves, A. (2001). Emotional geographies of teaching. *Teachers College Record, 103*(6), 1056–1080.

Hargreaves, A., & Fink, D. (2006). *Sustainable leadership.* San Francisco: Jossey-Bass.

Hargreaves, A., Moore, S., Fink, D., Brayman, C., & White, R. (2003). *Succeeding leaders? A study of principal rotation and succession.* Toronto, ON: Ontario Principals' Council.

Harris, A. (2009). Distributed knowledge and knowledge creation. In K. Leithwood, B. Mascall, & T. Strauss (Eds.), *Distributed leadership according to the evidence* (pp. 253–266). New York: Routledge.

Haskew, L. D. (1970). The state and educational policy. *Public Administration Review, 30*(4), 359–365.

Heck, R. (2007). Examining the relationship between teacher quality as an organizational property of schools and students' achievement and growth rates. *Educational Administration Quarterly, 43*(4), 399–432.

Heller, M. F., & Firestone, W. A. (1995). Who's in charge here? Sources of leadership for change in eight schools. *Elementary School Journal, 96*(1), 65–86.

Henderson, A., & Mapp, K. L. (2002). *A new wave of evidence: The impact of school, family, and community connections on student achievement. Annual Synthesis.* Austin, TX: Southwest Educational Development Lab.

Herman, J. L., & Haertel, E. H. (Eds.) (2005). *Uses and misuses of data for educational accountability and improvement* (The 104th yearbook of the National Society for the Study of Education, Part 2). Malden, MA: Blackwell.

Hess, A. (1999). Community participation or control? From New York to Chicago. *Theory into Practice, 38*(4), 217–224.

Hiller, N. J., Day, D. V., & Vance, R. J. (2006). Collective enactment of leadership roles and team effectiveness: A field study. *Leadership Quarterly, 17*(4), 387–397.

Ho Sui-Chu, E., & Willms, J. D. (1996). Effects of parental involvement on eighth-grade achievement. *Sociology of Education, 69*(2), 126–141.

Honig, M. (2006). *New directions in educational policy implementation: Confronting complexity.* Albany, NY: SUNY Press.

Honig, M. I., & Coburn, C. (2008). Evidence-based decision making in school district central offices. *Educational Policy, 22*(4), 578–608.

Honig, M., & Hatch, T. (2004). Crafting coherence: How schools strategically manage multiple, conflicting demands. *Educational Researcher, 33*(8), 16–30.

Hoover-Dempsey, K. V., & Sandler, H. M. (1995). Parental involvement in children's education: Why does it make a difference? *Teachers College Record, 97*, 310–331.

Hord, S., & Sommers, W. (2008). Leadership and professional learning communities: Possibilities, practice and performance. Thousand Oaks, CA: Corwin.

Hord, S., & Sommers, W. (2009). *Leadership and professional learning communities: Possibilities, practice and performance.* Thousand Oaks, CA: Corwin.

Hoy, W. K., & Sweetland, S. R. (2001). Designing better schools: The meaning and measure of enabling school structures. *Educational Administration Quarterly, 37*(3), 296–321.

Hutchins, E. (1996). Organizing work by adaptation. In J. R. Meindl, C. Stubbart, & J. F. Porac (Eds.), *Cognition within and between organizations,* (pp. 368–404). Thousand Oaks, CA: Sage.

Ikemoto, G. S., & Marsh, J. A. (2007). Cutting through the "data-driven" mantra: Different conceptions of data-driven decision making. In P. A. Moss (Ed.), *Evidence and decision making* (pp. 105–131). Malden, MA: Blackwell.

Ingram, D., Louis, K. S., & Schroeder, R. G. (2004). Accountability policies and teacher decision making: Barriers to the use of data to improve practice. *Teachers College Record, 106*(6), 1258–1287.

Jaques, E. (2003). Ethics for management. *Management Communications Quarterly, 17*(1), 136–142.

Jeynes, W. H. (2003). A meta-analysis: The effects of parental involvement on minority children's academic achievement. *Education and Urban Society, 35*(2), 202–218.

Jeynes, W. H. (2007). The relationship between parent involvement and urban secondary school achievement: A meta-analysis. *Urban Education, 42*(1), 82–110.

Joyce, B., Calhoun, E., & Hopkins, D. (2002). *Models of learning, tools for teaching.* London, UK: Open University Press.

Katz, S., Earl, L., and Ben Jaafar, S. (2009). *Building and connecting learning communities: The power of networks for school improvement.* Thousand Oaks, CA: Corwin.

Keith, N. Z. (1999). Whose community schools? New discourses, old patterns. *Theory into Practice, 38*(4), 225–234.

King, M. B., & Newmann, F. M. (2001). Building school capacity through professional development: Conceptual and empirical considerations. *International Journal of Educational Management, 15*(2), 86–93.

Kirschner, P. A., Sweller, J., & Clark, R. E. (2006). Why minimal guidance during instruction does not work: An analysis of the failure of constructivist, discovery, problem-solving, experiential, and inquiry-based teaching. *Educational Psychologist, 41*(2), 75–86.

Knapp, M. (1995). *Teaching for meaning in high poverty classrooms.* New York: Teachers College Press.

Koretz, D. (2005). Alignment, high stakes, and the inflation of test scores. In J. L. Herman & E. H. Haertel (Eds.), *Uses and misuses of data for educational accountability and improvement* (pp. 99–117). Malden, MA: Blackwell.

Kruse, S., & Louis, K. S. (in press). *Strong Cultures: A Principal's Guide to Change.* Thousand Oaks, CA: Sage.

Lambert, L., Walker, D., Zimmerman, D. P., Cooper, J. E., Lambert, M. D., Gardner, M. E., et al. (Eds.). (1995). *The constructivist leader.* New York: Teachers College Press.

Lee, J. S., & Bowen, N. K. (2006). Parent involvement, cultural capital, and the achievement gap among elementary school children. *American Education Research Journal, 43*(2), 193–218.

Lee, V. E., Bryk, A. S., & Smith, J. B. (1993). The organization of effective secondary schools. *Review of Research in Education, 19*, 171–267.

Leithwood, K. (2001). School leadership in the context of accountability policies. *International Journal of Leadership in Education, 4*(3), 217–235.

Leithwood, K. (2010). Characteristics of school districts that are exceptionally effective in closing the achievement gap. *Leadership and Policy in Schools, 9*(3), 245–291.

Leithwood, K., Strauss, T., & Anderson, S. E. (2009). How districts develop school leader efficacy. *Journal of School Leadership, 17*(6), 735–770.

Leithwood, K., & Beatty, B. (2007). *Leading with teacher emotions in mind.* Thousand Oaks, CA: Corwin.

Leithwood, K., Day, C., Sammons, P., Hopkins, D., & Harris, A. (2006, March 30). *Successful school leadership what it is and how it influences pupil learning.* Report to the U.K. Department for Education and Skills.

Leithwood, K., & Duke, D. (1999). A century's quest to understand school leadership. In J. Murphy & K. S. Louis (Eds.), *Handbook of research on educational administration* (pp. 45–72). San Francisco: Jossey-Bass.

Leithwood, K., & Jantzi, D. (1999a). The relative effects of principal and teacher sources of leadership on student engagement with school. *Educational Administration Quarterly, 35*(Supplemental), 679–706.

Leithwood, K., & Jantzi, D. (1999b). Transformational school leadership effects: A replication. *School Effectiveness and School Improvement, 10*(4), 451–479.

Leithwood, K., & Jantzi, D. (2005). A review of transformational school leadership research: 1996–2005. *Leadership and Policy in Schools, 4*(3), 177–199.

Leithwood, K., & Jantzi, D. (2006). Transformational school leadership for large-scale reform: Effects on students, teachers, and their classroom practices. *School Effectiveness and School Improvement, 17*(2), 201–227.

Leithwood, K., Jantzi, D., Earl, L., Watson, N., Levin, B., & Fullan, M. (2004). Strategic leadership for large-scale reform: The case of England's National Literacy and Numeracy Strategies. *Journal of School Leadership and Management, 24*(1), 57–80.

Leithwood, K., Jantzi, D., & Steinbach, R. (1999). *Changing leadership for changing times.* Buckingham, UK: Open University Press.

Leithwood, K., Louis, K. S., Anderson, S., & Wahlstrom, K. (2004). *How leadership influences student learning: A review of research for the Learning from Leadership Project.* New York: The Wallace Foundation.

Leithwood, K., & Mascall, B. (2008). Collective leadership effects on student achievement. *Educational Administration Quarterly 44*(4), 529–561.

Leithwood, K., Mascall, B., & Strauss, T. (Eds.). (2009). *Distributed leadership according to the evidence.* New York: Routledge.

Leithwood, K., Mascall, B., Strauss, T., Sacks, R., Memon, N., & Yashkina, A. (2007). Distributing leadership to make schools smarter: Taking the ego out of the system. *Leadership and Policy in Schools, 6*(1), 37–67.

Leithwood, K., & Riehl, C. (2005). What we know about successful school leadership. In W. Firestone & C. Riehl (Eds.), *A new agenda: Directions for research on educational leadership* (pp. 22–47). New York: Teachers College Press.

Linn, R. (2003). Accountability: Responsibility and reasonable expectations. *Educational Researcher, 32*(7), 3–13.

Little, J. W. (1996). The emotional contours and career trajectories of (disappointed) reform enthusiasts. *Cambridge Journal of Education, 26*(3), 345–359.

Locke, E. A., & Latham, G. P. (1984). *Goal-setting: A motivational technique that works.* Englewood Cliffs, NJ: Prentice-Hall.

Louis, K. S. (1989). The role of the school district in school improvement. In M. Holmes, K. Leithwood, & D. Musella (Eds.), *Educational policy for effective schools* (pp. 145–167). Toronto, ON: OISE Press.

Louis, K. S. (2006). Changing the culture of schools: Professional community, organizational learning, and trust. *Journal of School Leadership, 16*(4), 477–489.

Louis, K. S. (2007). Trust and improvement in schools. *Journal of Educational Change, 8*(1), 1–24.

Louis, K. S. (2009). Leadership and change in schools: Personal reflections over the last 30 years. *Journal of Educational Change* (10th anniversary special edition), *10*(2), 129–140.

Louis, K. S., Dretzke, B., & Wahlstrom, K. (2010). How does leadership affect student achievement? Results from a national US survey. *School Effectiveness and School Improvement, 21*(3), 315–336.

Louis, K. S., Febey, K., Gordon, M., & Thomas, E. (2008). State leadership for school improvement: An analysis of three states. *Educational Administration Quarterly, 44*(4), 462–592.

Louis, K. S., Leithwood, K., Wahlstrom, K. L., & Anderson, S. E. (2010). *Learning from leadership: Investigating the links to school improvement,* commissioned by the Wallace Foundation and produced by the Center for Applied Research and Educational Improvement at the University of Minnesota and the Ontario Institute for Studies in Education at the University of Toronto.

Louis, K. S., & Marks, H. M. (1998). Does professional community affect the classroom? Teachers' work and student experiences in restructuring schools. *American Journal of Education, 106*(4), 532–575.

Love, N. (Ed.). (2009). *Using data to improve learning: A collaborative inquiry approach.* Thousand Oaks, CA: Corwin Press.

Lucas, S. E. (2003). *The development and impact of principal leadership self-efficacy in middle level schools: Beginning an enquiry.* Paper presented at the annual meeting of the American Educational Research Association, Chicago, IL.

Lutz, F. W. (1986). Reforming education in the 1980s. *Peabody Journal of Education, 63*(4, Reforming Education in the 1980s), 1–5.

MacBeath, J. (2005). Leadership as distributed: A matter of practice. *School Leadership and Management, 25*(4), 349–366.

MacBeath, J. (2009). Distributed leadership: Paradigms, policy, and paradox. In K. Leithwood, B. Mascall, & T. Strauss (Eds.), *Distributed leadership according to the evidence.* New York: Routledge.

Macmillan, R. B. (1996). *The relationship between school culture and principal's practices at the time of succession.* University of Toronto, Toronto, ON.

Macmillan, R. B. (2000). Leadership succession, cultures of teaching and educational change. In N. Bascia & A. Hargreaves (Eds.), *The sharp edge of educational change: Teaching, leading and the realities of reform* (pp. 52–71). London, UK: Routledge/Falmer.

Macmillan, R. B., Meyer, M., & Northfield, S. (2005). Principal succession and the continuum of trust in schools. In H. Armstrong (Ed.), *Examining the practice of school administrators in Canada* (pp. 85–102). Calgary, AB: Detselig Enterprises Ltd.

Macneil, A. J., Prater, D. L., & Busch, S. (2007). The effects of school culture and climate on student achievement. *International Journal of Leadership in Education.*

Malen, B. (1994). Enacting site-based management: A political utilities analysis. *Educational Evaluation and Policy Analysis, 16*(3), 249–267.

Malen, B. (1999). The promises and perils of participation on site-based councils. *Theory into Practice, 38*(4), 209–216.

Malen, B., & Ogawa, R. T. (1988). Professional-patron influence on site-based governance councils: A confounding case study. *Educational Evaluation and Policy Analysis, 10,* 251–270.

Marks, H., & Louis, K. S. (1997). Does teacher empowerment affect the classroom? The implications of teacher empowerment for instructional practice and student academic performance. *Educational Evaluation and Policy Analysis, 19*(3), 245–275.

Marks, H., Louis, K. S., & Printy, S. (2002). The capacity for organizational learning: Implications for pedagogy and student achievement. In K. Leithwood (Ed.), *Organizational learning and school improvement.* Greenwich, CT: JAI.

Marks, H., & Printy, S. (2003). Principal leadership and school performance: An integration of transformational and instructional leadership. *Educational Leadership Quarterly, 34*(3), 370–397.

Marshall, C. (1988). Bridging the chasm between policymakers and educators. *Theory into Practice, 27*(2, Research, Policy, Practice: Where Are We Headed?), 98–105.

Marshall, C., Mitchell, D., & Wirt, F. (1986). The context of state-level policy formation. *Educational Evaluation and Policy Analysis, 8*(4), 347–378.

Marzano, R. J., Waters, T., & McNulty, B. A. (2005). *School leadership that works: From research to results.* Alexandria, VA: Association for Supervision and Curriculum Development (ASCD).

Marzano, R. J., & Waters, T. (2007). School district leadership that works: The effect of the superintendent leadership on student achievement. A working paper available at http://www.mcrel.org/topics/Leadership

Massell, D., & Goertz, M. (2002). District strategies for building instructional capacity. In A. Hightower, M. S. Knapp, J. Marsh, & M. McLaughlin (Eds.), *School districts and instructional renewal*. New York: Teachers College Press.

Mawhinney, H. B. (2004). Deliberative democracy in imagined communities: How the power geometry of globalization shapes local leadership praxis. *Educational Administrative Quarterly, 40*(2), 192–221.

Mayrowetz, D., & Smylie, M. (2004). Work redesign that works for teachers. In *Yearbook of the National Society for the Study of Education 103*(1), 274–302. Chicago, IL: University of Chicago Press.

Mazzoni, T. L. (1993). The changing politics of state education policy making: A 20-year Minnesota perspective. *Educational Evaluation and Policy Analysis, 15*(4), 357–379.

McCormick, M. J. (2001). Self-efficacy and leadership effectiveness: Applying social cognitive theory to leadership. *Journal of Leadership Studies, 8*(1), 22–33.

McDonnell, L. M. (2005). No Child Left Behind and the federal role in education: Evolution or revolution? *PJE. Peabody Journal of Education, 80*(2), 19–38.

McLaughlin, M., & Talbert, J. E. (2002). Reforming districts. In A. Hightower, M. Knapp, J. Marsh, & M. McLaughlin (Eds.), *School districts and instructional renewal*. New York: Teachers College Press.

MDRC (2007). *Instructional leadership, teaching quality, and student achievement: Suggestive Evidence from three urban school districts*. Available at http://www.mdrc.org/publications/470/overview.html

Mediratta, K., Fruchter, N., & Lewis, A. C. (2002). *Organizing for school reform: How communities are finding their voices and reclaiming their public schools*. New York: Institute for Education and Social Policy.

Mediratta, K., Shah, S., & McAlister, S. (2008). *Organized communities, stronger schools: A preview of research findings*. New York: Annenberg Institute for Reform, Brown University.

Meindl, J. R., Ehrlrich, S. B., & Dukerich, J. M. (1985). The romance of leadership. *Administrative Science Quarterly, 30*(1), 78–102.

Miles, M. B., & Louis, K. S. (1990). Mustering the will and the skill to change. *Educational Leadership, 47*(8), 57–61.

Miller, R. J., & Rowan, B. (2006). Effects of organic management on student achievement. *American Educational Research Journal, 43*(2), 219–253.

Miretzky, D. (2004). The communication requirements of Democratic schools: Parent-teacher perspectives on their relationships. *Teachers College Record, 106*(4), 814–851.

Miskel, C., & Cosgrove, D. (1984, April). *Leader succession: A model and review for school settings*. Paper presented at the annual meeting of the American Educational Research Association, New Orleans, LA.

Miskel, C., & Owens, M. (1983, April 11–15). *Principal succession and changes in school coupling and effectiveness*. Paper presented at the Annual Meeting of the American Educational Research Association, Montreal, Quebec.

Møller, J. (2006). Democratic schooling in Norway: Implications for leadership in practice. *Leadership and Policy in Schools, 5*, 53–69.

Mortimore, P. (1993). School effectiveness and the management of effective learning and teaching. *School Effectiveness and School Improvement, 4*(4), 290–310.

Mosenthal, J., Lipson, M., Torncello, S., Russ, B., & Mekkelsen, J. (2004). Contexts and practices of six schools successful in obtaining reading achievement. *Elementary School Journal, 104*(5), 343–367.

Murphy, J., & Hallinger, P. (1988). Characteristics of instructionally effective districts. *Journal of Educational Research, 81*(3), 175–181.

Nanavati, M., & McCulloch. (2003). *School culture and the changing role of the secondary vice principal.* Toronto: Ontario Principals' Council.

Nelson, B., & Sassi, A. (2005). *The effective principal: Instructional leadership for high quality learning.* New York: Teachers College Press.

Newmann, F. M., & Associates. (1996). *School restructuring and authentic student achievement.* San Francisco: Jossey-Bass.

Newmann, F., Smith, B., Allensworth, E., &. Bryk, A. (2001). Instructional program coherence: What it is and why it should guide school improvement policy. *Educational Evaluation and Policy Analysis, 23*(4), 297–321.

O'Donnell, R. J., & White, G. P. (2005). Within the account era: Principals' instructional leadership behaviors and student achievement. *NASSP Bulletin, 89*(645), 56–71.

Ogawa, R. T. (1991). Enchantment, disenchantment, and accommodation: How a faculty made sense of the succession of its principal. *Education Administration Quarterly, 27*, 30–60.

Ogawa, R. T. (1995). Administrator succession in school organizations. In S. B. Bacharach and B. Mundel (Eds.), *Images of schools: Structures and roles in organizational behaviour,* Thousand Oaks, CA: Corwin.

Opfer, V. D., & Denmark, V. (2001). Sorting out a sense of place: School and school board relationships in the midst of school-based decision making. *Peabody Journal of Education, 76*(2), 101–118.

Partlow, M. (2004). *Turnover in the elementary school principalship and factors that influence it.* Unpublished doctoral dissertation, University of Dayton.

Patrikakou, E. N., & Weissberg, R. P. (1998). *Parents' perceptions of teacher outreach and parent involvement in children's education.* Philadelphia: Temple University Center for Research in Human Development and Education.

Patterson, D., & Rolheiser, C. (2004, Spring). Creating a culture of change: Ten strategies for developing an ethic of teamwork. *Journal of Staff Development* (web exclusive), *25*, 1–4.

Pearce, C. J., & Conger, C. (2003). *Shared leadership: Reframing the hows and whys of leadership.* Thousand Oaks, CA: Sage.

Perkins, N. (1993). Person-plus: A distributed view of thinking and learning. In G. Salomon (Ed.), *Distributed cognitions: Psychological and educational considerations* (pp. 88–110). Cambridge, UK: Cambridge University Press.

Pescosolido, A. T. (2003). Group efficacy and group effectiveness: The effects of group efficacy over time on group performance and development. *Small Group Research, 34*(1), 20–42.

Pitner, N. (1988). The study of administrator effects and effectiveness. In N. Boyan (Ed.), *Handbook of research on educational administration* (pp. 99–122). New York: Longman.

Podsakoff, P., MacKenzie, S., Moorman, R., & Fetter, R. (1990). Transformational leader behaviors and their effects on followers' trust in leader satisfaction and organizational citizenship behaviors. *Leadership Quarterly, 1*(2), 107–142.

Popham, W. J. (2008). *Transformative assessment.* Alexandria, VA: Association for Supervision and Curriculum Development.

Pounder, D. (1999). Teacher teams: Exploring the job characteristics and work-related outcomes of work group enhancement. *Educational Administration Quarterly, 35*(3), 317–348.

Pounder, D. G., Ogawa, R. T., & Adams, E. A. (1995). Leadership as an organization-wide phenomena: Its impact on school performance. *Educational Administration Quarterly, 31*(4), 564–588.

Rebhun, G. (1995). If it's Tuesday, it must be P.S. 101. *Executive Educator, 17*(5), 21–23.

Reeves, D. B. (2006). *The learning leader: How to focus school improvement for better results.* Alexandria, VA: ASCD.

Reitzug, U., & Patterson, J. (1998). "I'm not going to lose you!" Empowerment through caring in an urban principal's practice with pupils. *Urban Education, 33*(2), 150–181.

Reynolds, C., White, R., Brayman, C., & Moore, S. (2008). Women and secondary school principal rotation/succession: A study of the beliefs of decision makers in four provinces. *Canadian Journal of Education, 31*(1), 32–54.

Riley, K., & Louis, K. (2004). *Exploring new forms of community leadership: Linking schools & communities to improve educational opportunities for young people*: University of London, National College for School Leadership.

Robinson, V. M., Lloyd, C. A., & Rowe, K. J. (2008). The impact of leadership on student outcomes: An analysis of the differential effects of leadership types. *Educational Administration Quarterly, 44*(5), 635–674.

Rosenholtz, S. J. (1989). *Teachers' workplace: The social organization of schools.* New York: Longman.

Ross, J. A., & Gray, P. (2006). School leadership and student achievement: The mediating effects of teacher beliefs. *Canadian Journal of Education, 29*(3), 798–822.

Rowan, B. (1990). Commitment of control: Alternative strategies for the organizational design of schools. *Review of Research in Education, 16*, 353–389.

Rowan, B. (1996). Standards as incentives for instructional reform. In S. H. Fuhrman & J. J. O'Day (Eds.), *Rewards and reform: Creating educational incentives that work.* San Francisco: Jossey-Bass.

Sammon, P. (1999). School effectiveness: Coming of age in the twenty-first century. The Netherlands: Swets & Zeitlinger.

Sanders, M. G. (1998). The effects of school, family, and community support on the academic achievement of African American adolescents. *Urban Education, 33*(3), 385–409.

Sarason, S. (1982). *The culture of the school and the problem of change.* Boston: Allyn & Bacon.

Schein, E. (1993). Defining organizational culture. In J. M. Shafritz and J. S. Ott (Eds.). *Classics of organizational theory* (pp. 369–376). New York: Harcourt College Publishers.

Scheurich, J. J. (1998). Highly successful and loving, public elementary schools populated mainly by low-SES children of color: Core beliefs and cultural characteristics. *Urban Education, 33*(4), 451–491.

Schlechty, P. (2009). *Leading for learning: How to transform schools into learning organizations.* New York: Wiley.

Schuller, T., Baron, S., & Field, J. (2000). Social capital: A review and critique. In S. Baron, et al. (Eds.), *Social capital: Critical perspectives* (pp. 3–38). Oxford, UK: Oxford University Press.

Scribner, J. P., Sawyer, R. K., Watson, S. T., & Myers, V. L. (2007). Teacher teams and distributed leadership: A study of group discourse and collaboration. *Educational Administration Quarterly, 43*(1), 67–100.

Senge, P. M. (1990, Fall). The leader's new work: Building learning organizations. *Sloan Management Review*, 7–23.

Sergiovanni, T. (2005). The virtues of leadership. *The Educational Forum, 69*(2), 112–123.

Serva, M. A., Fuller, M. A., & Mayer, R. C. (2005). The reciprocal nature of trust: A longitudinal study of interacting teams. *Journal of Organizational Behavior, 26*, 625–648.

Sharratt, L., & Fullan, M. (2009). *Realization: The change imperative for deepening district-wide reform.* Thousand Oaks, CA: Corwin.

Shaver, A. V., & Walls, R. T. (1998). Effect of Title I parent involvement on student reading and mathematics achievement. *Journal of Research and Development in Education, 31*(2), 90–97.

Sheldon, S. B. (2003). Linking school-family-community partnerships in urban elementary schools to student achievement on state tests. *The Urban Review, 35*(2), 149–165.

Sheldon, S. B. (2005). Testing a structural equation model of partnership program implementation and parent involvement. *Elementary School Journal, 106*(2), 171–187.

Silins, H., & Mulford, W. R. (2002a). Leadership and school results. In K. Leithwood & P. Hallinger (Eds.), *Second international handbook of educational leadership and administration* (pp. 561–612). Dordrecht, NL: Kluwer.

Silins, H., & Mulford, W. R. (2002b). Schools as learning organizations: The case for system, teacher, and student learning. *Journal of Educational Administration, 40*(5), 425–446.

Silins, H., & Mulford, W. R. (2004). Schools as learning organizations—effects on teacher leadership and student outcomes. *School Effectiveness and School Improvement, 15*(3–4), 443–466.

Silins, H. C., Mulford, W. R., & Zarins, S. (2002). Organizational learning and school change. *Educational Administration Quarterly, 38*(5), 613–642.

Slavin, R. (1987). Ability grouping and student achievement. *Review of Educational Research, 57*(3), 293–336.

Slavin, R., & Lake, C. (2008). Effective programs in elementary mathematics: A best-evidence synthesis. *Review of Educational Research, 78*(3), 427–515.

Smith, B. (1998). *It's about time: Opportunities to learn in Chicago's elementary schools.* Consortium on Chicago School Research. Chicago, IL.

Smith, T., Desimone, L., & Ueno, K. (2005). "Highly qualified" to do what? The relationship between NCLB teacher quality mandates and the use of reform-oriented instruction in middle school mathematics. *Educational Evaluation and Policy Analysis, 27*(1), 75–109.

Smith, W., Guarino, A. J., Strom, P., & Reed, C. (2003). Principal self-efficacy and effective teaching and learning environments. *School Leadership and Management, 23*(4), 505–508.

Smrekar, C., & Cohen-Vogel, L. (2001). The voices of parents: Rethinking the intersection of family and school. *Peabody Journal of Education, 76*(2), 75–100.

Smylie, M., Conley, S., & Marks, H. (2002). Exploring new approaches to teacher leadership for school improvement. In J. Murphy (Ed.), *The educational leadership challenge: Redefining leadership for the 21st century* (pp. 162–188). Chicago, IL: University of Chicago Press.

Smylie, M. A., & Wenzel, S. A. (2003). *The Chicago Annenberg challenge: Successes, failures, and lessons for the future: Final technical report of the Chicago Annenberg research project.* Chicago, IL: Consortium on Chicago School Research.

Snipes, J., Doolittle, F., & Herlihy, C. (2002). *Foundations for success: Case studies of how urban school systems improve student achievement.* Washington, DC: MDRC.

Snyder, J. (2002). New Haven Unified School District: A teaching quality system for excellence and equity. In A. Hightower, M. S. Knapp, J. Marsh, & M. McLaughlin, (Eds). *School Districts and Instructional Renewal.* New York, NY: Teachers College Press, 94–110.

Spillane, J. P. (1998). State policy and the non-monolithic nature of the local school district: Organizational and professional considerations. *American Educational Research Journal, 35*(1), 33–63.

Spillane, J. P. (2004). *Standards deviation: How schools misunderstand education policy.* Cambridge, MA: Harvard University Press.

Spillane, J. P. (2005). Primary school leadership practice: How the subject matters. *School Leadership & Management, 25*(4), 383–397.

Spillane, J. P. (2006). *Distributed leadership.* San Francisco: Jossey-Bass.

Spillane, J. P., Diamond, J., Burch, P., Hallett, T., Jita, L., & Zolmmers, J. (2002). Managing in the middle: School leaders and the enactment of accountability policy. *Educational Policy, 16*(5), 731–762.

Spillane, J. P., Halverson, R., & Diamond, J. B. (2004). Towards a theory of leadership practice: A distributed perspective. *Journal of Curriculum Studies, 31*(1), 3–34.

Spillane, J. P., Reiser, B. J., & Reimer, T. (2002). Policy implementation and cognition: Reframing and refocusing implementation research. *Review of Educational Research, 72*(3), 387–431.

Starbuck, W. H. (1996). Unlearning ineffective or obsolete technologies. *International Journal of Technology Management, 11*(7), 725–737.

Stein, M. K., & Coburn, C. E. (2007). Architectures for learning: A comparative analysis of two urban school districts. American Educational Research Association, Chicago, IL.

Stein, M. K., & Nelson, B. S. (2003). Leadership content knowledge. *Educational Evaluation and Policy Analysis, 25*(4), 423–448.

Stoll, L. (1999). School culture: Black hole or fertile garden for school improvement? In J. Prosser (Ed.), *School culture.* British Educational Management Series. London, UK: Sage.

Stolp, S. (1994). *Leadership for school culture.* East Lansing, MI: National Center for Research on Teacher Learning. (ERIC Document Reproduction Service No. 91).

Supovitz, J. (2006). The *case for district-based reform: Leading, building, and sustaining school improvement.* Cambridge, MA: Harvard Education Press.

Talbert, J. E., & McLaughlin, M. W. (1993). Understanding teaching in context. In D. K. Cohen, M. W. McLaughlin, & J. E. Talbert (Eds.), *Teaching for understanding: Challenges for policy and practice.* San Francisco: Jossey-Bass.

Tannenbaum, A. S. (1961). Control and effectiveness in a voluntary organization. *American Journal of Sociology, 67*(1), 33–46.

Tarter, C. J., Bliss, J. R., & Hoy, W. K. (1989). School characteristics and faculty trust in secondary schools. *Educational Administration Quarterly, 23*(3), 294–308.

Taylor, B., Pearson, D., Clark, K., & Walpole, S. (2000). Effective schools and accomplished teachers: Lessons about primary-grade reading instruction in low-income schools. *The Elementary School Journal, 101*(2), 121–165.

Timar, T. B. (1994). Politics, policy, and categorical aid: New inequities in California school finance. *Educational Evaluation and Policy Analysis, 16*(2), 143–160.

Togneri, W., & Anderson, S. E. (2003). *Beyond islands of excellence: What districts can do to improve instruction and achievement in all schools.* Washington, DC: Learning First Alliance and the Association for Supervision and Curriculum Development.

Townsend, T. (1994). Goals for effective schools: the view from the field. *School Effectiveness and School Improvement, 5*(2), 127–148.

Townsend, T., & MacBeath, J. (Eds.). (2011). *International handbook of leadership for learning.* New York: Springer.

Tschannen-Moran, M. (2001). Collaboration and the need for trust. *Journal of Educational Administration, 39*(4), 308–331.

Tschannen-Moran, M. (2004). *Trust matters: Leadership for successful schools.* San Francisco: Jossey-Bass.

Tschannen-Moran, M., & Hoy, W. K. (2000). A multidisciplinary analysis of the nature, meaning, and measurement of trust. *Review of Educational Research, 70*(4), 547–593.

Tschannen-Moran, M., Woolfolk Hoy, A., & Hoy, W. K. (1998). Teacher efficacy: Its meaning and measure. *Review of Educational Research, 68*(2), 202–248.

Tsoukas, H. (2005). *Complex knowledge.* Oxford, UK: Oxford University Press.

Tymms, P., Merrell, C., Heron, T., et al. (2008). The importance of districts. *School Effectiveness and School Improvement, 19*(3), 261–274.

Wagner, T., Kegan, R., Lahey, L., Lemons, R. W., Garnier, J., Helsing, D., et al. (2006). *Change leadership: A practical guide to transforming our schools.* San Francisco: Jossey-Bass.

Wahlstrom, K., & Louis, K. S. (2008). How teachers experience principal leadership: The roles of professional community, trust, efficacy, and shared responsibility. *Educational Administration Quarterly, 44*(4), 458–495.

Wahlstrom, K. L., Louis, K. S., Leithwood, K., & Anderson, S. E. (2010). Investigating the links to improved student learning. Executive Summary of Research Findings. Center for Applied Research and Educational Improvement at the University of Minnesota and the Ontario Institute for Studies in Education at the University of Toronto.

Walberg, H., & Fowler, W. (1987, October). Expenditure and size efficiencies of public school districts. *Educational Researcher*, 5–13.

Waters, T., & Marzano, R. J. (2006). *School district leadership that works: The effect of superintendent leadership on student achievement.* Denver, CO: Mid-continent Research for Education and Learning (McREL).

Waters, T., Marzano, R. J., & McNulty, B. (2003). *Balanced leadership: What 30 years of research tells us about the effect of leadership on pupil achievement. A working paper.* Denver, CO: Mid-continent Research for Education and Learning (McREL), p. 10.

Wayman, J. C., Cho, V., Jimerson, J. B., & Snodgrass Rangel, V. W. (2010, May). *The data informed district: A systemic approach to educational data use.* Paper presented at the 2010 Annual Meeting of the American Educational Research Association, Denver, CO.

Wayman, J. C., Jimerson, J. B., & Cho, V. (2010). *District policies for the effective use of student data.* Paper presented at the 2010 convention of the University Council for Educational Administration, New Orleans, LA.

Wayne, A. J., & Youngs, P. (2003). Teacher characteristics and student achievement gains: A review. *Review of Educational Research, 73*(1), 89–122.

Weick, K. (1976). Educational organizations as loosely coupled systems. *Administrative Science Quarterly, 21*(1), 1–19.

Wenger, E., McDermott, R., & Snyder, W. M. (2002). *Cultivating communities of practice.* Boston: Harvard Business School Press.

Wenglinsky, H. (2002). How schools matter: The link between teacher classroom practices and student academic performance. *Education Policy Analysis Archives, 10*(12).

Wenglinsky, H. (2004). Review: From practice to praxis: Books about the new principal preparation. *Educational Researcher, 33*(9), 33–37.

White, R., Cooper, K., & Brayman, C. (2006). *Case study of principal rotation and succession policies: An international perspective.* Toronto, Ontario: Ontario Principals' Council.

Wiley, S. D. (2001). Contextual effects on student achievement: School leadership and professional community. *Journal of School Change, 2*(1), 1–33.

Wilson, D. (2004). Assessment, accountability, and the classroom: A community of judgment. In D. Wilson (Ed.), *Towards coherence between classroom assessment and accountability* (103rd Yearbook of the National Society for the Study of Education) (pp. 1–19). Chicago, IL: University of Chicago Press.

Wilson, S. M., & Peterson, P. (2006). *Theories of learning and teaching: What do they mean for educators?* Washington, DC: National Education Association.

Wiske, M. S. (Ed.). (1998). *Teaching for understanding: Linking research with practice.* San Francisco: Jossey-Bass.

Wohlstetter, P., Datnow, A., & Park, P. (2008). Creating a system for data driven decision making: Applying the principal-agent framework. *School Effectiveness and School Improvement, 19*(3), 239–259.

Wong, K. K. (1991). State reform in education finance: Territorial and social strategies. *Publius, 21*(3), 125–142.

Yammarino, F., Dionne, S., Chun, J., & Dansereau, F. (2005). Leadership and levels of analysis: A state-of-the-science review. *Leadership Quarterly, 16,* 879–919.

York-Barr, J., & Duke, K. (2004). What do we know about teacher leadership? Findings from two decades of scholarship. *Review of Educational Research, 74*(3), 255–316.

Yukl, G. (1994). *Leadership in organizations* (3rd ed.). Englewood Cliffs, NJ: Prentice-Hall.

Yukl, G. (2002). *Leadership in organizations* (5th ed.). Upper Saddle River, NJ: Prentice Hall.

Zaccaro, S. J., Blair, V., Peterson, C., & Zazanis, M. (1995). Collective efficacy. In J. E. Maddux (Ed.), *Self-efficacy, adaptation, and adjustment: Theory, research and application.* New York: Plenum.

Zavadsky, H. (2009). *Bringing school reform to scale: Five award-winning urban districts,* Harvard Education Press: Cambridge, MA.

Zembylas, M. (2003). Interrogating "teacher identity": Emotion, resistance, and self-formation. *Educational Theory, 53*(1), 107–127.

INDEX